DATE DUE

X 9 X X X9 X98X		
MAY XX X 1969		
X X X X X9X		
X X X X X97X		
XJUL 3 X 19XX		
SEPX X X97X X		
X X X X X X9X X X		
SEP X 0 3 1976 X X X		
XDG X X X XX X		

Poverty and Progress

A Publication of the
Joint Center for Urban Studies
of the Massachusetts Institute of Technology
and Harvard University

POVERTY AND PROGRESS

SOCIAL MOBILITY
IN A NINETEENTH CENTURY CITY

BY STEPHAN THERNSTROM

HARVARD UNIVERSITY PRESS

CAMBRIDGE, MASSACHUSETTS · 1964

TO MY MOTHER AND FATHER

ACKNOWLEDGMENTS

This book has been in gestation some five years now. For generous financial support during those years I am indebted to the Graduate School of Arts and Sciences and the Frederick Sheldon Fund, Harvard University, and to the Joint Center for Urban Studies of the Massachusetts Institute of Technology and Harvard. Two Faculty of Arts and Sciences grants and a Frederick Sheldon Travelling Fellowship financed the original research. A Samuel A. Stouffer Research Fellowship awarded me by the Joint Center for Urban Studies provided, in addition to the funds for a year of full-time writing, an ideal environment for creative work—a quiet office and lively colleagues. Some of my ideas were profitably exposed to critical scrutiny at two seminars sponsored by the Joint Center, and I am particularly grateful to Martin Meyerson, then director of the center, and to Lloyd Rodwin, chairman of its Faculty Committee, for their stimulating criticism.

For reading the manuscript and contributing valuable comments I am indebted to the following: Norman Birnbaum, Martha Derthick, Karl DeSchweinitz, Jr., Marc Fried, Oscar Handlin, P. M. G. Harris, Ira Lapidus, N. Gordon Levin, Jr., Barrington Moore, Jr., David Riesman, Maurice Stein, and Sam B. Warner, Jr. P. M. G. Harris was exceptionally helpful in reviewing the statistical chapters and suggesting a procedure for retabulation of the mobility data. My greatest debt is to Oscar Handlin, who has kindly and patiently guided this work through each of its many stages, from the initial formulation of the topic to the final revision. Something of my obligation to his pioneering scholarship in American social history will be apparent from the citations below, but what I have learned from him is far more than footnotes can convey.

The staffs of many libraries made my task easier, but I owe a special word of thanks to Katherine Kuechle of the Newburyport Public Library. The Essex Institute in Salem, the Massachusetts State Archives, the Newburyport City Treasurer, and the Newburyport Superintendent of Schools allowed me access to indispensable documents. Leon M. Little of Boston graciously helped me to obtain permission from the officers of the Institution of Savings for Newburyport and Vicinity to examine bank records for the 1850-1880 period. Vivian Gruder, Judy Diekoff, and Judith Walzer provided helpful editorial advice. My wife Abigail took time from her own work to cast a sharp eye over the manuscript, improving the final product in both style and substance.

S. T.

Cambridge, Massachusetts
May 1964

CONTENTS

TABLES

Poverty and Progress

Introduction

Men of literary taste . . . are always apt to overlook the working-classes, and to confine the records they make of their own times, in great degree, to the habits and fortunes of their own associates, and to those of people of superior rank to themselves, of whose sayings and doings their vanity, as well as their curiosity, leads them most carefully to inform themselves. The dumb masses have often been so lost in this shadow of egotism, that, in later days, it has been impossible to discern the very real influence their character and condition has had on the fortune and fate of the nation.

Frederick Law Olmsted (1859)

American legend has it that the United States has long been "the land of opportunity" for the common man. No other society has so often celebrated social mobility, none has made a folk hero of the self-made man to quite the same degree. The idea of the distinctive fluidity of our social order has been a national obsession for more than a century.

This has been the myth. How has it squared with social reality? The literature on social mobility in contemporary America is abundant, but social scientists have made few efforts to examine the problem in historical depth. One of the most glaring gaps in our knowledge of nineteenth century America is the absence of reliable information about the social mobility of its population, particularly at the lower and middle levels of society. It was this gap which made recent discussions of the question "are social classes in America becoming more rigid?" so inconclusive and superficial. A satisfactory verdict could hardly be arrived at when so little was known about the actual extent of social mobility in the United States prior to 1900.

This study of the social mobility of working class families in a nineteenth century city thus ventures into unexplored territory. Virtually the only systematic mobility research in America which extends back into the nineteenth century has dealt with the social origins of members of the American business elite.[1] Valuable as this research has been, it does not provide a satisfactory basis for estimating the openness of the nineteenth century class structure. What is an "open" society? A society of five millionaires and ten million paupers, for instance, cannot be so described merely because the former are recruited from the ranks of the poor by some process of free competition which selects individuals purely on merit. As Americans have understood the term, an open society is one with room at the middle as well as at the top, a society in which mobility opportunities are widespread.

The business elite studies deal with social advances which were, if often dramatic, necessarily atypical. Almost nothing can be learned about the range of mobility opportunities at the great base of the social pyramid from a survey of the class origins of the elect few who climbed to its very pinnacle. It is by now well established that the great majority of American millionaires, Wall Street bankers, and corporation presidents in both the nineteenth and twentieth centuries have come from middle class homes, but surely these are dubious grounds on which to assert that the American social structure as a whole has been relatively closed. A more relevant question for research is whether it was easy, difficult, or impossible for a laborer or a laborer's son to become a grocer, a foreman, or a farm owner in the United States a century ago. About opportunities at this social level we know dismayingly little. The plea that American history be written "from the bottom up" has been often voiced but rarely heeded.[2]

This volume deals with the lives of hundreds of obscure men who resided in a New England community in the latter half of the nineteenth century. It traces the changing social position of unskilled manual laborers and their families, and suggests some hypotheses about working class social mobility in other American cities of the period. These families stood at the very bottom of the social ladder by almost any criterion. Living at the margin of subsistence, they suffered from the classic disabilities of the depressed social group: unemployment, illiteracy, bad housing, poor diets. It would be impressive testimony to the fluidity of the social structure if many of these unskilled workmen and their sons actually climbed to a higher social level. Certainly they represent the least favorable case with which to test the validity of popular American beliefs about widespread opportunities.

Newburyport, Massachusetts, a city already well known in the annals of American social science, was the site of this research. Only a generation ago a massive inquiry into "the social life of a modern community" was conducted in Newburyport. W. Lloyd Warner's "Yankee City" series was a pioneering work in the genre which includes such books as *Black Metropolis, Caste and Class in a Southern Town, Streetcorner Society, Elmtown's Youth,* and *Middletown.*[3] The five Yankee City volumes provide an exhaustively detailed portrait of the Newburyport class structure as it appeared to Warner and his assistants in the 1930's, a portrait which notably in-

fluenced subsequent field studies of social stratification in
American communities. For this reason Newburyport
seemed a promising setting for my own research into class
and mobility in a nineteenth century city. It offered the
possibility of an unusual confrontation between the historical and sociological approaches to a community. Their
ahistorical methodological preconceptions made the Yankee City investigators misunderstand the Newburyport
past, and this misunderstanding seriously distorted their
portrait of the community in the 1930's. Since a solid
historical foundation is conspicuously lacking in many
products of American social science today, a concrete
demonstration of how a grasp of the historical context can
illuminate the modern community should be of considerable value. The concluding chapter of this book and an
appendix deal with this matter.

To find a body of evidence from which to reconstruct
the lives of men who left no written monuments behind
them seemed at first a hopeless task. William F. Whyte
could take a room in Boston's North End and observe the
"street corner society" of working class youth by partic-
ipating in it, but the method of direct observation is
obviously unavailable to the historian.[4] The essays, novels,
memoirs, speeches, sermons, and editorials of the nineteenth century were not produced by those who made a
living with their hands. And few writers, as Frederick
Law Olmsted remarked, felt any inclination to portray
their social inferiors. Even the investigators employed by
the Massachusetts Bureau of the Statistics of Labor were
forced to report in 1872: "Of unskilled out-door laborers
but little information can be gathered, save that they are
poor, live poor, and remain poor, as a rule."[5]

It is hardly surprising, therefore, that such groups as

Philadelphia's "business aristocracy" and the merchants of colonial New England have received greater attention from scholars, or that specialists in labor history have concentrated so narrowly on workmen organized in trade unions. Labor unions were of negligible importance in the United States until this century—as late as 1901 only 7 percent of the labor force was organized—but at least the early unions provided the historian with a wealth of written source material. The millions of American workmen who remained untouched by the labor movement seem lost to history.

Fortunately there is one source of information about the economic and social situation of ordinary, unorganized laborers: original manuscript schedules of the United States Census. Starting in 1850, when a new method of census-taking was initiated, manuscript census schedules provide the historian with a primitive social survey of the entire population of a community; occupation, place of birth, property holdings, literacy, and other useful information about every inhabitant is listed. These skeletal facts, supplemented by data from contemporary newspapers and other sources, made it possible to fix the social position of the unskilled laboring families of Newburyport at decade intervals, and to measure how much social mobility they experienced in the period 1850-1880.[6]

The selection of this particular time period was fortuitous (census data were unavailable before 1850 and after 1880) but not unfortunate, for these three decades were of decisive importance in the social history of Newburyport. It was in just these years that the community, still a sleepy preindustrial town of 7000 in 1840, experienced the sudden shock of rapid population growth, mass immigration, and economic transformation. The initial impact of urbanization and industrialization upon the social life of the community, and particularly its working class, is analyzed in the first two chapters of this book. Nineteenth century beliefs about the social mobility opportunities open to the common workman are then set forth, providing a framework against which to evaluate the findings of the social mobility inquiry reported in Chapters Four, Five, and Six. With this detailed knowledge of the actual social experiences of Newburyport working class families in the three decades following 1850, it will be possible to re-examine the community at the end of this period and to explain the stable social patterns which had taken shape by 1880.

This is a book about a single community, yet it hopes to reveal something of importance about the larger society of which Newburyport was but a small part, and to trace the effects of large-scale social changes which took place in other American cities as well. Inferences about "American society" or "American cities" based on happenings in one small community are obviously perilous, a fact too often forgotten by the authors of some of the classic sociological community studies. No simple solution to this problem is advanced here, but I have been conscious of it throughout this work, and have attempted to suggest relevant comparisons and contrasts with other American cities wherever possible. The concluding chapter will discuss the problem of Newburyport's representativeness at length, and will show how the findings of this inquiry can be used to help answer the question of whether or not mobility opportunities for men at the bottom of the social ladder are declining in present-day America.

The limits of the evidence upon which this book is based, it must be repeated, are severe and inescapable.

The task of the historian who takes as his subject the common citizens of a nineteenth century community seems at times to resemble that of the archaeologist, who seeks to breathe life into scattered artifacts from a long-dead civilization. This exercise in reconstruction was often painfully uncertain, and my interpretations are open to challenge at many points. But I hope that it will be suggestive, and that it will convince some readers of the potentialities of history written "from the bottom up."

I · *Laborer and Community at Mid-Century*

"The most remarkable social phenomenon of the present century is the concentration of population in cities," an American scholar noted in 1899.[1] The rise of the modern city was the product of a series of economic, political, and social changes of far-reaching significance. If sprawling giants like New York, Chicago, Pittsburgh, and St. Louis revealed these changes most dramatically, the same forces were at work in Lowell, New Haven, Rochester, and dozens of other similar communities which burgeoned in those years. These small and medium-sized cities are easily overlooked, but from the point of view of population growth and industrial expansion they were as important as the glamorous metropolitan centers. The factory system, indeed, first grew up largely outside the established commercial capitals, in communities like Pawtucket, Lowell, and Lawrence. Smaller cities like these displayed, on a scale that could be grasped, the changes wrought by vast impersonal forces. To observe nineteenth century Newburyport is not to view New York in microcosm, but this small New England community can serve as a valuable case study of the social effects of processes which affected New York and every other American city to a greater or lesser degree.

The Transformation of the Newburyport Economy

In the opening years of the nineteenth century a series of economic disasters overtook the once flourishing port at the mouth of the Merrimack River. A rich European and West Indian trade, supplemented by fishing, shipbuilding, and commerce with the interior, had made Newburyport one of the wealthiest communities in the young republic.[2] Years of embargo, blockade, and war disrupted this foreign commerce, and European peace in 1815 permanently deprived the American neutral trader of his special advantages. A further calamity came in 1811, when a fire leveled Newburyport's entire business district, destroying 250 stores and homes. The building of the Middlesex Canal was the ultimate blow. The canal allowed Boston to siphon off the town's trade with northern New England, and interrupted the supply of New Hampshire timber used by local shipbuilders. Newburyport, wrote Caleb Cushing in 1826, "has withered under the influence of Boston."[3] The total valuation of property in the town declined by almost 50 percent between 1807 and 1815, and it was still lower in 1820. Newburyport's population fell from 7634 in 1810 to 6852 in 1820 and 6375 in 1830, while the physical deterioration of the community became a legend: "Everything grew old and rusty and dead. Nobody thought to paint a building, and there were so many of them empty that rent was nothing . . . If an old fence blew down, there it lay unless it was picked up to burn; and when a pump-handle broke, no more water came from that well."[4]

In the 1840's the dormant town suddenly awakened. After thirty years of genteel decay Newburyport became a bustling manufacturing center; its population and wealth doubled in little more than a decade. The fifth decade of the century opened with the forging of a rail link between Newburyport and Boston, and closed with the construction of a second rail line, designed to recapture the trade of the northern New England hinterland for the city's merchants. By 1850 Newburyport could boast five large cotton factories, as well as new gas works and dozens of new business buildings. Its population, static or declining for a third of a century, increased by 80 percent between 1840 and 1851; nearly 600 new houses were erected to accommodate the newcomers.

England's industrial revolution of the last half of the eighteenth century "was repeated in New England in the first half of the nineteenth."[5] Dramatic improvements in transportation, the growth of a national market, the spread of the factory: all these played a part in the transformation of dozens of villages and small towns into humming industrial cities. Only six cities with more than 10,000 inhabitants could be found in the United States in 1800; the number increased tenfold in the half century that followed. The connection between population growth and industrial expansion is suggested by the figures for Massachusetts. The population of the Commonwealth, the leading state of the union in both textile and shoe production, doubled between 1830 and 1860.

The tempo of urbanization and industrialization in Massachusetts was particularly rapid to the north of Boston, in Essex County. The striking growth of Newburyport in the fifth decade of the century was matched by Salem and Lynn, Haverhill and Salisbury.[6] The decline of shipping and maritime industries had released capital, and entrepreneurs were beginning to seize new investment opportunities in manufacturing and transportation. Residents of Essex County found a vivid portent of the future in the great dam thrust across the Merrimack River at

Deer Jump Falls in 1848. The quiet fields along the river became the site of Lawrence, a textile city of 16,000 in less than a decade.

As in England, the textile industry played a strategic role in the process of industrial transformation. An important change in the technology of textile production was beginning in the 1840's. Before that, America's only successful wool and cotton mills had used water power to drive the spindles. A handful of early experiments with steam-run mills were costly failures; in the absence of an efficient rail network coal proved too expensive to transport.[7] Under these circumstances the industrial ambitions of communities which lacked swiftly running rivers seemed doomed by the economics of location. Caleb Cushing, no man to deprecate his native town, painfully confessed in 1826 that "as Newburyport possesses no site with water power, it does not afford facilities for the establishment of those manufactories which require the application of a great moving force to complicated machinery." The entrepreneurs of the town, he reluctantly concluded, would be well advised to resign themselves to their accustomed role as builders of ships and distillers of rum.[8]

Cushing was soon proved wrong. From the 1840's on it became increasingly evident that the steam engine fed with cheap coal could provide highly economical power. The declining seaport, possessing an idle labor force and the cheapest of all forms of transportation, suddenly found itself in a strategic position. The final proof of the superiority of the steam mill came only after the Civil War, in Fall River and New Bedford, but the most important American experiment with the steam-run mill prior to the war was carried out in Newburyport.

The sudden burst of entrepreneurial energy which awakened the slumbering city in the forties was released after the arrival of America's leading prophet of the steam mill, General Charles T. James. A brilliant engineer, James came to Newburyport an evangelist in the cause of steam. He impressed his contemporaries as a man "full of power, and energy, and enterprise, who had studied machinery until he himself was one of the most powerful machines; who had been among steam engines till he was a perfect steam engine himself." James had "an influence over the opinions and purses" of Newburyport's "staid old capitalists that no other man possessed for a long time"; he left behind him, as testimony to his persuasive powers, five large steam mills, three of which he had designed and built himself.[9]

Newburyport, according to James, offered the entrepreneur three great assets: cheap raw materials, a cheap power supply, and cheap labor. A pamphlet by James, published in Newburyport in 1841 under a pseudonym, elaborated these advantages. The economies of water transportation would assure cheap coal and cheap cotton. As to the labor force, the declining port had "an abundance of help." Its residents would not move to new jobs in another city "without the inducement of high wages," but they would "readily and gladly go into mills in their immediate vicinity" at a subsistence wage.[10] Had James written a few years later, he doubtless would have heralded the rich opportunities for wage reduction afforded by the mass influx of destitute Irish immigrants.

The Bartlett Steam Mill, a rugged four-story brick building built to James's specifications, was erected in Newburyport's central business district in 1838, a few yards from the proud spire of the Unitarian Church. The

James Steam Mill followed in 1842, the Essex in 1843, the Globe and the Ocean factories in 1845. By 1850 Newburyport's five mills were capitalized at one and a quarter million dollars, and employed 1500 persons to produce eleven million yards of cloth annually.[11] In capital value the Bartlett, Globe, and James factories ranked among the forty-one largest cotton textile mills in the United States.[12]

The imposing structures which housed the five new mills, reflected one citizen, embodied an "overbearing spirit" which he found disturbing.[13] These buildings were only the most dramatic of the physical proofs that a fundamental change in the character of the community was taking place. Eight hundred and six houses had been counted in Federalist Newburyport in 1800; only twenty-six more were reported in the Census of 1840.[14] The whirlwind of new construction which increased the number of buildings in town by more than two thirds during the fifth decade of the century was a vivid measure of change. New residential housing was built at a feverish pace; six hundred homes were erected in Newburyport during the forties, most of them during the latter half of the decade.[15] In the central business district new shops, whole new business blocks, were created. At this time State Street "doffed its old exterior of small windows, carefully curtained, lest the sun or customers should see the goods intended for sale, and in their place appeared large plate glass, granite fronts, and liberal display of colors, in cheerful contrast to the old secretive way of doing business."[16] The tracks of two railroads now pierced the center of town, and there were new passenger depots, freight offices, railroad bridges.

A number of other changes signified growth and progress to the residents of Newburyport at mid-century. A telegraph office was established in 1847. A new gas company was formed in 1850, and construction began on a building to house the gasworks. A second daily newspaper, the *Daily Evening Union*, appeared in 1849 to compete with the *Herald*. The town's streets and sidewalks were greatly improved, and a program to beautify the city by planting trees was begun. Houses were given numbers for the first time in 1849.[17]

On July 4, 1850, the cornerstone for a spacious new town hall was laid with appropriate ceremony. By the time the hall was completed, a year later, Newburyport had been granted a charter as a city. Its population had grown by a third during the forties, from 7161 to 9572. An extension of the community's boundaries, taking in part of Newbury, added three thousand more to the Newburyport total in 1851.[18] In the space of a few years, a stagnant town of seven thousand had become a booming city of almost thirteen thousand. Who was to say that its growth would stop there? "You will find the place entirely changed from what it was thirty years ago," the mayor was proud to advise the "sons of Newburyport" who returned for a reunion in 1854. The city, boasted the newspaper, was "like a new place."[19]

The Situation of the Laborer

A new and bigger place, it seemed, was a better place. Yet it was difficult for the Newburyport citizen to greet with unqualified delight the social changes which accompanied the city's economic advance. The rationale given for the publication of the community's first *Directory* in 1849 was revealing. "Since the introduction of the railroad," stated the preface, "the erection and operation of cotton mills, the influx of strangers and the floating character of a portion of its inhabitants . . . Newburyport is not what it was ten, or even five years since. We have been gradually losing that social knowledge of each other's residences and occupations."[20]

The language is mild, for this loss of "social knowledge" was symptomatic of a dramatic change in the character of the community. Optimists could gaze with pleasure at the aggressive factory towers competing with the steeples of an earlier age for dominance of the skyline. But the changes in the composition of the Newburyport population and in the relationship between groups within the community which the new mills symbolized awakened troubling doubts.

These doubts took many forms, but they had as a common origin the new situation of the lower class within the community. Newspaper editors might proclaim that "the working classes" of the town "are like the body of citizens, and . . . God has neither given them riches or poverty. From this city and the surrounding country, they come from good families with the benefit of a common school education."[21] This claim, however, was too patently false to be reassuring—as any reasonably observant citizen could see. The working class of Newburyport at mid-century was not made up chiefly of natives of "good" family; the bulk of its members had not received a thorough education in a common school; and poverty was by no means a stranger to it.

The same newspaper provided a more recognizable image of the laborer when it described his existence as "a continued round of working and sleeping, and sleeping and working; and it is the life of a brute and not a man."[22] The lot of the laborer in preindustrial Newburyport, of course, had been far from idyllic; laboring occupations had been at least as brutish and degrading in 1800 as they were in 1850. What was decisively new in the community was not the depressed position of the working class, but its increased visibility and the weakening of older mechanisms of subordination and social control. The coming of the new industrial order had the double effect of making the Newburyport lower class less easily ignored and less easily controlled.

The social position of the working class of industrial Newburyport may best be understood by examining in detail an occupational group small enough to permit intensive study; the unskilled manual laborers of the city were chosen for this purpose.[23] A "laborer" is defined as any male resident of Newburyport so listed in the schedules of the United States Census. There were 191 laborers in the community in 1850, 310 in 1860—roughly a tenth of the male labor force. The common laborers ranked at the bottom of the Newburyport social hierarchy, but in many ways their situation was analogous to that of servants, operatives, and the other unskilled or semiskilled workers of the city.

What kind of work was performed by the common laborer in the nineteenth century community? No simple explanation of his function can be given. The position of the laborer, Oscar Handlin has observed, was defined not in terms of a specific function, but rather in terms of a lack of specific function.[24] The content of laboring jobs varied widely—digging, sawing wood, shoveling snow, lifting and hauling. Figures for three of the city's five textile plants reveal that they consumed 3800 tons of coal and 1,680,000 pounds of cotton annually; unloading these vast quantities at the docks and hauling them to the factories required the services of several dozen laborers.

Similarly, boards and bricks had to be carried and foundations dug for the 600 new buildings constructed in Newburyport in the forties. The Highway Department of the city provided dollar-a-day jobs for twenty-five to thirty laborers through the spring, summer, and fall.[25]

Two characteristics were constant in these laboring jobs. First, engagements were short and casual. The job might be for an hour, a day, a week. The employer could terminate it at his pleasure, and the laborer had no choice but to look elsewhere for work. Second, no skill was required to perform the task. Any reasonably able-bodied male would do. Selection was more or less at random.[26]

The level of wages paid to ordinary laborers was governed by simple Malthusian laws. European travelers during this period often claimed that unskilled labor was in short supply in America, and that the United States was a paradise of high wages for the ordinary workman.[27] This probably was true in the West; it emphatically was not the case in Newburyport at mid-century. When an employer in a city a few miles to the north of Newburyport advertised in Boston and New York papers for 200 laborers at good wages, for example, so numerous were the applicants that he was able to hire 200 at seventy-five cents a day, and that sum payable in overpriced goods from his store rather than cash.[28]

There were, of course, shortages of certain types of labor in various communities at peak seasons. But at mid-century the steady drift of farm boys into the Eastern cities and the sudden arrival of masses of Irish immigrants made the labor market highly unfavorable for the laborer. Efforts to restrict the supply and hence raise the price of unskilled labor were doomed to failure. Trade unions could be established in some of the skilled trades, for skilled craftsmen who withdrew their services from an employer could not easily be replaced. But anyone could perform the task of the unskilled worker, and usually there were more seekers after work than jobs available.

The market situation of the unskilled laborer was summed up in the experience of 100 Irish laborers who were employed in a Boston icehouse in 1847. They successfully struck for higher wages twice, choosing moments when their services were in great demand. Their third challenge to their employer—a strike in support of demands for a ten-hour day—met with a different response. The firm immediately hired 100 New Hampshire farm youths and the Irish found themselves unemployed.[29]

The famous Amesbury textile strike of 1852 revealed the same balance of power. The argument of the operatives against management was persuasive, winning them considerable public sympathy throughout the state. But the market position of these semiskilled laborers was terribly weak. They were dispensable—their jobs could be learned in a few hours by immigrants who were desperate for work and willing to accept lower wages and inferior working conditions. The same bitter lesson was administered to the operatives in Newburyport's Bartlett Mills in 1858. This first strike in the city, a protest against an increase in working hours coupled with a 22 percent cut in weekly pay, lasted a mere eight days.[30]

Emerson, observing the Irish laborers of Concord, grasped the economics of the situation perfectly: "Now the humanity of the town suffers with the poor Irish," he wrote Thoreau, "who receive but sixty or even fifty cents, for working from dark till dark, with a strain and a following up that reminds one of negro-driving." But what could be done to improve their lot "as long as new applications for the same labor are coming in every day? These of course reduce the wages to the sum that will suffice a bachelor to live, and must drive out the men with families."[31]

The annual earnings of the unskilled laborer were miserably low; precisely how low is difficult to estimate. The 1850 Census returns for Newburyport reported $1.33 as the typical daily wage for unskilled labor, and other contemporary sources indicated a range from 75 cents to $1.50. The great difficulty lies not in estimating the daily wage, but in judging how many days each year the laborer was likely to find work. The first scientific studies of unemployment and underemployment in Massachusetts, conducted in the 1870's, revealed that the common laborer generally worked no more than 230 or 240 days per year; this probably held true in Newburyport at mid-century as well.[32]

The common laborer might be thrown out of work at any time; he was nearly certain to be out of work during much of the winter. Laboring jobs were outdoor jobs, many of them difficult or impossible to perform in bad weather. There was only a limited amount of snow to shovel and wood to saw during the winter—and very little else for the laborer to do. Each winter the papers complained of hundreds of laborers loitering on street corners and in the market, "watching for four-penny jobs." The winter of 1857-1858 was particularly bad; the city's regularly unemployed workmen had assigned leaning places along the wall in Market Square.[33] Thomas Wentworth Higginson, newly appointed minister of the First Religious Society, conducted an informal investigation of poverty in Newburyport during December 1850. He reported numerous cases of able-bodied males walking the streets all day in search of work, finding "once in a fortnight a chance to saw a cord of wood."[34] It was not merely bad luck, but the structure of the labor market which accounted for cases like that of John McFeaing, a man arrested in January of 1850 for stealing wood from the wharves. McFeaing pleaded necessity. An investigation revealed that he had been unable to find work, and that his wife and four children were living "in the extremity of misery. The children were all scantily supplied with clothing, and not one had a shoe to the feet. There was not a stick of firewood nor scarcely a morsel of food in the house, and everything betokened the most abject want and misery."[35]

Want and misery, of course, had always accompanied the New England winter. The community always had its share of poor widows, fishermen at the end of a bad season, laborers without work; and these had been taken care of in time of need. Two to three hundred Newburyport citizens had customarily sought assistance each year —3 to 4 percent of the population. About two thirds of these were home-relief cases who were given firewood, food, and sometimes small amounts of cash. The almshouse existed for the less respectable paupers, particularly those with an excessive fondness for strong drink. Thus the Overseers of the Poor voted on April 9, 1827, to discharge one Jacob Cutter from the almshouse as soon as he had finished whitewashing a fence: "This by request of his wife and two sons and he promises to be temperate."[36]

At mid-century, however, the problem of poverty in Newburyport took on new dimensions. The total number of persons receiving public aid tripled between 1850 and 1851, and rose by another 241 the next year. The increase in the community's population accounted for only a small portion of the rise in applicants for relief. In 1850, 3.1 percent of the city's residents received aid; the figure for 1851 was 7.9 percent, and by 1853 it had passed 10 percent. About half of the new paupers were foreign-born; most of these were Irish who had fled from the potato famine. Despite the combined efforts of the Overseers of the Poor and the newly created Ladies General Charitable Society, the newspapers printed repeated complaints that beggars were flocking the streets, going from door to door asking alms.[37]

The typical common laborer in Newburyport earned perhaps $300-350 annually; even the fortunate laborer who found relatively steady employment could earn at most $450.[38] A single man might live on such an income, but not a family, except in conditions of dismal poverty. A defining characteristic of the life style of the unskilled laborer, therefore, was that he was *unable to support his family unassisted.* A series of case studies of Massachusetts working class families conducted by a state agency in 1875 decisively established this fact, and all the Newburyport evidence indicates that it held true there a quarter century earlier. Work performed by the laborers polled accounted for only two thirds of family income; the other third was earned by their wives and children. Almost 20 percent of the expenditures made by these families was financed by income from the labor of children under fifteen years of age.[39]

The relentless pressure of poverty—stemming from the depressed wage level for common labor and from sharp seasonal fluctuations in employment opportunities—forced the children of Newburyport's laborers into the job market at an early age. Sometimes a laborer went several weeks without earning a cent; then the four dollars a week his twelve-year-old son earned as a bobbin boy was the family's sole source of support.[40] Opportunities for formal education past the age of ten or eleven, as a result, were effectively nil for working class children. No more persistent theme appeared in the successive reports of the School Committee during this period than the low enrollment, and still lower attendance rate, in the public schools. Some statistics for 1857 provide a precise measure of the dimensions of the problem. There were 2853 children between five and fifteen years of age living in Newburyport; only 1841 of these were enrolled in the public schools, and the mean attendance at these schools was 1383; an additional 250 attended private academies. Thus roughly 750 children were not registered in school at all, and several hundred others attended classes infrequently.[41]

Equally decisive evidence to show the exact relationship between class status and school attendance is not available, but the children of the laboring class were clearly the locus of the problem. In the 1850 Census it was asked whether the respondent's school-age children had been enrolled in school at some time during the year; 40 percent of the replies by laborers were negative. Even an affirmative answer was no proof that the child was substantially exposed to the influence of the school. There was some temptation to lie to a representative of the government, who would be presumed to look with disfavor on the failure to send a child to school. In any case, a truthful affirmative answer meant only that a child had been enrolled, even if for but a single eleven-week term. Actual school attendance was fully 25 percent below enrollment, and absences by lower class children accounted for much of the truancy.[42]

A major obstacle to the education of laborers' children in Newburyport was that by 1850 a majority of them were Roman Catholic, and Protestants controlled the public school system. Teachers were Protestant, the Protestant version of the Bible was read aloud each day. It was feared—perhaps not entirely without reason—that the schools were used to lure Catholic children away from their faith. But in 1850 the Catholic community within Newburyport could not yet afford to operate its own schools. In these circumstances, many working class parents decided that no schooling was preferable to Protestant schooling.[43]

Another, more subtle, barrier further reduced educational opportunities for these children. Consider this report of an interview with an Irish laborer in the 1870's. This father of three, who had earned $442 during the previous twelve months, "never attended school, and thinks his children will have sufficient schooling before they reach their tenth year; thinks no advantage will be gained by longer attendance at school; so children will be put to work as soon as able."[44] Why a child should receive more education than his father must have puzzled many workmen. Nearly 20 percent of Newburyport's laborers reported in the Census of 1850 that they were unable to read or write; a majority of the remainder were probably no more than semiliterate.

In any case, it mattered little whether or not laboring parents were persuaded of the truth of Horace Mann's dictum that the well-educated workman "earns more money, commands more confidence, rises faster and to higher posts in his employment than the uneducated workman can."[45] Education for *their* children was simply a luxury the family could rarely afford. An encounter between a Newburyport working class family and the secretary of the Ladies General Charitable Society well illustrates the fact. The good lady had admonished the family to take their young son out of the textile mill and send him back to school, where his "true talents" might properly be developed. The family in question, reported the dismayed lady, viewed this well-meaning request as "quite as unreasonable as if we had asked of them a hundred dollars for some charitable purpose."[46] She quite failed to understand that to a family living on the margin of subsistence, the demand that a child capable of earning his keep be sent to school was precisely equivalent to a demand for a gift amounting to a fifth or a quarter of its annual income.

When a Newburyport worker could not pay for food, rent, or firewood—his children might lose their jobs at a time when he could find no work, or he might have no children old enough or strong enough to work—the options were simple: he might take charity from the government or a private association, he or his children might beg on the streets, or he might steal. The laboring family in need usually survived on a combination of these expedients.

Charitable assistance was penurious in the extreme: the city's per capita expenditure on its 1023 paupers in 1851 was exactly $7.54, and the figure for the General Charitable Society was even lower.[47] For the immigrant the prospect of going on relief was made even less attractive in the mid-fifties. A new law forbade relief to alien paupers except in a few grim State almshouses, especially designed to discourage malingerers.[48] This Massachusetts equivalent of the New Poor Law was not strictly enforced, and some humane efforts were made to counteract it—a special concert to raise funds for local relief of the foreign-born was held in Newburyport in 1856, for instance—but these were largely unavailing.

Without employment or sufficient charity, it was natural to turn to begging. The papers continued to report that "a multitude of beggars . . . daily perambulate our streets, asking alms from door to door . . . ragged children, with clothes insufficient to cover their nakedness, shivering with cold and borne down with weighty loads." The small returns of begging were supplemented with wood picked up along the wharves or coal stolen from the coal yard.[49]

In a Yankee community which prized self-reliance, one out of ten families lacked the resources to support itself the year round. This radical change was doubly distressing to old Newburyport residents because so many of the destitute were immigrants from an alien land: it was a shock when the Census of 1850 revealed that one out of seven persons living in the city had been born outside the United States. More than half of the newcomers had been born in Ireland; nearly all the rest listed England or Canada as their place of birth, and the great majority of these were of Irish parentage.[50]

Old Newburyport had been tolerant of foreigners. Ships from a dozen lands had docked there, and their crews had been well treated. Immigrants had occasionally drifted into town and settled, experiencing no exceptional difficulties in adjusting to the community. The sudden avalanche of poverty-stricken Irish which began in the late forties, however, was unprecedented. Driven from their homeland by famine, the newcomers had desperately fled to the New World. A few arrived in ships which happened to call at Newburyport; most were dropped in Nova Scotia or New Brunswick, and, drifting toward

Boston, got as far south as Newburyport before halting for a time.[51]

The newly arrived Irish brought neither capital nor useful skills. Most of these uprooted peasants lacked even the customary skills of the farmer. The agricultural system of Ireland used men as it used livestock: "All they know how to do is to dig," observed an Irish M.P.[52] Naturally the newcomers found themselves confined to menial and ill-paid occupations. Two thirds of the common laborers in Newburyport in 1850 were born outside the United States, nearly all of them Irish; the concentration of the foreign born in low-paid occupations was even more marked in 1860. "There are several sorts of power working at the fabrick of this Republic," remarked an Irish journalist: "water-power, steam-power, horse-power, and Irish-power. The last works hardest of all."[53]

Newburyport's first response to the news of the Irish famine had been generous. A series of sympathy meetings were held, at which ten large cases of clothing and $2002.07 were collected for Irish relief. Some reservoir of good will and democratic optimism still existed for the first Irish settlers in Newburyport. The Democratic paper, the *Union*, was especially eager to insist that the Irish were "quiet, industrious, and good citizens" and were making "constant advancement."[54]

These friendly voices were soon drowned out in a rising chorus of complaints against the newcomers. A series of unfavorable stereotypes of the immigrant began to recur in the press. The typical Irishman was portrayed as a shiftless laborer, noted for his "lack of enterprise, self-denial, systematic industry, and other qualities" essential to civilized living. He was usually drunk, and when drunk, exceedingly quarrelsome. Reports of a foolish Irishman downing a quart of rum on a bet and dying of its effects were a staple item. Another standard story was something like the following: "While the Roman Catholic population of England is but one out of twenty-one of the whole population, it furnishes one seventh of all the prisoners, producing three criminals where all other classes, religious or irreligious, produce but one." The next column in this issue of the *Herald* informed Newburyport citizens that thirty-eight of the forty prisoners in the House of Correction in South Boston were Roman Catholics. The *Herald* delighted in items with leads like "were it not for our Irish population, we are inclined to believe that the wheels of justice would grow rusty," or "James Enright, Daniel Leahy, and Michael Coffee, being desirous of having their names immortalized in the police record, where the names of so many of their countrymen appear." The tone of these stories varied from whimsical condescension to frightened contempt. The effect, in either case, was to build up community distrust of the newcomer, and to make immigration synonymous with the influx of "paupers, criminals, and intriguing Jesuits."[55]

The lowly status of the laborer, whether immigrant or native, was reflected in his housing. Home ownership was rare. Only 18 of the 191 laborers resident in Newburyport in 1850 owned any real property, and this small number includes some individuals who, despite their census classification, were not ordinary unskilled laborers. Peter Landsford's holdings of $3000, for example, consisted of a house and barn, several acres of arable land, and livestock. Several of these property owners in the laboring group were actually farmers who hired themselves and their teams out in busy seasons and accordingly reported their occupations as "laborer." The extent to which the purchase of a farm was a characteristic vehicle of working class social mobility in Newburyport will be discussed in a later chapter. Suffice it to say here that the overwhelming majority of common laborers in the city at mid-century owned no property at all, and that the few who did generally held very small amounts—the median figure for the group was $600.[56]

The laborer with surplus income to invest in a home was thus a rare exception in 1850. The ordinary worker paid rent each month for his lodgings. Anywhere from $60 to $100 annually might go for rent. In return, the laborer and his family had the use of a few rooms, or sometimes a small house. A state investigator's description of one tenement occupied by a Newburyport laborer suggests the quality of these dwellings. The tenement was situated on a narrow street. The rear of the house was "very disagreeable," with "the sinkwater" running through a yard heaped with ashes and rubbish. "The inside of the house is nearly as disagreeable as the outside, for the floors are bare and furniture scanty." A more lurid report, by Thomas Wentworth Higginson, described two families —one of five persons, one of six—living in two adjacent rooms. The heads of both families were out of work, and there was no money for firewood. All eleven inhabitants were consequently huddled together in one room, around a fire built of chips and shavings picked up at the wharf. In many cases the laborer's large family was increased by a pig or two, an economic but not a sanitary asset.[57]

By the mid-fifties it had become fairly common for Newburyport landlords to discriminate against the immigrants, and to advertise houses "for Americans only."[58] More important than this overt ethnic segregation, however, was the pattern of residential segregation by social

class which was taking shape at the same time. A map of
the residential distribution of laborers in 1850 shows many
streets where laborers never lived, others where they
clustered together in large numbers. The highest concentration of laboring families was in the shacks and back
rooms of Merrimack and River streets. From this central
cluster along the river the line of settlement ran up the
short streets going down to the river—Salem, Ship,
Federal, Independent, Winter, Warren. A substantial
number of laborers lived in the central business district,
above stores and warehouses. Others made their homes in
cramped cottages in short lanes or alleys near the
factories. Some of these streets—Smith's Court, next to the
James Mill, is one instance—seem to have been expressly
designed to meet the growing demand for cheap working
class housing. Closer to High Street, the finest street in
the city, the number of laborers fell sharply. None lived
on High Street itself, and few on adjacent streets.[59]

There were now distinctly "bad" neighborhoods in the
town, shunned by respectable people. The papers often
reported incidents of assaults, name-calling, and rowdyism
on these streets at night. Citizens demanded the installa-
tion of streetlights for the first time. Liberty Street was
dubbed "Misery Row," in honor of its rum shops. When
the General Charitable Society divided the city into ad-
ministrative districts, it was clearly established that poverty was not randomly distributed throughout the city, but
was, instead, concentrated in working class neighborhoods. A newspaper writer, seeking a convenient way of
labeling persons of high and low status, contrasted "persons born on High Street" with "persons born on Ann
Street."[60]

A final observation about the situation of the laborer can be made on the basis of a close inspection of Newburyport's earliest city directories. Volumes purporting to list every family in the community were published in January 1849 and January 1851. These have been compared with a list of all laborers resident in Newburyport taken from the Seventh United States Census. Fully 45 percent of the laboring families found by the diligent census-taker in September and October of 1850 cannot be located in either directory.

This was partly due to the exceptional geographical mobility of unskilled laborers; many of the missing families apparently moved into the city after January 1849 and moved away before January 1851. One of the most important features of the new industrial community was that a portion of its population was "floating," as the editor of the first local directory remarked. As we shall see later, a great many of the common laborers who drifted into Newburyport in the period 1850-1880 were unable to form a stable economic connection which could hold them in the community. Buffeted about from city to city within the New England labor market, these men were permanent transients, helpless before the vicissitudes of a rapidly changing economy.

The Newburyport laboring population, however, was not nearly volatile enough to account for all of these omissions. It is clear that the compiler of the directories either did not know about or did not choose to include many working class families in his volumes. A similar selective process influenced the contents of the local press. At mid-century men at the bottom of the social ladder were noticed only when they disturbed the peace or swelled the relief rolls. Whether the explanation of this silence be ignorance or hostility, the consequence was the same: many laborers lived in the city of Newburyport at mid-century, but they were not "members of the community."

2 · *The Problem of Social Control*

Late in 1856 the Newburyport *Herald* devoted a long earnest editorial to the topic "WHERE WE ARE—WHAT DO WE NEED?" The paper had just sponsored an agricultural fair, declared the editor, out of a longing to see the citizens have "for a day at least, a common object, a common enjoyment." Why were the men of Newburyport so separated and estranged from each other? Why were satisfying "social relations" between them "so few"? The city had "no aristocratic notions to keep the people apart," no "class pride and family dignity that make strangers of men." Yet it was "a positive fact" that "*we don't know each other.*" What was urgently needed was to "renew the spirit of former times," and nothing short of "a return to the social life of those days" was required to achieve this.[1]

This suggestive passage hints at anxieties felt by many Americans of the age. "We don't know each other"; "we have been gradually losing that social knowledge of each other's residences and occupations"; we must "renew the spirit of former times"—these became commonplace utterances as the forces of change reached into quiet villages and towns across the land. The warmth and security of a vanished organic community was an attractive image to set against the realities of the present—the factory, the immigrant, the reign of the market. Wendell Phillips, for example, sounded this chord when he recalled an idyllic New England town "with no rich man and no poor man in it, all mingling in the same society, every child at the same school, no poorhouse, no beggar, opportunities equal, nobody too proud to stand aloof, nobody too humble to be shut out."[2]

The beguiling image of such a preindustrial community was often invoked by critics of the nineteenth century city, and it has influenced such popular sociological constructs as the *Gemeinschaft-Gesellschaft* and *solidarité méchanique–solidarité organique* dichotomies. To grasp the impact of urbanization and industrialization in a particular community, however, it will be necessary to abandon cherished stereotypes and to examine historically the social life of the community in its preindustrial phase. A sketch of the main features of the Newburyport social system at the close of the eighteenth century will dispel some common illusions about the character of "the old New England town," and will provide essential perspective on the social disorganization visible at mid-century.

The Social System of Federalist Newburyport

At the close of the eighteenth century Newburyport bore little resemblance to the democratic paradise depicted by Wendell Phillips and his nostalgic contemporaries. Great wealth and extreme poverty existed in Federalist Newburyport, and opportunities were far from equal. The community was sharply divided into social classes, and it contained, in Henry Adams' phrase, "a social hierarchy in which respectability, education, property, and religion united to defeat and crush the unwise and vicious."[3] Preindustrial Newburyport was indeed a tightly knit organism, but it was integrated on an almost medieval pattern. An intricate combination of circumstances allowed the survival of older corporate forms of social organization and facilitated the rule of an elite and the subordination and deference of the lower classes.

The early settlers of Massachusetts made determined efforts to transplant older European forms of social organization to the New World. These forms included the traditional household and the institutions of "family government." The traditional household had been "an all-encompassing entity within which were united familial, religious, and economic activities."[4]

The seventeenth century Puritan family had been not only "a little church and a little commonwealth," but also "a school wherein the first principles and grounds of government and subjection are learned."[5] Every member of the community had to belong to some family, the agency through which social stability was maintained. This accounted for the wealth of Puritan legislation decrying "the dissolute lives and practices of such as do live from under family government."[6] In 1668 the Commonwealth of Massachusetts ordered each town to draw up a list of young persons living "from under family government, viz., do not serve their parents or masters as children, apprentices, hired servants, or journeymen ought to do, and usually did in our native country, being subject to their commands and discipline."[7] An Essex County court commanded a Haverhill resident, indulging in the "sin and iniquity which ordinarily are the companions and consequences of a solitary life," to settle himself promptly "in some orderly family in the town, and be subject to the rules of family government."[8] Indeed, so great was the determination to insure order through family government that the officers of the Massachusetts Bay Company, dismayed by the fact that the bulk of settlers in the early years were unmarried male servants, went so far as to create artificial families. The company informed the deputy governor of the colony in April 1629 that: "For the better accommodation of businesses, wee have devyded the servants belonging to the Company into severall famylies." It was urged that "spetiall care" be taken to select as "cheife" of each family someone with proper religious training, so that "morning and evening dutyes may be duely performed, and a watchfull eye held over all in each famylie . . . soe that disorders may bee prevented, and ill weeds nipt before they take too great a head."[9]

This pattern of household production and the system of family government based upon it showed a good deal of resilience in the New World. The Puritan attempt to build a theocracy was doomed to failure, and within a generation of the original settlement "declension" began.[10] But towns like New Haven, Salem, and Newburyport were relatively insulated from the disruptive influences of the frontier, and elements of traditional European forms of social organization remained important there down to the end of the eighteenth century. If Newburyport was in certain respects a distinctively American community by 1800, on the whole its social organization still resembled seventeenth century Exeter more than twentieth century Muncie.[11]

Roughly a quarter of the men of preindustrial Newburyport belonged to the merchant and professional class. Among them were the "merchant aristocracy," a group of less than 200 men who effectively controlled the community; the lower fringes of this class took in a variety of petty merchants, traders, and shipmasters. Below them ranked the artisans, who made up almost half of the labor force. Sharply marked off from these two groups were the "laboring poor," the laborers, servants, sailors, and vagrants who made up the bottom quarter of the population.[12]

The dominance of the merchant elite and the deference of lower status groups was insured by a number of circumstances. The fact that the household was the primary locus of activity, the absence of the separation of workplace from home characteristic of the industrial city, meant that the residential pattern facilitated control of lower class elements. The town was small—about six thousand in 1800—and its residents were packed into an area less than a mile square. The distinct class-segregated neighborhoods of the modern city did not yet exist. There were no working class ghettos, nor had the merchant and professional class abandoned the central business district as a place of residence. True, by 1800 the merchant elite had erected some of the great Federalist mansions along High Street, and an incipient slum was forming along the waterfront, with taverns and flophouses for sailors. But it is significant that Joseph Marquand, Esq., also had his home near the docks, close to Marquand Wharf. Great merchants like Marquand, William Bartlett, and William Coombs lived at or near their places of business, and shopkeepers frequently lived above their stores. Apprentice, journeyman, and master often slept under the same roof; servants and laborers lived in or near the household of their master and were subject to surveillance and discipline. If a few drifters lived entirely apart, their numbers were small and they had little effect on the affairs of the community.[13]

The church was a primary source of stability in the Federalist community. The Newburyport of 1790 or 1800 was not the ideal Puritan city "set on a hill." The pious memory of this period by a local clergyman must be discounted: "Their moral precepts were all drawn from one book . . . The Bible was read from lisping infancy to purblind decrepitude."[14] But religion was still a powerful mechanism of social integration. There was, as yet, no religious anarchy, no multitude of competing denominations. The community in 1780 contained but four churches —two Congregational, one Episcopal, one Presbyterian. The ministers of these churches were men of unquestioned elite status, and spokesmen for the entire community. Members of their congregations were seated according to social status.[15] Merchant, craftsman, laborer, and servant, each in his appropriate pew, heard sermons which identified the Newburyport social system with the will of God. The Lord had created the existing class structure, and "His providence presided over the affairs of men, to preserve the various orders, ranks, and conditions of society."[16] As Henry Adams observed, the strength of the Federalist social system rested heavily on this "cordial union between the clergy, the magistracy, the bench and bar, and respectable society throughout the State."[17]

Nor was religious performance left to individual whim; irreligion was a threat to community stability. The office of tithing man, created by the General Court in 1679, was symbolic of the mutual dependence of church and state. Armed with long black sticks tipped with brass, tithing men prowled the streets of Federalist Newburyport in search of vice and immorality, paying special attention to immoderate imbibers, disorderly children and servants, and "those who absent themselves from the public worship of God on the Lord's day."[18] "Of all the arrangements for maintaining a rigid surveillance over the habits of the people, perhaps none was so effectual" as the appointment of tithing men.[19] This office existed in Newburyport until 1838, though the institution had fallen into disuse some time earlier. Another important social recognition of "the expediency of those religious obligations which are generally supposed to hold society together" survived until 1834, when compulsory taxation for the support of churches was abolished in Massachusetts.[20]

Here was a community pattern in which every citizen was closely bound to other members of the community by familial, religious, recreational, economic and political ties. The social hierarchy was clear; a series of institutions supported that hierarchy; and the community was so compact that it was difficult to escape the vigilant surveillance of the dominant class. A historian of early Salem described preindustrial Newburyport as well when he concluded: "Everybody had a pretty clear idea of what everybody else amounted to."[21]

The hierarchical assumptions implicit in a classic expression of Federalist political thought in Massachusetts—the "Essex Result" of 1778, written by Newburyport's Theophilus Parsons—were the natural product of these conditions. "The idea of liberty has been held up in such dazzling colours," complained the Essex Result, that certain unruly individuals were no longer willing to "submit to that subordination necessary in the freeest States." These wicked radicals had forgotten the "united interest," had "fancied a clashing of interests among the various classes of men," and had "acquired a thirst of power, and a wish for domination over some of the community."[22]

The offenders who disturbed Parsons' peace of mind were not local citizens but outsiders—restless farmers from Western Massachusetts, and Boston artisans, pre-

sumably. Within Newburyport itself there was little un-
seemly "clashing of interests" to interfere with the subordination the Federalists demanded. Even the formally
democratic town meeting, where social conflict in Newburyport might have been expressed, was a major instrument of social control, bulwarking community stability
and perpetuating the system of social stratification.

That only property owners were allowed to vote in the
Newburyport town meeting was not the most important
limitation on dissent. In 1773, when only 59.8 percent of
the adult males resident in the town had the franchise,
the property requirement was indeed an obstacle of considerable significance. The great majority of merchants
and professionals could vote then, of course, but barely
half of the maritime artisans and less than 40 percent of
the laborers. But in the closing years of the eighteenth century suffrage became more widely extended in Newburyport. A lowering of the property requirement and growing
prosperity combined to make 86 percent of the town's
adult males eligible to vote in 1785, and the figure increased to 92 percent in 1807.[23]

This growth in the percentage of qualified voters, however, was of slight consequence. Democracy as practiced
in the town meeting rarely provided significant political
choices because of the Federalist institutional framework
within which it operated. When economic, social, and
religious conditions promoted the rule of an elite and the
subordination of "the lower orders," politics served largely
as a vehicle for engineering consent. To be sure, the journeyman carpenter with enough property to vote was formally free to stand up in the town meeting to oppose a
measure favored by the owner of the shipyard in which
he worked, by the minister of his church, and by the rest

of the most powerful men in the community. But the social system of Federalist Newburyport provided persuasive sanctions against the exercise of this freedom.

Local pressures for conformity produced a pattern of *deference voting*, in which the lower orders pliantly followed the lead of their superiors. Only this habit of deference voting can account for the striking unanimity with which the town meeting so often acted on the bitterly disputed issues of the day. In 1798, for example, the Newburyport town meeting passed a sharp anti-French petition "without a dissentient voice" and dispatched it to John Adams.[24] Twenty years earlier the town unanimously rejected a proposed draft of a state constitution, and endorsed instead the recommendations contained in the Essex Result.[25] The "bulk of the people" sorely lack "wisdom, firmness, consistency and perseverance," asserted the Essex Result; these qualities were reserved to "men of education and fortune."[26] A suitable constitution was defined as one which would insure the continued rule of that elite which alone was fit to rule. The conservative Massachusetts constitution of 1780 was more to the liking of the Federalists and was unanimously approved by the Newburyport town meeting, despite the fact that less prosperous men who presumably voted for it were in effect voting to disfranchise themselves![27] It is difficult to imagine a more vivid proof of the powerful social control exercised through the institutions of preindustrial Newburyport.

To what extent similar social patterns prevailed in other American communities of this period is a matter for speculation. Federalist Newburyport probably was an extreme of one type. By the time of the Revolution, New York, Boston, Philadelphia, and a few other large cities had already left this form of social organization far behind. The small agricultural towns of the interior were probably less closed and hierarchical, though a recent study of an eighteenth century Connecticut frontier town shows some important similarities to Federalist Newburyport. Early New Haven followed precisely the Newburyport pattern, and Salem seems not to have differed in essentials. Certainly hierarchy, religiously sanctioned elite rule, and institutionalized deference were not peculiar to the small New England community under scrutiny here.[28]

Social Control in Industrial Newburyport

Under the social system of Federalist Newburyport, the "mutually connected and dependent" classes of the community were bound together by a web of institutions which insured the rule of an elite and the "natural" subordination of the lower classes.[29] This social order was already beginning to disintegrate as the new century opened, but its final collapse was delayed until the 1840's, when industrialization and sudden urban growth drastically altered the composition of the Newburyport population and the relationship between the community's social groups. A new basis of order and new mechanisms of social control would eventually develop in industrial Newburyport, but at mid-century the shock of change was fresh and the new order still untested.

The greatest element of uncertainty, the source of the sharpest anxieties, was "the poor and the working classes of the city."[30] Important changes in both the composition of this group and the institutional setting impeded its integration and disturbed the patterns of "natural" subordination prevalent in preindustrial Newburyport.

By 1850 the household economy of the old community

had disappeared, and a freely fluctuating market for labor had been established. In the household-based economy even the lowliest laborer was customarily attached to a particular master. The coming of the factory and the mass influx of floating workmen brought a new anonymity and impersonality to the labor contract. General James, described by an admirer as a man who "had been among steam engines until he was a perfect steam engine himself," spoke the language of the new age when he sharply calculated the dollars and cents value of the "abundance of help" Newburyport possessed.[31] Employers had come to think less of individual laborers, more of "labor" as an abstraction, a pool to be dipped into when market conditions made it profitable to do so.

In industrial Newburyport the ordinary workman was much less subject to round-the-clock surveillance by an acknowledged social superior. He was freer to express discontent, and in certain respects he had greater cause for discontent, for his subsistence had become less certain. The sudden tripling of relief applicants at mid-century was a startling indication. The immediate cause of much of this new poverty was Irish immigration, but immigration only accelerated a process already underway. A freely fluctuating labor market was a concomitant of industrialization, and it had begun to take shape in Newburyport even before the Irish arrived. Inherent to the unregulated market economy was the problem of recurrent unemployment for the manual labor force. When market conditions became the exclusive determinant of whether a man was paid well or badly, or whether or not he found employment at all, a decisive social transformation had taken place.[32]

Doubtless the laborer's opportunity to earn a high daily

wage was better in the new industrial order—when business was booming. But the price of new prospects of gain was greater exposure to the fluctuations of the market. The common laborer of Federalist Newburyport had worked out of doors, and had also faced the problem of seasonal unemployment in bad weather. But the fixed personal relationship between laborer and master had provided a modicum of protection; the master's knowledge that the man who lived in the room over the stable had five children to feed in the winter as well as the summer was some incentive to find work for that man. The severing of this tie and the substitution of market criteria for hiring sharply intensified the problem of unemployment and underemployment. Laborers had found themselves out of work before, but never had the search for a few hours' or a few days' employment been such a frequent and desperate necessity. In a casual labor market, notes an economic theorist coolly, "the time which it takes to find a job becomes closely comparable with the time a job lasts when it is found."[33] The long lines of workers crowding the Newburyport market district when business was bad were vivid proof that whatever the fruits of progress, greater security for the ordinary workman was not one of them. Here was a fertile potential for the social unrest and "clashing of interests" which the institutions of the old community had so effectively suppressed.

The striking increase of the Newburyport population in the 1840's and the new distribution of its residents further undermined the old system of social control, which had depended on a tight network of direct personal relationships among members of the community. The mere fact that a large portion of the working class at mid-century was made up of recent arrivals to the city limited the possibilities of this kind of discipline. And the new residential pattern contributed to the same end by limiting contact among social classes. In contrast to the preindustrial community, class-segregated neighborhoods were now visible. A distinct clustering of lower class persons in certain areas of the city had occurred. The "teeming lanes and alleys" of these districts, with their floating population, were becoming unknown territory to most middle class citizens. Since less was known of the people who resided there, it was natural to view them in invidious stereotypes. Lower class neighborhoods were portrayed as breeding grounds of drinking, crime, fornication, and other immoral activities.[34]

In the old community, religious institutions had played a central role in enforcing unity and order. By 1850 three developments had impaired the stabilizing influence of religion. One of these was the growing secularization of community life. The most obvious manifestations of this trend were the new liberties taken on the Sabbath. In Federalist Newburyport, some said, it was a sin to smile on the Sabbath. In the new city, an officer of the Ladies General Charitable Society gloomily reported, individuals had been discovered washing, ironing, even repairing shoes on the holy day. Some Irish children had the temerity to play out on the street, and on Sunday evenings scores of young men could be seen prowling the downtown area "smoking the offensive cigar."[35]

Whether the secularization of the community was reflected in a decline in either church attendance or inner religious conviction may be debated, but there can be no doubt that the nineteenth century witnessed a new separation between religion and other spheres of life. The Reverend George D. Wildes accurately complained, in

1854, that "these days we are quite too much in the habit of identifying religion only with the sentiments and tastes. We practically dissociate it from its political and social relations."[36] Ministers might still enjoin their flocks to be moral and obedient, but none spoke about secular matters with the tremendous authority of their predecessors in Federalist days. The political and social power of the eighteenth century divine could survive only so long as men drew no sharp distinctions between church, polity, and economy. In the new industrial city such divisions were clear, in thought and in behavior.

Closely connected with the growth of secularism was a second change: the splintering of the religious community into a multitude of competing sects. It would be foolish to imply that a climate of religious harmony had prevailed in Federalist Newburyport, a community periodically torn by violent theological disputes. But an absence of harmony was not equivalent to a state of anarchy; the drift of the nineteenth century community appeared to be toward religious anarchy. In 1780 Newburyport had only four churches, representing three denominations: Congregational, Episcopal, and Presbyterian. In 1826 Cushing reported seven churches of five denominations. A quarter of a century later there were fifteen churches of ten denominations. During that quarter century a new church came into being on the average of once every three years! The community had become split into Baptists, Unitarians, Methodists, Congregationalists, Episcopalians, Adventists, Christians, Presbyterians, Universalists, Roman Catholics and nonbelievers—and the end was not in sight. Still more churches were founded in the fifties. When the *Herald*, in 1856, called attention to the effects of the striking proliferation of religious sects, it remarked with dismay: "If our *twenty* churches could *all* meet together . . ."[37]

A third development in Newburyport religious life fostered separation between social groups and further undermined the social system of the old community. It is difficult to imagine Newburyport's twenty churches responding to the *Herald's* appeal and meeting together, but all at least were products of a common tradition of American Protestant Christianity—all, that is, but one of them. The Roman Catholic Church, overwhelmingly the church of the new lower class, was impossible to fit into the old scheme of things. There had been but a handful of Catholic families in Newburyport until the early forties; the community had no resident priest until 1848. After that church membership increased precipitously, and within a few years Roman Catholics were the largest denomination in the city. The crowds of worshipers soon overflowed the temporary church building; even in the winter, it was noted in the press, a hundred or more of the devout could often be seen kneeling on the church steps or out in the yard.[38]

Not everyone in Newburyport took the simple view of Catholicism expressed by the carpenter who confided to his diary: "It has long been understood that the Catholicks of this country, are bound to do what they can, to put the government of this country into the hands of the Pope of Rome, there is no doubt of it."[39] There were many expressions of community sympathy and good will toward both individual Catholics and the church itself.[40] But who was certain in his heart that the carpenter was wrong? A note of fear sometimes crept into even friendly gestures. The new church was so different, so alien—and it appeared to fulfill none of the traditional social functions of religious institutions. Its leaders were not members of the local elite; they came from outside the city, usually from outside the United States. Rather than an instrument of community integration, the church seemed an agency of separation; instead of reinforcing working class obedience to the local system of authority, it extended protective isolation from the Protestant elite and directed the allegiance of its communicants elsewhere. Perhaps, Newburyport citizens began to reflect, there was "no hidden alchemy in the air of the United States" which could Americanize "Jesuitical institutions" and make them compatible with democratic ideas.[41]

Not only had the religious unity of Federalist Newburyport dissolved; the striking growth of the Roman Catholic population also signified an end to the ethnic homogeneity of the community. The Catholics were Irish immigrants, almost to a man, and the adjustment of the Irish to the traditions and mores of the New England community seemed problematical at best. Economic and social pressures, as well as their own preferences, operated to separate the Irish into ethnic enclaves. These were generally in the "bad" neighborhoods, and blame for the vice prevalent in these districts was often attached to all who resided there. The image of the Irishman projected in the press at mid-century was becoming increasingly negative and increasingly threatening.

Violations of community moral norms, by Irish and natives alike, were certainly more widespread in the eighteen-fifties than at any previous time. The old constraining network of religious, economic, political, and personal controls had become weakened; the charitable, educational, and legal institutions on which the burden of social control now fell seemed feeble substitutes. A voluntary association like the Ladies General Charitable Society, for instance, sought to police community morals, but its earnest efforts had only marginal influence. The Society's reports were sprinkled with remarks like: "An Irish woman who applied for assistance was judged unworthy after inquiries were made concerning her character, and her case was accordingly dismissed," and "one woman of Indian origin, who had long absented herself from public worship, has been induced to attend the Baptist Church." The benevolent ladies required more than cleanliness, hard work, and elevated morality from those they aided. A description of one Negro laundress, whom they evidently regarded as the ideal recipient of assistance, placed great emphasis on her passivity and sense of submission. These rigorous standards and limited funds kept the scale of the society's activities small; it reached less than a hundred families annually.[42]

Public charitable assistance was similarly aimed at inducing the poor to abide by middle class standards of behavior, and it had a much larger public to influence. But city officials did not have quite the same freedom to reward the moral and obedient and to refuse aid to the deviant. Once a person was able to lay claim to legal residence in Newburyport, it was difficult to remove him from the relief rolls. The power the official might wield against the drifting needy laborer from Vermont or Dublin, however, was great. A change in state poor legislation in the early fifties in effect restored the old "warning-out" power to towns. Paupers without an established local residence could be committed to one of the grim new state almshouses. No records which show how often the Newburyport Overseers of the Poor availed themselves of this opportunity can be located, but a sharp decline in requests for charity in 1854 and 1855 suggests the deterring effects of the change.[43]

Higher hopes were attached to public education as a means of integrating and disciplining the lower classes. "In this day of agitation and violence," the Newburyport School Committee warned portentously in 1844, the passions of the ignorant mob posed a grave threat to "the permanence of that system to which we are indebted for the security of our rights—the defense of our property, our persons and character." The appropriate "antidote for this evil" was "the diffusion of general information" to the masses; the chosen instrument of diffusion was the schools, those "moral and intellectual machines, which spin and weave the very 'warp and woof' of a well-regulated and order-loving community."[44]

Education was a means of uplifting "all classes of the population," and it served to "diminish the vice, crime and moral degradation" which resulted from "the influx of a population which has not been trained up under a system of popular education." Just how education achieved these lofty aims was little discussed. The "diffusion of general knowledge" was thought a sufficient condition of social stability. Sometimes, however, it was bluntly stated that the central function of the school was to discipline pupils to abide by the moral standards of the community without hesitation. "School days are those emphatically in which the individual is taught obedience." The failure to inculcate community norms in every pupil would result in "restlessness" and "a constant straining to escape from law" among the lower elements of society. The school was one of the few remaining pillars of order in a turbulent time; "unless . . . obedience were demanded and enforced somewhere, society could not long hold together, and would soon come tumbling in pieces around us." A proper sense of obedience and submission could not be instilled in the pupil by coddling him. The Committee had "none of that superfine confidence in the plasticity and docility of children which would always withhold corporal punishment from them ... Pupils need governing, and this, in the last analysis, always means coercing, compelling."[45]

"Popular education," however, simply was not popular enough in Newburyport at mid-century to be a powerful instrument of social control. However devoted to discipline teachers may have been, nearly half of the children in the community were rarely or never inside a classroom. The compelling economic considerations which kept the sons and daughters of laborers out of school have already been discussed. Eleven weeks of schooling each year for children under fifteen employed in manufacturing was mandatory in Massachusetts, but the statute had little discernible effect in Newburyport.[46] The task of educating working children fell largely to the Free Evening School, established by Thomas Wentworth Higginson in 1851. Supported by private donations and an occasional twenty-five-dollar subsidy from the School Committee, the school had a sporadic existence in the fifties and sixties. Dependent on voluntary teachers, it collapsed whenever the spirits of a few local reformers flagged. Even had these evening classes been held more regularly, the impact of a few dozen hours of education spread out over a year was sorely limited. Some knowledge of the rudiments of reading and writing might be imparted; the sustained influence necessary to induce children of the laboring class to assimilate middle class norms was impossible.[47]

With the breakdown of the old order and the relative futility of these new efforts, the task of establishing order in the community fell increasingly on the formal institution of social control—the law. This specialized institution was a feeble substitute for the old network of personal authority relations. For one thing, its sanctions were more distant, less immediately applicable to the offender. Furthermore, the law could be applied only against the limited number of offenses which were defined as "criminal," rather than more broadly against any breach of local custom.

A third important limitation on the social control which could be exercised through the law stemmed from the fact that in a democratic society law is supposed to represent "the will of the people." But who was to control "the people" if a majority of them were disobedient, immoral, lower class ruffians? The Newburyport resident who doubted that "a hidden alchemy in the air of the United States" could dissolve all social problems was particularly fearful of the political power which might soon be grasped by the alien mob. These dark fears were not entirely without substance, for there had indeed been a major change in the character of the Newburyport political system. In the eighteenth century community the political structure encouraged habits of obedience and deference, habits promoting stability and unity. Parties were abhorred, "factions" despised. Repeated unanimous votes in the town meeting revealed the powerful centripetal influence of local political institutions.

At mid-century the town meeting disappeared; the size and complexity which made Newburyport a city demanded a more rationalized, impersonal form of government. Voting became an anonymous act, and social constraints supporting political deference were thereby weakened. Party competition was now fierce and chaotic. The Whig party, legitimate heir of the Federalists, was the majority party in Newburyport at mid-century, but its dominance was becoming increasingly uncertain. A Democratic daily was established in 1849 to compete with the *Herald,* and the Democratic vote began to climb. Newburyport was still a Whig town, but it no longer possessed a single unquestioned hierarchy of political authority.

The competing political parties were not sharply polarized along class lines in 1850, and both were controlled by respectable middle class citizens. The Whigs attracted a disproportionate number of the oldest and wealthiest residents, but the Democrats drew none of their leaders from the lower class. Not a single laborer was included on an 1852 list of the seventy-two members of the Democratic vigilance committees in the wards.[48] The lower class was politically passive; laborers and operatives exercised their franchise less frequently than citizens of higher status. The *Union* printed a table of voting by wards in the 1851 city elections with the observation: "The smallest wards in voters are not the least populous, but the difference is occasioned by the factory operatives and foreign residents" being there.[49]

There were signs, however, of an imminent change. The local Democratic party was strongly committed to the strategy of wooing the labor vote. The *Union* was sometimes eloquent about "the rights of labor," and more sympathetic to the poor and the immigrants than its competitor.[50] The heated local elections of the fifties were certainly not expressions of community solidarity behind a political elite. Workingmen were being gradually drawn into the political arena, at a time when the old pressures to defer to their betters were weakening. Sixty Irish immigrants qualified to vote in the 1853 elections, and there were hundreds more potential voters from among their ranks. Three years later the increased participation of the laboring class may have been the factor which shifted the political balance in a furiously contested mayoralty election. "Rum and money were freely used to buy voters with," cried the Whigs.[51] The *Herald's* neighborly nostalgia for the intimate, harmonious social relations of Federalist days appeared in a new light. A savage editorial charged that Democratic demagogues had reached "down in the lowest mud to pull up the remnants and wrecks of manhood and inspirit them for the occasion." In the secure, well-ordered social system of Federalist Newburyport, the lower class could never get out of hand so dangerously. The editorialist summoned all his contempt for the new state of affairs in an imaginary dialogue: the scheming politician knocks and asks, "Does Mr. Timothy O'Flarety live here?" The Irishman "straightened up; he had never been called Mister before in his life, and probably never will be again except on 'lection day." Asked to take part in the election, "Tim looked more surprised; he had never taken part before with anybody, except in digging gravel."[52]

Most of the *Herald's* overt fears, in this case, were prompted by the Irish. But, in fact, the separation of the Irish from Newburyport life was part of a larger social process which severed the entire lower class, foreign and native, from its traditional bonds to the community. The immigrant was naturally the most vulnerable target of the stereotypes: "When the paupers, criminals, and intriguing Jesuits are poured in upon us, then let every true-blue American show all such the way they should be received."[53] The facile coupling suggested the ease with which a further equation could be made. Perhaps the impoverished and the immoral, the immigrants and the drifters, the coal porters and the gravel diggers were all part of the same *class*. If in fact only the foreign-born members of this class were, strictly speaking, "alien," in a deeper sense all were coming to be seen as alien to the traditional values of the community. Caleb Cushing's Fourth of July oration for 1850 included one revealing passage. Pleading for the preservation of the Union through compromise on the slavery issue, Cushing evoked an apocalyptic vision of the disaster which would follow a split between North and South: "And then, with productive industry paralyzed, with passions inflamed by political disasters, comes that crisis of domestic conflict" which destroyed Greece and Rome, the bloody struggle between "the *Have-alls* and the *Lack-alls*" which would end in either anarchy or tyranny.[54]

The stability and organic unity of Federalist Newburyport had vanished. The economic, political, religious, and social pillars of the old order had been overturned. A series of disturbing new problems had appeared, problems to which the experience of the community fathers provided no guide. Amidst the hundreds of utterances celebrating the increase in population and wealth, a profoundly pessimistic note was sometimes sounded. The imminent exhaustion of America's free land, it was suggested, would mean that "the great safety valve of our prosperity will be forever closed." Then, as land became concentrated in the hands of "the strongest class," "the most indolent class" would be driven off the land and forced into the cities. In the sprawling cities, "the strife of competition" would become "a hundred fold more severe," and the gulf between "exaltation" and "degradation" would grow ever wider.[55] What was to prevent Cushing's class war between the "have-alls" and the "lack-alls" from engulfing and destroying civilization?

These lurid fears rested on the premise that the "lack-alls" of America were a permanent class, with a consciousness of their separate identity and a determination to fight for their interests. But such fears were only rarely expressed by residents of Newburyport at mid-century, because few men were willing to believe that fixed social classes could exist in the United States. The condition of the working class of the community was distressing, they conceded, but it was temporary. The troubling social problems of the present could be explained away with the aid of a new ideology. The rise of the city and the spread of the factory across America was accompanied by a new social creed. According to this complex of ideas, American society was a collection of mobile, freely competing atoms; divisions between rich and poor could not produce destructive social conflict because the status rich or poor was not permanent. If society was in a state of constant circulation, if every man had an opportunity to rise to the top, all would be well.

3 · *The Promise of Mobility*

Edward Marvel, an unskilled laborer, has been without work for some weeks. After another day pacing the London streets in search of a job, he returns to his dingy rooms. "The native independence of my character revolts at our present condition," he tells his wife Agnes. There is no opportunity for the enterprising laborer in England; "every avenue is crowded." What was to be done? Readers of this story in a Newburyport paper of the 1850's might easily have anticipated Agnes' reply: "There is another land where, if what we hear be true, ability finds employment and talent a sure reward." Edward looks up: "America!" The happy couple arrange passage on the next boat, and sail away to the Land of Promise.[1]

The message of this story—the promise of mobility in the New World, where talent "finds a sure reward"—was a central cultural theme in America at mid-century. Editorials, news stories, political speeches, commencement addresses, sermons, popular fiction: for all their variety, they displayed a striking convergence on certain fundamentals. A complex of attitudes and beliefs about the American social order, the position of the working class, and the prospects for individual progress was consistently disseminated.

These ideas constituted an "ideology," a set of ideas which served to "direct activity toward the maintenance of the existing order."[2] The traditional Federalist image of society was unable to provide a satisfactory orientation to the new age. The function of the ideology of mobility was to supply the citizens of nineteenth century America with a scheme for comprehending and accommodating themselves to a new social and economic order. According to this doctrine, a distinctively open social system had appeared in the United States. The defining characteristic of this open society was its perfect competitiveness, which guaranteed a complete correspondence between social status and merit. The wealthy and privileged could occupy their superior position only so long as their performance warranted it; the talented but low-born were certain to rise quickly to stations befitting their true worth.

That this ideology was appealing and reassuring to the middle class opinion makers who propounded it is obvious. More open to question is the response of individuals at the bottom of the social ladder, persons not already predisposed to believe in the equity of the existing hierarchy. A general acceptance of the mobility ideology by the lower class would have served to integrate workmen into the social order, minimizing discontent and directing it against targets other than the society itself. The repetition of success stories would have nurtured the hope that opportunity was just around the corner—if not this week, then next; if not for oneself, then for one's children. Were belief in mobility widespread, the failure to succeed in the competitive race would have seemed proof of individual inadequacy rather than social injustice. Politically explosive resentment would thus have been transformed into guilt and self-depreciation.[3]

This is an interesting hypothesis, but to demonstrate its relevance to working class life in nineteenth century America is difficult. Direct evidence on lower class attitudes about mobility opportunities is unobtainable; dead men cannot be interviewed, and humble workmen left no written testimony behind for the historian's use. Despite these severe limitations, however, it is possible to advance some well-grounded inferences about this problem by comparing the claims of the mobility ideology with the actual mobility experiences of laborers in a nineteenth century community. The relationship between the realities of their social situation and the promises of the mobility mythology will provide some valuable clues as to the plausibility of the doctrine to ordinary American workmen.[4]

From Farm to Factory

Few of the separate strands of the mobility ideology were inventions of the nineteenth century. Many of its components had roots in an older America. Benjamin Franklin's *Advice to Young Tradesmen* had much in common with Horatio Alger's advice to the youth of his day, and even Cotton Mather penned sentences which could have delighted Russell Conwell.[5]

A sharp distinction, however, must be drawn between these early seeds and what flowered in the nineteenth century. The older conception of the "gentleman" disappeared, for example, and the rewards of success were increasingly portrayed in secular rather than religious terms.[6] Most important was the change in the frequency and intensity with which these doctrines were voiced. The mobility ideology which grew up in the nineteenth century was not a few occasional maxims, but a complex of related ideas which were expounded with passionate intensity. As such, it played a strategic role in the evolution of American social attitudes, serving to overcome certain traditional hostilities toward the city and the factory, and to allay the fears of many who saw urbanization and industrialization as a threat to American democratic values.

Thomas Jefferson's early belief that democracy depended on the agrarian virtues is well known. Commerce and industry bore with them the corruptions of Europe—teeming cities, restless mobs, massive immorality. Jefferson later took a more complicated view, and half-embraced the industrial transformation sparked by the War of 1812.[7] Nevertheless, his fears of its social effects never wholly vanished. These fears were shared by many of his contemporaries, even by some of the first important American entrepreneurs. Thus the founders of Lowell, Massachusetts, America's first great textile center, apparently believed that "the operatives in the manufacturing cities of Europe were . . . of the lowest character, for intelligence and morals." Allegedly, the question of whether "this degradation" of the laboring population was an inescapable concomitant of the industrial way of life was "deeply considered" by Nathan Appleton and his partners.[8]

The Lowell solution was a curious blend of agrarian nostalgia and commercial realism. The hunger for industrial wealth was to be satisfied without creating a permanent urban proletariat. The factory labor force would consist of a steady "succession of learners."[9] Laborers would be lured to Lowell from the countryside by high wages; after a few years in the mills they would save enough to purchase a farm out West; their place in the factory would then be taken by other newcomers from rural New England. The city and the factory were fatal to republican virtue, but only in large doses: "While most of our operatives are born and bred in virtuous rural homes, and, after working for a few years in the mills, return to agricultural pursuits, the interests of Lowell will rest secure; for, as Jefferson remarks . . . 'corruption of morals in the mass of cultivators, is a phenomenon, of which no age nor nation furnishes an example.' "10

The Lowell solution was a halfway house, not a viable rationale for a new way of life. American industry could not rest on the foundation of a labor force made up of "a succession of learners." Immigrants, small-town boys, and farm lads had to come to the new manufacturing cities to stay. The return to the countryside promised by the Lowell publicists became increasingly unlikely. If the free movement of labor was to prevent the creation of a European proletariat in America, a redefinition of move· ment in social rather than physical terms was required. Instead of heading for the Western frontier, the laborer with talent had to be urged to make his conquests on the urban frontier. High status within the urban industrial order had to be substituted for the plot of land in the West. When this was achieved, when Thomas Jefferson was assimilated to Horatio Alger, the full-fledged ideology of mobility was born.

The New World and the Open Race

The first premise of the ideology of mobility was that America was radically different from the Old World. The most striking difference was in the impact of industrialization on the common people of the two civilizations. The horrors of the Industrial Revolution in Europe were portrayed in lurid terms. Lyons and Paris, London and Manchester were filled with "ignorance," "imbecility," and "squalid misery." The peoples of Europe were generally "poor, miserable and starving." Revolutionary upheaval, therefore, could be expected in these countries at any time.[11]

Misery and anarchy, however, were not the necessary companions of industrialization. The growth of cities and the establishment of factories were not themselves evil; the problems created by the Industrial Revolution in the Old World were the result of circumstances peculiar to Europe. The mobility ideology was vague about the character of these circumstances; to label the Old World evil, stagnant, decaying was usually sufficient. But implicit in the dogma was a critique of the European social system. A society in which class barriers were rigid was unjust; economic advance, in such a setting, necessarily enriched the elite and further degraded the common people.

In old New England, said the Newburyport *Herald*, and in Europe still, "every thing depended on the accidents of family, station, and possession—the three that were blended in one, and confined to the few, while for them the masses labored and died."[12] The lowly position of laborers in England, explained a publicist from nearby Lowell, was due chiefly to the European "feeling of caste, which operates strongly to keep every man in the same social position which he has hitherto occupied . . . and children in the social position occupied by their parents."[13] Francis Bowen took the same line in his popular *Principles of Political Economy*. America had its rich and poor, Bowen observed, but these were quite unlike the gentry and laboring poor of England, for the latter were "true castes," and "nothing short of a miracle can elevate or depress one who is born a member of either."[14]

There were neither castes nor classes in America. Differences in social status could be discerned, but these were not "artificial," inherited, or permanent. America was the

Robinson Crusoe's island conjured up by the laissez-faire economists, Adam Smith's Eden. America was a truly "natural" society—a collection of millions of competing atoms, held together by enlightened self-interest. These atoms were in a state of constant motion; the never ceasing "up and down" of American communities, "like the waves of the sea," served to "purify" society.[15]

Life in America was thus an endless race open to all, one in which all began on an equal footing, regardless of social background and training. Inherited wealth or established position were only seeming advantages. In the long run, "men succeed or fail . . . not from accident or external surroundings," but from "possessing or wanting the elements of success in themselves."[16]

All contestants began the race on the same footing, but not all could be victorious. "Necessarily society has its higher and lower grades—its ruling and its ruled. When the influential are so from real merits, and their ranks are open to all, not being founded on birth or wealth but virtue and intelligence . . . it is proper and right."[17] "Virtue" and "intelligence" being unequally distributed by nature, the rewards of victory would also be unequally distributed. The chief reward was money. Wealth was the universally acknowledged symbol of superior status in the United States; Francis Bowen found it "the only distinction that is recognized among us."[18] The nineteenth century American seems to have found nothing offensive in the patent medicine advertisement which read: "The first object in life with the American people is to get rich; the second, how to retain good health. The first can be obtained by energy, honesty, and saving; the second, by using Green's August Flower."[19]

The doctrine of the open race sanctioned sharp differences in wealth and social status, for these resulted from a free and fair contest, in which superior merit inevitably triumphed. In testimony before a state investigating committee, a Lawrence operative stated the faith perfectly: "There is no reason for discontent. Every man in Lawrence is paid exactly what he is worth and no more."[20] On the other hand, there was an explicit rejection of the classic conservative assumption that virtue could be concentrated in an elite social class and transmitted by blood over generations. The mobility ideology rested on the equalitarian premise that talent was distributed at random throughout the population. This made the repeated running of the race conducive to progress; the open society could tap the energies of all its members by allowing all to compete freely.

How to Succeed—the Poor Man's Guide

The ideas of the New World and the open race constituted the basic framework of the mobility ideology; yet they were explicitly discussed much less than a more pedestrian and practical topic. The mobility creed, as it was presented to the working man, emphasized the subject of immediate personal concern: What did it take to succeed? The race was fair, and every man was "the architect of his own fortune," "the master of his fate." Choice of the appropriate virtues would insure victory. Precisely what were these virtues, and how might a working man acquire them?

The answer was, at first glance, somewhat confusing. Almost any socially desirable quality was useful in the race: honesty, sobriety, courage, charity, foresight, inventiveness, kindness, and a dozen others. Despite the bow paid to honesty, charity, and the rest, however, a closer inspection reveals a central preoccupation with two other related traits: in the practice of industry and economy lay the secret of success.

The good citizen was endlessly industrious. "Idle men and women are the bane of any community. They are not simply clogs upon society, but become, sooner or later, the causes of its crime and poverty . . . Every family motto should read: 'Be somebody. Do something. Bear your own load.' "[21] A characteristic news item, "Business First, and then Pleasure," told of a very rich man who had risen from lowly origins: "My father taught me never to play till all my work for the day was finished . . . If I had but half an hour's work to do in a day, I must do that the first thing, *and in half an hour* . . . It is to this habit that I now owe my prosperity."[22]

In an open society there could be no obstacles insuperable to the industrious man. However unfavorable the economic and social circumstances in which he might find himself, an act of will and determination could improve his situation. Dogged industry was a constant imperative: "If Washington had whined away his time after the defeat on Long Island, he would never have been victor at Yorktown; but he put himself to work to make up his losses."[23] The story of Peter the bookbinder yielded the same moral. Times were hard; Peter lost his job and was too proud to perform unskilled tasks, for that would "lower him in the social scale." Lacking the proper industry to take the lowly jobs which were available, Peter and his shopmates devoted their energies to "whining for work." Peter fortunately mended his shiftless ways, and was persuaded to take a position as a common laborer. His reward was immediate; an employer, impressed by Peter's diligence, singled him out for a superior position in bookbinding.[24]

What were the much talked-about "rights of labor," demanded an editorialist. The answer was simple. The poor had one indubitable right—the right to "labor diligently." The industrious workman who exercised this right was sure to succeed.[25]

Even more important than industry was a second trait. The central injunction of the mobility creed to the working man was the advice: *spend less than you earn and you are certain to rise in the world.* The poor were not poor because they earned too little, but because they squandered what they did earn; a rich man was simply a poor man who had learned to control his impulse to spend foolishly. Improvident workers "look out so little ahead that even though employed ten months in the year at double wages, yet if cast out of employment the other two months they would suffer. For such incapacity," it was certain, "there is no remedy—and this class of people must always be poor in dull times, and need the assistance of those to whom God has given better faculties and more powers of self-denial." The poor were poor because of their own "habits of extravagance."[26]

So great was the improvidence of the working classes that there was doubt that they were fully human. Frequent contemptuous references were made to workers' "animal impulses towards an undue multiplication of their species" and to their gross "indulgence in animal appetite."[27] The most common and pernicious indulgence was fondness for the demon rum. Drink was the single most important cause of poverty. Newspaper stories reporting the total number of charity cases in a given year frequently specified what percentage of these individuals "were reduced to poverty by intemperance"; the figure was invariably well over 50 percent.[28]

The theory of economy rested on the ascetic distinction between "artificial wants" and "real wants." The key to success was to satisfy economically one's real wants, and to suppress artificial wants. How could this be done? The mobility ideology attempted to provide a detailed answer, a manual on saving designed to show wise workingmen with "prudent wives" how to "rise above poverty and reach independence."[29]

Some of this advice was foolish, some of it cruel, setting superhuman standards of economy for presumably sub-human workers. Consider the model laborer of the story "The Mechanic's Home." Earning only $1.25 a day, the virtuous hero nevertheless supported his family in what was described as "great comfort." How? By not drinking or smoking, by not eating meat, and by keeping a small mill on which he ground his own flour, the basis of the family diet! "Go thou and do likewise," advised the author cheerily.[30] Another typical enjoinder to the laborer was the following: "Look well to the mode of spending your Sabbaths. The Sabbath is generally the most expensive day in the week to the poor who do not attend church. It is the harvest day of the stable keepers, and the patronage of the poor makes it such. The cheapest place to spend the Sabbath is in the house of God. He who cannot afford to be there can afford no other place."[31] Advice of this character served less to educate the working class than to reassure the middle class that its superior economic position was warranted by its superior morality.

The gospel of thrift, however, did not consist exclusively of such mean exhortations. A substantial amount of practical information on household management and budgeting was conveyed in mobility writing. The newspapers of the fifties were filled with stories titled something like "January Bills."[32] This flourishing fictional genre dramatized the necessity of strict budgeting of family income and prompt payment of debts. While the extraordinary rewards the practice of economy brought fictional heroes were not very plausible, the advice the stories offered about economical living was, on the whole, sensible and educational.

Two Definitions of Success

Through the practice of industry and economy, the working man could escape poverty and attain success. But what constituted success? Two different answers could be found in the ideology of mobility. The more common defined success as mobility out of the status of manual laborer. To succeed was to move into a new type of job—as foreman, clerk, manager, professional, or business owner. The enterprising laborer in the factory, it was sometimes said, might become a mill overseer, and from there rise to a high managerial position.[33] Surprisingly, however, the possibilities of upward movement within the factory hierarchy rarely captured the imagination of mid-century propagandists. A far more promising route of upward mobility, according to them, was the golden road to success via small business. Any man was free to take his chances in business. The chief difference between capitalist and laborer, after all, was that the capitalist practiced scrupulous economy and the laboring man did not. The determination to economize was an act of will anyone was free to perform, and it was the cardinal requisite for business success. The successful businessmen of America "have not become rich by earning much, but by saving little, and then a little more, and then a little to the end of that."[34]

Francis Bowen outlined the transmutation of workmen into businessmen. To save "small sums"—even fifty cents a month—was the first step. If these pennies were not allowed to "dribble away," the accumulation of interest over the years transformed them into capital. The workman could then invest in tools, machinery, or "a stock in trade," and venture out on his own. Returns of 10 to 12 percent per annum were almost certain to follow; the original stock of capital hence would double every six or seven years. The happy result of the process was that "he who began life as a common laborer, often drives about in his own carriage before its close . . . At least half of the wealthy men in Boston," added Bowen, "rose thus."[35] Success was thus occupational mobility.

A second definition held out a more modest reward to the enterprising laborer. Instead of asserting that the laborer was perfectly free to change his occupational status, this doctrine redefined status. Whether a man worked with his head or his hands, for someone else or for himself, was no longer the chief determinant. The criterion became whether or not he owned property. Saving money was a prerequisite for occupational mobility, accordingly to the first theory; to save money was itself to change status, according to this one.

This is what John Aiken meant when he said that in America "almost every free laborer has begun to be a capitalist as soon as he has begun to labor."[36] The term "capitalist" was broadened to include any man, whatever his occupation and income, who owned property or had a savings account. Even $100 in the savings bank was considered capital, and its owner was something more than a mere laborer. There was a lower class in America, conceded one writer, but as soon as "a man has saved something, he ceases to belong to this class."[37] The propertyless lower class man was in fact "but half a man." By contrast, "the man who owns the roof that is over his head and the earth under his dwelling, can't help thinking that he's more of a man than though he had nothing, with poverty upon his back and want at home; and if he don't think so, other people will."[38]

Local Boy Makes Good

According to a story cherished in Newburyport folklore, the distinguished Federalist lawyer Tristram Dalton sought one day to have his carriage repaired. An enterprising young carriage maker, Moses Brown, surprised the town by refusing to wait for Dalton's servant to haul the carriage to Brown's shop. Impatient to begin work immediately, undismayed at getting his hands dirty, Brown repaired the carriage speedily and efficiently. Such virtue, of course, found reward. Dalton died not long after; his son squandered the fortune he had inherited, while Brown scrimped and steadily added to his capital. In a few years, Brown became one of the wealthiest men in Massachusetts; soon he purchased the old Dalton mansion on High Street, where he lived until his death.[39]

Such stories had a central place in the ideology of mobility. Persuasive as the exploits of a fictional hero or the exhortations of an editorialist might be, nothing lent greater plausibility to the creed than the dramatic instance of local success which seemed to prove that it could happen here. Newburyport opinion makers were fully aware of the possibilities Russell Conwell exploited so shrewdly on his lecture tours across America during this period. There are "acres of diamonds" to be found "in this city, and you are to find them," Conwell told more than six thousand audiences, accumulating a fortune in lecture fees.[40] The Newburyport papers labored to supply Conwell with numerous footnotes on this theme.

A typical report told of one Balch, who bought a seemingly worthless stony field not far from town and managed to farm it profitably. If Balch could wring a good living from a few acres of sand and stone, any poor laborer could surely do likewise. Better land in the vicinity was available for a song. "There are hundreds of poor men in Newburyport who might, if energetic," provide a comfortable income for their families in this manner. "Energy and industry is all that is needed."[41]

A commencement address by the editor of the *Herald* was sprinkled with examples to prove the same point. The door of opportunity was open, in politics as in business: "The men who govern the world are those who when boys went barefooted, wore ragged trousers and crownless hats." This was true at every level of power: "We nominate a railsplitter for President, we have a bobbin boy for governor, a shoemaker for Senator, and a brick-layer for mayor—men who have made themselves by their own energy and skill."[42] In the same vein was a paean to two of the richest men in town: "They were both men of humble origin, and thrown early in life on their own resources. They were . . . architects of their own fortune . . . men of integrity, industry, and of indomitable perseverance, and they succeeded—of course."[43]

The conclusion of a popular study of *The Rich Men of Massachusetts*, published in 1851, seemed definitive proof that opportunities for social elevation were abundant in Newburyport. After listing thirty-seven local citizens who possessed more than $50,000 worth of poverty, the authors of this study asserted: "Unlike what we might naturally expect of this ancient town, very little of its wealth comes by inheritance, or accident of any kind. Almost all the names in the preceding list belong to persons once poor, of the common people, and, in not a few instances, from the lowest walks of life. They are the artificers of their own fortune."[44] The local papers gave enthusiastic reports of these conclusions.

The fluid social structure of Newburyport was considered the guarantee of stability and prosperity. The "mighty change" in the character of the population caused by immigration and economic change would not be destructive, for equal mobility opportunities were open to all. A bright future could be predicted for children born in even the worst sections of the city. It seemed quite possible that "the proportion of persons born in Ann St. in 1853, that shall become learned, and useful, and wealthy by 1883, will not fall below those born at the same time on High St." The Tom MacDonalds and Patrick O'Harrigans would "doff their old hats, and knock off their linsey woolsey," and emerge as "Captain Thomas Donald, and Patrick Harrigan, Esq."[45] Anyone could emulate the example of Moses Brown. This was the promise of mobility which Newburyport held out to its working men.

Environment and Institutions

Distressed by the lack of community facilities in Newburyport, a local writer printed a short story designed to dramatize "The Influence of Public Libraries." In the first section he described two youths; lazy and shiftless Tom, and Frank, a teacher's pet with pure morals and high ambition. Ten years later we find the two young men again. Shiftless Tom has been "gradually ascending the social ladder," and is now considered "one of the most promising young men around here"; Frank is in jail! What was the explanation? It was all a matter of environment. Tom happened to become apprenticed to a master in another town, where the public library was "the favorite resort of the young men," and this healthy influence transformed him. Frank, by contrast, was unable to find a sufficiency of good books and respectable companions. He kept low company, married a slovenly woman, and was dragged down into poverty and oblivion.[46]

The story is extremely significant, for it suggests a major complication in the mobility ideology. Here were some of the basic elements of the mobility creed woven together so as to lead to reformist conclusions quite different from the harsh laissez-faire ideas surveyed above. The point is important, for it has often been implied that an acceptance of such notions as the New World and the open race dictated a monolithic Malthusian attitude toward specific problems, such as the treatment of the poor, government welfare, and educational activities. In fact, however, there was some diversity and flexibility of opinion about these matters in Newburyport at mid-century. In addition to the usual hard version of the mobility ideology, a more humane interpretation of this creed was sometimes advanced.

Consider attitudes toward the problem of poverty. For many Newburyport residents, the logic of the mobility ideology led to a "just deserts" rationalization. The matter was simple, according to a local editor: "We declare it a vice and a sin for a man to be poor, if he can help it." And the typical poor man in America could help it. It was "not a want of means, but a want of will—of real manliness and self-control" which accounted for the bulk of poverty.[47] The "deserving poor"—old maids, widows with young children to tend, and workers seriously ill—might legitimately request outside assistance if suitably moral, frugal, and temperate in their habits. But only a fraction of the applicants for charity actually met these criteria. There was grave danger that indiscriminate aid would tempt many strong but slothful men into a life of pauperism. The community must be ever vigilant, lest these morally weak people take advantage of its generosity. The *Union* solemnly disclosed that handbills announcing "Massachusetts is a paradise for paupers" were being circulated in Europe.[48] The Manchesterian arguments which produced the English New Poor Law were echoed in support of the new policy of sentencing paupers without local residence to state workhouses.

Such was the predominant view of poverty in Newburyport at mid-century, but it was by no means the only view. It was occasionally suggested that social obstacles—the fluctuating labor market, for instance—unfairly hampered worthy laborers in their struggle against want, and that a more generous and helpful attitude toward the poor was appropriate until the "defective state of society" could be remedied. Men were sometimes enmeshed in "a web of circumstances" which effectively limited their opportunities to better themselves.[49] "Had the birth and training of many who occupy respectable positions in society been as unfortunate as many of those who are objects of charity or slaves of sin," asked a report of the Ladies Charitable Society, "would they have risen superior to the circumstances which surrounded them and become useful and valued members of society?"[50] A thoroughgoing environmentalism, of course, would have contradicted too many basic assumptions of the mobility ideology to be acceptable. No one thought of denying entirely the ability of the individual with strong character and resolute will to master hardship. Yet at times the community seemed to be groping toward recognition that environment and institutions could significantly increase or limit the possibilities for individual mobility.[51]

Should this deviation from the "just deserts" theory of poverty be considered an abandonment of the mobility ideology? To argue this is to take too narrow a view of the nineteenth century mobility creed.[52] It is a mistake to suggest that from a few general premises about the American class system a single attitude toward a concrete problem could always be deduced. On the problem of poverty, for instance, the "just deserts" theory was the most common, but not the only possible position which the adherent to the mobility creed might take.[53] The mobility ideology did not hold that all societies at all times gave genuinely equal opportunities to all men; the race was thought truly open only in the New World at a specific point in its history, a point at which two sets of conditions were fulfilled. First, the absence of European fetters on the individual—monarchy, aristocracy, feudal customs—was necessary. Second, and less obviously, the mobility ideology assumed the presence of certain American institutions which facilitated individual mobility. Even the most extreme proponents of the hard version of the mobility doctrine, after all, were not anarchists. They recognized, at a minimum, that good government was necessary to insure stable conditions under which the race for success might be conducted. If government, why not public schools to help American youths compete more effectively, public libraries to do the same for adults, even welfare programs to alleviate the effects of poverty and give a fresh start to the unfortunate? A whole series of questions was raised by even the partial admission that positive public action could sometimes make an open class system operate more smoothly and equitably. The door was open to the argument later formulated by Theodore Roosevelt when he asserted that "the present rules" under which the race was run were unjust, and that these rules should be changed to promote "a more substantial equality of opportunity."[54]

Within the broad framework of the ideology of mobility, in short, there could be debate over what measures were necessary to maintain an environment conducive to individual mobility. Extreme conservatives might call for a laissez-faire "policeman state"; reformers could derive support from this same creed for various kinds of institutional changes.

The concrete proposals of reformers in Newburyport at mid-century were admittedly mild. They urged a more generous attitude toward the relief of the poor, suggested provision of public employment for unemployed workers, and placed great hopes on the uplifting effects of a proposed community center and reading room for education and recreation. By far the most important agency of improvement (as well as the least controversial), felt the reformers, was the public school system.

The career of Horace Mann reveals how easily the mobility creed could be exploited in a campaign to extend and democratize the educational system. At a Lyceum lecture in Newburyport in 1845, Mann launched a violent attack on the principle of "caste" in English life. The absence of social mobility, resulting in stagnation and exploitation, he attributed to "the systematic denial of the means of knowledge to the common people," who were "compelled to drudge as beasts of burden for the

wealth and pleasure of the highest classes."[55] Four years
later, Mann coupled the same indictment of the English
class system with the charge that class stratification was
becoming dangerously rigid in Massachusetts. "The distance between the two extremes of society is lengthening
instead of being abridged"; a new industrial feudalism
was taking shape. His solution, as always, was to perfect
the system of universal education: "If education be
equably diffused, it will draw property after it," thereby
preventing the establishment of permanent class divisions.[56]

The school was the chief instrument by which society
equipped its citizens with the skills and values necessary
to compete effectively. By it "the key is furnished which
opens every secret shut up in books, and this is the main
thing which the individual can demand of society. Open
the doors of knowledge to all, and those who have the
capacity and the ambition will do the rest for themselves."[57] Within the school, every pupil was free to
develop his talents to the fullest. "The goal has been
pointed out," remarked the School Committee proudly,
and the students "have entered the race, aware that the
prize was equally before all, and attainable only by
personal exertion."[58]

A surprisingly pessimistic corollary was implicit in this
line of argument. To insist that it was essential for "the
doors of knowledge" to be open to all was also to say that
those to whom the doors of knowledge had been closed
competed under a severe handicap. It would have been
heretical to explore the full implications of this idea, but
some recognition of it appears in much of the contemporary writing, particularly in the distinction often drawn
between intra-generational and inter-generational mo-

bility. In discussing the Irish working class, writers frequently distinguished between the situation of "the present generation" and the possibilities open to the next generation.[59] As the old Newburyport families decline on the social scale, they said, "the teeming lanes and alleys will send their sons and daughters to take possession of their empty mansions on the upper streets."[60] The pressures of environment, in other words, might so stifle an illiterate laborer that the promise of mobility was really meaningful only for his children. The laboring parent still had an important function to perform, in providing his children with a suitable home environment to nurture and cultivate the traits conducive to success; but to the first generation the rewards of mobility would be largely vicarious. A promotional book on *The Irish in America* was careful to say that in the New World "the rudest implements of labour may be the means of advancement to wealth, honour, and distinction, *if not for those who use them,* at least for those who spring from their loins."[61] The mobility creed remained an essentially optimistic and individualistic doctrine, but this version of it was considerably chastened by its recognition of the potent influence of environment and institutions.

A restatement of the mobility ideology by a great Irish-American orator revealed a similar modification through experience, less in its explicit claims about opportunity than in its selection of imagery. America was no longer a race track but a crowded corridor, in which there was "no turning back": "Some in this crowd may have their pockets picked or their ribs broken, or their corns trampled; but they must go on, with ribs broken or pockets full or empty. The rich and poor, the weak and strong, the native and the stranger, are all thrown mercilessly upon themselves, in the Common School of American experience."[62]

The bitter experience of the Irish sometimes provoked graver doubts, calling into question the validity of fundamental tenets of the mobility ideology. "If the school of adversity is the best place to learn," observed the Boston *Pilot* dryly, "few will be disposed to question the great opportunities enjoyed by us to acquire a knowledge of mankind."[63] On the basis of knowledge gained in "the school of adversity," the paper mounted an assaut on the myth of America as "the paradise of the poor man." Just how was the lot of "the poor man in America superior to the poor man in Austria or Italy?" The trinity of poverty, misery, and vice had been exported to the United States with eminent success. The braggart's "boastful tongue is silenced . . . in hard times like these." And even in times of great prosperity, not more than "five or ten out of a hundred may rise in the world, while the ninety-five will live and die in the condition in which they were born."[64]

Perhaps the social problems of the new age were not merely temporary disturbances, momentary interruptions in the steady upward march toward equality and abundance for all. Perhaps, in the New World as in the Old, a portion of the community was fated to live as a permanent degraded class. Perhaps, in short, the promise of mobility was an illusion, a deception.

4 · *The Dimensions of Occupational Mobility*

John R. Fowle was an ordinary workman of Newbury-port, nothing more. Born in New Hampshire in 1802, Fowle was listed variously as "laborer," "gardener," and "porter" in the census schedules and local city directories of the 1850-1880 period. Nor did he display any great talent for saving money; the census and the tax assessor's records show him without any property holdings during these years. Fowle had five daughters and four sons; none of them received much education. Two of the sons left Newburyport while still youths. A third started work as a common laborer, but after a few years of unskilled labor, and a few more as an operative in a shoe factory, he was able to open a small grocery; the shop was rented, and his inventory was valued at $300.

John Fowle's youngest son, Stephen, had a more striking career. Where he obtained the capital for his first venture into business is unknown. In 1856, a lad of twenty-two, he paid only a poll tax. Two years later tax records show him the owner of a house and lot valued at $1100, and the city directory lists him as a "newsdealer." His news agency prospered, and Stephen was willing to take risks. He sold the house for $1250 in 1862, and looked for new possibilities. Not long after, with the aid of $4500 borrowed from the Institution for Savings, he entered into a series of transactions which gained him a home just off the best residential street (High) and a shop on the main business thoroughfare (State). His real estate holdings reached $8000 by the time of the Census of 1870; his inventories of periodicals, fruit, and sundries approached $2000. The Fowle store is still doing well on the same site after ninety years, though the family itself has disappeared from the city.

Michael Lowry, born in Ireland in 1815, came to the New World in the great exodus following the famine. Lowry settled in Newburyport in the late forties, and worked there as a day laborer the rest of his life. His eight sons were put to work as soon as they were able, but the family remained propertyless, living in rented quarters along the waterfront. One son, James, had a minor success; he saved $450 out of his wages as a mariner to purchase a house. None of the other children appear to have advanced in the slightest; all were unskilled laborers or seamen in 1880, lacking property holdings or savings accounts. Thomas Lowry did embark on certain ventures which might have produced a considerable income, but his brief career as a housebreaker ended with five years behind bars.

Pat Moylan was one of the few laborers in Newburyport who owned his own home in 1850. Moylan too was Irish, but he had immigrated to America well before the Great Famine, and had married a native-born girl. His successes over this thirty-year period were moderate, but they were sufficient to allow his children greater career opportunities than was common at this social level. Sometime in the 1850's Moylan found the job he was to hold until his death—night watchman at a textile mill. If his daily wages were not much higher than they had been as a common laborer, he was now sure of steady employment. His Olive Street home, valued at $700, made it unnecessary to pay out a large portion of his income in rent; he reported an additional $300 in personal property on the Census of 1870. Moylan's children were freer than most of their companions from compelling pressure to enter the labor market at the earliest possible age. Two of his five daughters graduated from the Female High School, a rare achievement for a working class girl at this time. Moylan's eldest son became a factory operative at sixteen, but during the Civil War decade acquired the skills of a blacksmith. Albert and James entered more promising situations; one was employed as a clerk in a cotton mill in 1880, while the other was still studying at Brown High School.

William Hardy, like John Fowle, was a native-born day laborer; like Fowle, Hardy never succeeded in accumulating any property. Hardy's two eldest sons did little better; one became a seaman, the other a factory operative. His two younger boys, however, were able to move into a skilled manual calling. Neither James, a machinist, nor Frank, a molder, could claim any property holdings in 1880, but each had entered occupations with earning opportunities well above those for unskilled labor.

The families of Michael and Jeremiah Haley achieved impressive property mobility without any occupational mobility at all. Michael and Jeremiah were recorded as common laborers in the Eighth, Ninth, and Tenth United States Censuses. In 1860 Michael owned property on Monroe Street worth $700; Jeremiah had none. In 1864 Jeremiah, who had three young children working to supplement his income, bought a half share in the Monroe Street house for $400; Michael used this sum to purchase another lot. Michael added steadily to his holdings; by 1880 he paid taxes on $1700 in real estate. In 1870 Jeremiah sold his half share back to Michael, and invested in a larger place on Dove Street, valued at $900 in 1880. The two brothers between them had five sons, none of whom entered any skilled or nonmanual occupation. One of Jeremiah's sons, Pat, did save enough money to build a small house next door to his father's, but he too remained but an ordinary unskilled manual laborer.[1]

These few sketches make one thing quite clear. The situation of the hundreds of Newburyport residents ranked common laborers on the United States Census of 1850, 1860, and 1870 had seemed bleak: these men and their families shared a common plight as members of the lowest social stratum in the community. As these cases reveal, however, not all of these families remained at the very bottom of the Newburyport social ladder. Some, like the Lowrys, were trapped in poverty and illiteracy; others were socially mobile in a variety of ways. This much can be established by examining the life histories of a few families. But a handful of instances cannot reveal what *proportion* of the laboring population of Newburyport reaped the benefits of social mobility, nor can it indicate what *avenues* of social advance were of particular significance to the working class. Perhaps the Lowry family was typical, and the Fowles a curious exception; perhaps the embittered editor of the Boston *Pilot* was right that 95 out of 100 workmen in America were fated to "live and die in the condition in which they were born."[2] Or was Stephen Fowle a representative man, an example of the opportunities open to a wide segment of the working class? To answer the question requires a statistical analysis of social mobility.

Social mobility refers to the process by which individuals alter their social position. But to say this, unhappily, is to say nothing until social position has been

defined. The terms social status and social class raise
perilously complex and disputed problems of definition.
A brief comment at this point will clarify the approach
taken here; the subject will be considered further in a
later chapter. One major sociological school—represented
by W. Lloyd Warner and his followers—emphasizes the
prestige dimension of class; the study of social mobility
becomes the study of the subtle "climbing" tactics by
which the ambitious manipulate others in an effort to improve their prestige rank. Status is measured by polling the
community social elite; great emphasis is placed on the
intricacies of etiquette. Whatever the merits of this subjective approach to social class and social mobility, it is of
little value to the historian, for historical records rarely
yield the information necessary to apply prestige categories systematically to societies of the past.[3]

The historical study of social mobility requires the use
of objective criteria of social status. The most convenient
of these is occupation. Occupation may be only one
variable in a comprehensive theory of class, but it is the
variable which includes more, which sets more limits on
the other variables than any other criterion of status.[4] An
analysis of the occupational mobility of unskilled laborers
and their sons in Newburyport, therefore, is an appropriate starting point.[5] But such an analysis must take into
consideration the changing composition of the Newburyport laboring class.

Men on the Move: The Problem of Geographical Mobility

Observers of cities have too often treated the modern
community as a self-contained entity with a stable population core. A city like Newburyport, whose total population has varied little in the past century, is particularly

conducive to such illusions. It is hardly surprising that Lloyd Warner's volumes on Newburyport social life miss the significance of migration in and out of the community and view social mobility exclusively as a reshuffling of its inhabitants into different social classes.

A careful scrutiny of the composition of the Newburyport laboring class in the 1850-1880 period suggests how misleading the myth of stability can be. The most common, if most easily overlooked, form of mobility experienced by the ordinary laborers of nineteenth century Newburyport was mobility out of the city. Slightly less than 40 percent of all the unskilled laborers and their children living in the community at mid-century were still listed there in the Census of 1860; of the 454 men in this class in 1860, but 35 percent were to be found in the city a decade later; the comparable figure for 1870-1880 was 47 percent. (Local health records indicate that deaths accounted for few of these departures.) The first generalization to make about the "typical" Newburyport laborer of this period, it appears, is that he did not live in Newburyport very long! Contemporary observers were correct in characterizing the new working class as floating. For a majority of these permanent transients, Newburyport provided no soil in which to sink roots. It was only one more place in which to carry on the struggle for existence for a few years, until driven onward again.

Even before the effects of occupational and property mobility are taken into account, therefore, it is evident that Newburyport did not develop a degraded proletarian class with fixed membership in the 1850-1880 period. The founders of Lowell had thought of the factory labor force as being made up of "a succession of learners"; to a striking extent this was true of the lowest stratum in

Newburyport. A large and steady stream of working class men poured out of the community during these years. Their places were taken by masses of newcomers. Ireland was a continuing source of fresh unskilled labor throughout this period; a smaller but still important group came from the stagnant farms of Vermont, New Hampshire, and Maine. These streams of migration in and out of the community resulted in a turnover of more than half of the local unskilled labor force each decade.

Two of the chief social trends of nineteenth century America—the mass influx of immigrants from the Old World, and the drift of population from country to city—thus appear on our small stage. This volatile society made a hero of the man on the road, heading for the Great West or the Great City.[6] And American folklore equated movement with success—the hero was on the make as well as on the move. A few shreds of evidence from recent sociological inquiries support this old belief that geographical mobility and upward social mobility are positively related, but whether the myth had any foundation in fact in nineteenth century America is unknown.[7]

This whets our curiosity about the subsequent career patterns of the hundreds of laborers who worked in Newburyport for a short time in the 1850-1880 period and then moved on. It is quite impossible, let it be said immediately, to trace these individuals and thereby to provide a certain answer as to how many of them later won fame and fortune. Without a magical electronic device capable of sifting through tens of millions of names and locating a few hundred, there is no way of picking out former residents of Newburyport on later national censuses. We do know something, however, about the experiences of these men in Newburyport, about the circumstances in which they departed from the community, and about the New England labor market at this time. On the basis of this information we may venture certain inferences about their future with a degree of confidence.

In only a handful of all these cases was the laborer migrating from Newburyport in a particularly strategic position to take advantage of new opportunities in another community. For instance, if the son of a laborer, unencumbered as yet with family responsibilities, was fortunate enough to possess a substantial savings account and perhaps a high school education or some experience in a skilled or nonmanual occupation, his employment prospects after migration were obviously excellent. Such cases, however, were rare. The great majority of laborers who left Newburyport departed under less auspicious circumstances. Without financial resources, occupational skill, or education, frequently with heavy family responsibilities, the range of alternatives open to these men in their new destination was slender. Laborers like these were not lured to leave Newburyport by the prospect of investing their savings and skills more profitably elsewhere; they left the city when the depressed state of the local labor market made it impossible for them to subsist where they were. As a result of the collapse of 1857, for example, Newburyport suffered a population decline estimated by the *Herald* at "more than one thousand." Most of these departures, it was thought, were cases of workers moving to "locations where work is more abundant."[8]

That the geographical mobility of such laborers dramatically improved their opportunities for upward social mobility seems highly unlikely. The telling objection which has been advanced against the famous "safety valve" theory of the frontier applies here.[9] Migrant laborers from the city rarely had the capital or the knowledge necessary to reap the benefits of the supply of "free land" at the frontier. It seems to have been largely artisans, schoolteachers, farmers, and unsuccessful businessmen who sought their fortunes in Illinois wheat or California gold. The Newburyport newspapers of the 1850-1880 period reported but a single instance of a local laborer who successfully settled in the West, and his was not a case of which Horace Greeley could be proud. The *Herald* of June 22, 1878, carried news of a letter from one Michael Welch, then in Nevada. Welch, the son of a local laborer, had been the treasurer of one of Newburyport's volunteer fire companies; when he left for the frontier he took the treasury with him! Welch advised his parents that he was doing very well in Nevada, and would soon repay the stolen funds. Few workmen in the city, needless to say, found capital to finance a trip west so readily available.[10]

Neither were laborers migrating from Newburyport likely to discover acres of diamonds on the urban frontier. The community fell within the orbit of Boston, which became a great industrial center in the middle decades of the century partly because of the vast reservoir of cheap labor provided by immigration. The unskilled labor market which was centered in Boston included Lowell, Lawrence, Lynn, and smaller cities like Newburyport and Chicopee. There was a high rate of labor mobility from city to city within this market, the flow varying with local fluctuations in the demand for unskilled workers.[11] In these circumstances, differences not only in wages and working conditions but in promotion opportunities as well probably were marginal. Certainly it is doubtful that a workman without capital or skills would have found it markedly easier to advance himself in Boston than in Newburyport. The great metropolis offered alluring opportunities at the top to those with the proper requisites, but to the common laborer who drifted there from Newburyport it probably meant only more of the same. Indeed, occupational opportunities for the unskilled may have been somewhat less in a great city like Boston, where many of the most helpless and destitute members of the working class tended to cluster.

The social mobility study described below necessarily gives disproportionate attention to the settled minority of workmen who remained within the community for a decade or more and whose careers could therefore be traced. It is highly improbable, however, that our lack of precise knowledge of the later careers of migrants from Newburyport has led to an underestimation of the upward mobility eventually achieved by laborers in the sample. The circumstances in which they departed and the character of the unskilled labor market in New England make it unlikely that large numbers of these workmen were more successful in their new places of residence than were their counterparts who remained in Newburyport.

An inquiry of this kind, in fact, is biased to some degree in the opposite direction. To analyze the social adjustment of workmen who settled in a particular city long enough to be recorded on two or more censuses is to concentrate on laborers who were most resistant to pressures to migrate, and these tended to be men who had already attained a modicum of economic security in the community. Thus four fifths of the local unskilled laborers who owned real property in 1850 were still living in

Newburyport in 1860, a persistence rate of 80 percent; the comparable figure for propertyless laborers in this decade was 31 percent. Migration was, in this sense, a selective process. Masses of unskilled newcomers—from rural areas and from abroad—streamed into the nineteenth century city. Large numbers of these men were unable to establish a secure place for themselves in the community. Unemployment was always a possibility, and all too often a grim reality. When jobs were too few to go around, the rumor of work in Lawrence, or Lynn, or Holyoke was enough to draw these men on. Workmen who remained in Newburyport for any length of time were therefore a somewhat select group, because to find sufficiently stable employment to maintain a settled residence in a community was itself success of a kind to the laborer. In tracing the changing social position of groups of Newburyport workmen we must keep this relationship between geographical mobility and social mobility clearly in mind. The process of internal migration within the unskilled labor market removed many of the least successful laborers from the community; the following analysis of occupational and property mobility in Newburyport applies primarily to a settled minority from the total unskilled laboring population which passed through the community between 1850 and 1880.

The Nature of the Occupational Hierarchy

To speak of occupational mobility presupposes the social gradation of occupations, a gradation implied in such phrases as the social ladder and the occupational pyramid. The question we should now turn to is, in effect, how to justify the use of these metaphors in a specific historical context. The sociologist is able to go about this task more directly than the historian; by various polling devices he may ask the members of the society he studies how they rank various occupations.[12] While the historian may extrapolate certain of these findings back into the past, he must rely chiefly on indirect evidence to support his judgments as to the nature of the occupational hierarchy.

The occupational classification scheme used in this study is simple, designed to make possible some immediate generalizations from the census data. Occupational mobility is defined as a move from one to another of the four broad categories: unskilled manual occupations, semiskilled manual occupations, skilled manual occupations, and nonmanual occupations. Moves within these categories, involving more subtle changes in status, will be ignored for the present; they will receive some attention at a later point.

The superior ranking of nonmanual occupations seems incontestable. Status differences between manual and nonmanual callings have narrowed somewhat in recent years, with some overlapping between highly skilled manual jobs and certain routine nonmanual occupations. In the nineteenth century, however, the gulf between the two was wide. The annual income of the ordinary white collar worker was at least twice that of the typical laborer.[13] Newburyport papers of the period spoke of "the general belief" that manual work was undesirable; it was often complained that far too many young men were irrationally eager to become clerks and professionals, that not enough were willing to learn a secure manual trade.[14]

Within the broad category of manual labor, three levels of occupational status must be distinguished. If the social distance between these three was less than that between manual and nonmanual occupations as a group, status distinctions within the working class occupational world were nonetheless important. At the top of the manual laboring group stood the skilled craftsmen, artisans, and mechanics—carpenters, caulkers, sailmakers, master mariners, tailors, butchers, and so forth. (Some Newburyport artisans in this period were self-employed and owned significant amounts of capital; these were considered small businessmen and placed in the nonmanual category.) Certain of these trades were prospering during these years, while others were declining from changes in technology and market structure. Even the stagnating trades, however, remained markedly superior to other sources of manual employment. The artisan possessed a special skill; he had a "vocation," a "calling," rather than a mere "job." His earnings, as Tables 1 and 2 clearly show, were much higher than those of the semiskilled or unskilled workman; his wife and children were under much less pressure to enter the labor market themselves to supplement the family income.

Status differences between unskilled and semiskilled occupations were less dramatic, but they did exist. The situation of the ordinary unskilled manual laborer of Newburyport at mid-century was analyzed at length in Chapter Two. The common laborer was, to an extreme degree, at the mercy of the harsh uncertainties of the casual labor market. Without a specific economic function to perform regularly for a predictable reward, he was forced to take his chances daily in the competition for temporary employment. His wages were invariably below those of his fellow workmen in other occupations, and his children were the first to be forced to seek work to keep the family going.

TABLE 1. Occupational differences in employment and annual earnings, Essex County, Massachusetts, 1875[a]

	Number in sample	Days worked[b]	Mean annual earnings
Skilled occupations			
machinist	135	272.4	$601.94
blacksmith	68	260.0	567.60
carpenter	359	218.0	534.40
mason	101	177.6	524.02
cotton spinner (male)	14	280.5	523.75
shoecutter (male)	254	243.1	521.05
painter	108	207.8	474.79
Semiskilled occupations			
shoecutter, undesignated	883	234.3	418.68
factory operative, undesignated (male)	191	249.6	379.62
Unskilled occupations			
common laborer	412	230.6	358.68

[a] Compiled from the Massachusetts Bureau of Statistics of Labor, *Seventh Annual Report*, pp. 122-199.

[b] On the basis of a six-day week, without considering holidays, the number of possible work days in a year is 312.

By the criteria of earnings, skill required, and definiteness of function, semiskilled jobs were a cut above this. The ordinary operative in a shoe factory or textile mill, the gardener, or the night watchman did not perform as complex a task as the spinner, shoecutter, or mason, and his wages were correspondingly lower.[15] But it would be a mistake to suppose that such jobs required no "skill" at all, and that they were in no way superior to common laboring positions. The semiskilled workmen of Newburyport had a somewhat more secure and respected position than the general laborers. Their function was more clearly defined, their wages were a bit higher and a bit more

TABLE 2. Occupational differences in annual wages and proportion of family income earned by family head, Massachusetts, 1874[a]

	Number in sample	Mean annual wage of family head	Percent of total family income
Skilled occupations			
machinist	41	$746.54	89.5
carpenter	44	716.57	86.6
teamster	6	646.67	86.2
Semiskilled occupations			
mill hand	13	594.31	71.9
shoemaker	22	527.41	68.4
Unskilled occupations			
laborer	43	414.42	56.8

[a] Compiled from the Massachusetts Bureau of Statistics of Labor, *Sixth Annual Report*, pp. 221-354. The wage levels here, it will be noted, are consistently higher than those reported for Essex County a year later (Table 1). This is largely because the 1874 sample was gathered in a way which biased the findings toward the more prosperous representatives of each occupation. We are interested in relative differentials here, so the bias is unimportant.

regular, and they were better able to support their families on their own income.[16]

One further question about the Newburyport occupational hierarchy must be considered. The shape of a community's occupational structure is obviously a prime determinant of the range of occupational mobility opportunities there. Consider an extreme case—a city in which 95 percent of the labor force holds unskilled jobs, with only 5 percent in the higher occupational categories. Even if the occupants of these few high status positions were continually recruited from the bottom class, the majority of men in this community would remain laborers all their lives. The opposite polar type would be a city with only a small fraction of its residents in lowly occupations; here a much slower turnover of personnel in high status jobs would mean relatively greater mobility opportunities for lower class persons. The significance of data about occupational mobility in a given community cannot be grasped without some sense of the range of mobility which could be "expected" within that community.[17]

The Newburyport occupational structure at mid-century resembled the second polar type more closely than the first. Only about 8 percent of the labor force held unskilled jobs; three times as many occupied nonmanual positions of some kind. Approximately one quarter of the employed males of the city were semiskilled workers, while almost 40 percent were skilled laborers. The diversity of skilled trades was striking—thirty-nine varieties of artisan could be counted on the local census schedules for 1850. It is misleading to classify mid-century Newburyport a "mill town"; its occupational structure was not heavily weighted toward unskilled and semiskilled callings. The community had a highly diversified craft economy, with almost two thirds of its labor force in the top two occupational categories and less than a tenth at the very bottom.

Between 1850 and 1880 the main outlines of the Newburyport occupational structure did not change drastically. A distinct shrinking of employment in the skilled trades did occur, matched by a moderate expansion of both semiskilled and nonmanual callings. But the local economy, which had reached a plateau after the rapid growth of the 1840's, did not undergo large-scale technological changes which fundamentally altered the opportunity structure. The declining proportion of skilled positions in the city, and the expansion of semiskilled and white collar occu-

pations reflect national trends of the period, but in Newburyport these tendencies manifested themselves more
slowly than in other more dynamic nineteenth century
cities.[18] The local occupational structure offered a relative
abundance of high status positions in 1850; its general
shape seemed equally favorable to upward occupational
mobility in 1880.

Intra-generational Occupational Mobility, 1850-1880

The career patterns of hundreds of unskilled laborers of
nineteenth century Newburyport are summed up in
Table 3. A simple generalization immediately suggests
itself: less than half of the unskilled laborers listed in the
city on the Census of 1850, 1860, or 1870 remained there

TABLE 3. Occupational and geographical mobility of three groups
of laborers, 1850-1880

Year	Occupational status attained				Rate of persistence[a]	Number in sample
	Un-skilled	Semi-skilled	Skilled	Non-manual		
1850 Census group						
1860	64%	16%	15%	5%	32%	55
1870	36	39	9	15	64	35
1880	57	21	7	14	40	14
1860 Census group						
1870	74	12	8	5	33	74
1880	69	19	6	6	65	48
1870 Census group						
1880	79	6	10	5	41	102

[a] This column provides a measure of the geographical mobility of
workmen in the sample. The rate of persistence of a group for a
particular decade is defined as that proportion of the group recorded on
the census at the start of the decade that is still present in the community
at the end of the decade. Thus 32 percent of the unskilled laborers of
1850 still lived in Newburyport in 1860; 64 percent of the men in this
group as of 1860 still lived in Newburyport in 1870, and so forth.

for as much as a decade, and only a minority of those who did attained a higher status occupation.* The experiences of these obscure workmen, however, were sufficiently varied and complex to merit closer scrutiny.[19]

Of the 171 common laborers employed in Newburyport in 1850, fully two thirds had disappeared from the city by 1860. A few of these had died; most had moved away. Of those who remained, almost two thirds were still ordinary unskilled laborers after a decade. Only 5 percent had risen into a nonmanual calling. Upward mobility was restricted almost entirely to the skilled and semiskilled occupations; a sixth of these men acquired semiskilled positions by 1860, a slightly smaller proportion found skilled employment.

During the Civil War decade, however, this group fared better. Its members were older, and more securely settled in the community; the persistence rate of the group for 1860-1870 was twice that for 1850-1860. Their occupational adjustment improved markedly in one respect. While two thirds of them had made no occupational gains at all between 1850 and 1860, by 1870 only one third of the group still held completely unskilled laboring jobs.

Almost all of the upward mobility attained by these men in the Civil War decade involved one small step up the occupational ladder. The dramatic shift out of the un-

---

* A word of warning is in order here. The discussion which follows is based on a series of tables which display in percentages the changing occupational distribution of several groups of men and boys. Scrutiny of the absolute numbers from which these percentages were calculated will reveal that, in some instances, occupational shifts by relatively few men appear as a rather dramatic percentage change. These changes in the occupational adjustment of even a small group of individuals are suggestive, but the reader must recall that this is an interpretative essay based on fragmentary data, not a large-scale, definitive statistical study.

skilled occupations was accompanied by only a small expansion of the nonmanual category and by an actual decrease in the skilled category. By far the most widespread form of upward mobility was into positions of only slightly higher status than unskilled labor—semiskilled jobs of various kinds.

Occupational opportunities for the immigrants from rural New England and abroad who arrived in Newburyport *after* 1850 were somewhat less favorable. The laborers first listed in Newburyport in the Census of 1860 remained more heavily concentrated in unskilled jobs ten and twenty years later than the men of the 1850 group. Three quarters of them attained no occupational mobility after a decade in the community, and nearly 70 percent were still common laborers after two decades. One laborer in twenty from those who stayed throughout the Civil War decade obtained a nonmanual position of some kind by 1870; no further gains of significance were made in this category during the seventies. The prospects of moving into a skilled manual job were also remote: only 8 percent held skilled positions after a decade in the city, and the proportion fell to 6 percent by 1880. The most marked difference between the attainments of the 1850 and 1860 groups, however, was in the semiskilled occupations. The unskilled laborer who came to Newburyport after 1850 had fewer prospects of attaining the very modest advance in status involved in becoming a fisherman, a factory operative, a gardener, a night watchman.

The shrinkage of semiskilled opportunities is even more evident from the experiences of the laborers first listed in the Census of 1870. Some two thirds of the men in the 1850 group remained trapped in the unskilled category after a decade; the comparable figure for the 1860 group was three fourths; in the case of the 1870 group, four out of five men remained laborers for at least a decade. This unfavorable trend, however, did not mean the appearance of new barriers against movement into the skilled and nonmanual occupations. The prospects of becoming a grocer or a mason were quite similar for members of all three groups. The chief advantage of the more successful group was that they enjoyed superior access to jobs of a semiskilled character.

It is tempting to conclude flatly that a change somewhat unfavorable to common laborers occurred in the Newburyport occupational structure during these years. But a different explanation of the pattern of declining opportunities can be conceived. We know that the industrial transformation of the Newburyport economy coincided with the arrival of masses of impoverished Irish peasants, and that the proportion of foreign-born men in the local working class rose steadily through the 1850-1880 period. It is possible that foreign laborers had fewer opportunities than their native counterparts throughout this period and that the two later groups had a larger proportion of immigrants than the 1850 group.

Did Yankee workmen climb into higher status occupations more easily than immigrant laborers in these years, as many observers believed, or were ethnic differences in mobility opportunities actually negligible? The relationship between occupational mobility and ethnicity is displayed in Table 4; while the absolute numbers from which these distributions were calculated were tiny in some instances, the uniformity of the pattern which emerges is impressive. The immigrant workman in Newburyport was markedly less successful than his native counterpart in climbing out of the ranks of the unskilled

Table 4. Ethnic differences in intra-generational occupational mobility

Year	Unskilled		Semiskilled		Skilled		Nonmanual		Number in sample	
	Native	Foreign	Native	Foreign	Native	Foreign	Native	Foreign	Native	Foreign
1850 Census group										
1860	47%	72%	32%	8%	15%	14%	5%	6%	19	36
1870	15	55	77	14	0	14	8	18	13	22
1880	25	70	25	20	25	0	25	10	4	10
1860 Census group										
1870	50	83	30	5	5	10	15	2	20	54
1880	50	74	30	15	10	5	10	5	10	38
1870 Census group										
1880	60	84	15	4	15	9	10	4	20	82

in the 1850-1880 period. In each of the three groups at each census disproportionately high numbers of the foreign-born remained concentrated at the bottom of the occupational scale. The disadvantages of the newcomers were reflected, to some extent, in their underrepresentation in the skilled and nonmanual callings. But the sharpest difference in mobility opportunities was not in the two highest occupational categories but in the semi-skilled field. The distribution of the 1850 group in 1870—with 77 percent of its native-born members and 14 percent of its immigrants holding semiskilled jobs—is only the most dramatic illustration of a tendency evident throughout Table 4. Evidently many local employers shared Francis Bowen's belief that "the rude labor" to which the newcomers had become accustomed had "so incapacitated them for higher tasks" that a factory could not be profitably run if more than a third of its labor force was made up of immigrants. "Foreigners generally, and the Irish in particular," wrote Bowen, "cannot be employed at all" in the factory, "except in that small proportion to the total number of hands which will make it possible to restrict them to the lower or less difficult tasks."[20] In the Newburyport factories of this period the proportion of immigrant workmen on the payroll was kept well below that supposedly dangerous level.

The shrinking of opportunities in the semiskilled occupations, therefore, was intimately connected with the changing ethnic composition of the Newburyport laboring class. The proportion of foreign-born men in the community labor force was steadily rising, and in these years the immigrants had particularly restricted access to employment in the occupations most open to the ambitious common laborer. It is noteworthy, however, that the special handicaps of immigrant laborers do not fully account for the inferior showing of the 1860 and 1870 groups. When the occupational experiences of native and foreign laborers are tabulated separately—as in Table 4— the pattern of declining mobility shows up in the figures for both groups.

A few general conclusions about the mobility patterns of common laborers in Newburyport in the 1850-1880 period can now be suggested. The composition of the community's unskilled laboring force was extremely fluid: a majority of the men registered as laborers on a United States Census in these years left the city before a second census was taken. These high rates of migration from the community significantly affected occupational adjustment; the improved occupational distribution of the three groups was partly due to the simple fact that unsuccessful laborers were quicker to leave Newburyport than successful ones.

Surprisingly, however, variations in the flow of migrants from the city were not closely related to variations in occupational opportunities there. The persistence rates of the 1850 and 1860 groups (Table 3) were almost identical —32 and 33 percent respectively the first decade, 64 and 65 percent respectively in the second decade—even though the occupational gains of the two were not. The 1870 group departed somewhat from the pattern; 41 percent of its members remained in Newburyport for at least a decade. This instance hints at a mild negative relationship between group persistence and occupational mobility, since the most stable of the three groups was also the least mobile occupationally. Ethnic differences in migration seem to have followed no consistent pattern. Foreign-born laborers were less successful occupationally than their native competitors throughout these three decades; the persistence rates of the newcomers, however, were lower in 1860 and 1870 and much higher in 1880. The rate of emigration, therefore, was an independent variable which strongly influenced the occupational adjustment of unskilled laborers; it did not vary in response to changes in occupational mobility opportunities in the community.

The common workman who remained in Newburyport in these years had only a slight chance of rising into a middle class occupation, even if "middle class" is generously defined to include the ownership of a subsistence farm. Only one laborer in twenty succeeded in making this advance during his first decade in the city. In the case of the 1850 group this proportion increased to three in twenty after two decades, but the two-decade figure for the 1860 group remained one in twenty. Moreover, neither politics nor religion, often assumed to have been important channels of upward mobility for immigrant groups, provided any opportunities for these men. Not one instance of ascent of this kind was recorded in the 1850-1880 period. The climb into a nonmanual occupation was not impossible for the unskilled workman, but it was achieved by only a tiny minority.

It is perhaps not very surprising that men without capital, education, or special training of any sort should have had limited access to nonmanual occupations. More noteworthy is the fact that these laborers found so little opportunity to enter skilled manual occupations. Approximately a third of the total Newburyport labor force in this period was made up of artisans and craftsmen of various sorts, but few laborers found openings here.

In none of the groups of laborers did as much as a quarter of the men succeed in obtaining either skilled or non-manual positions in the period studied. From 75 to 85 percent of them remained near the bottom of the social ladder in the low-skill, low-pay occupational universe. The great majority continued to work as day laborers; most of those who did change occupations became semi-skilled workmen, performing simple manual tasks at slighty higher wages and with somewhat more regular employment than they had previously enjoyed.

The opportunity to take this very modest step upward into the semiskilled category varied in two significant ways—according to the laborer's nativity and to his time of arrival in the community. Compared to the Yankee, the foreign-born workman was generally underrepresented at all occupational levels above unskilled labor, but his chief disadvantage was not at the top of the occupational ladder but at the second rung. Similarly, the growing tendency of laborers who arrived in Newburyport after 1850 to remain fixed in unskilled occupations involved a relatively small reduction in mobility into skilled and non-manual positions; most of the change was due to the restriction of employment opportunities in the semiskilled category.

Inter-generational Occupational Mobility, 1850–1880

If nineteenth century Americans were optimistic about the laborer's chances of "pulling himself up by his own bootstraps," they were more optimistic still about his children's prospects for success. The following analysis of career patterns of sons of Newburyport laborers will help to determine to what extent such optimism was justified.

Intra-generational mobility is computed by comparing men's occupations at two or more points in their career, but the task of estimating inter-generational mobility is rather more complicated. A comparison of the status of two different individuals—father and son—is sought. At what point in the careers of the two is it appropriate to make the comparison? Half of this problem has been solved here by arranging the data on sons' occupations by age group, so that the occupational status of sons at varying stages of their careers is displayed (Table 5). Control for age is particularly important in this case because most boys entered the labor market in their early teens, and there is good reason to doubt that the jobs they held at that tender age provide a reasonable measure of inter-generational mobility. It is obviously important to determine how closely the adult occupations of these sons corresponded to the occupations they held while in their teens. One recent study revealed that well over half of a sample of white collar and professional workers in Oakland, California, had worked in a manual laboring position at some point in their early career, persuasive evidence of the dangers of ignoring intra-generational mobility in a study of inter-generational mobility.[21] By utilizing age groups in analyzing the career patterns of laborers' sons this danger can be avoided.

There remains the difficulty that not all of the fathers of these men continued to be unskilled laborers through the entire period of the study. Some, we have seen, moved up the occupational ladder themselves. How did a father's mobility or lack of mobility influence his son's prospects for occupational advance? This question will be considered at a later point. For the present it will simplify matters to ignore occupational advances made by the father and to consider all fathers laborers. Most of them did in fact remain laborers, and, as we shall see later,

TABLE 5. Occupational and geographical mobility of sons of laborers, 1850-1880[a]

Year	Occupational status attained				Rate of persistence	Number in sample
	Unskilled	Semiskilled	Skilled	Nonmanual		
	Youths born 1830-1839					
1850	39%	56%	6%	0%	—	18
1860	10	76	7	7	29%	41
1870	11	48	30	11	56	27
1880	11	42	37	11	63	19
	Youths born 1840-1849					
1860	11	84	2	4	54	57
1870	28	45	17	10	32	58
1880	21	46	17	17	33	24
	Youths born 1850-1859					
1870	23	59	11	7	54	95
1880	33	40	20	8	44	76
	Youths born 1860-1869					
1880	25	60	7	8	56	73

a The reader may be surprised to see the number of youths in a group increasing from decade to decade in some instances, at the same time that the persistence rate figure indicates that half to two thirds of the group members left Newburyport each decade. The explanation is that large numbers of youths were coming *into* the city during these years as well, and that these have been included in the analysis.

those who did climb a notch or two upwards had little success in passing on their advantage to their offspring.

Perhaps the most important question to ask about the hundreds of laborers' sons whose careers are recorded in Table 5 is whether or not they customarily inherited the occupation of their fathers and themselves became unskilled day laborers. The answer is apparent in a glance. In none of the age groups at any of the four censuses between 1850 and 1880 did a majority of sons hold unskilled jobs. The most frequently chosen occupation in every instance was in the semiskilled manual category. More often than not, it has been shown, the unskilled Newburyport workman remained an unskilled laborer throughout this period; more often than not the son of such a man became a semiskilled worker.

The really dramatic opening up of semiskilled employment opportunities to laborers' sons occurred in the 1850's. Even in 1850 a slight majority of the handful of sons old enough to be employed held semiskilled positions, but the extent of direct occupational inheritance was still quite high for this group—close to 40 percent. A decade later the situation was strikingly different: almost 85 percent of the boys in the teen-age group held semiskilled jobs, and 75 percent of the youths aged 20-29; only a tenth of the members of either group were mere common laborers! Very few, on the other hand, had climbed more than one rung up the status ladder. Barely 5 percent of the teen-agers working in 1860 had entered skilled or nonmanual callings. The comparable figure for youths in their twenties was higher, but even this meant no more than that one in thirteen held a skilled job and one in thirteen a nonmanual job. By far the most common form of inter-generational mobility evident by 1860 was into semiskilled occupations.

After 1860 there continued to be a heavy concentration of laborers' sons in semiskilled callings, but a significant tightening up occurred. Eight-five percent of the teen-agers in 1860 held semiskilled jobs, less than 60 percent of the teen-agers in 1870. For the group aged 20-29 in 1860 the drop was from 76 percent to 45 percent. A great wave of working class children entered the labor market during the Civil War decade, and the local employers hiring semiskilled labor did not expand their activity sufficiently to absorb all of them. Indeed, one major source of semiskilled employment began to dry up during this decade. Almost half of the laborers' sons who held semiskilled jobs at the time of the Census of 1860 listed themselves as "fisherman" or "seaman." Both the fishing industry and the coasting trade carried on out of New-buryport experienced a sharp decline during the sixties; by 1870 the maritime industries accounted for only a quarter of the semiskilled jobs held by these youths and by 1880, less than 15 percent. Semiskilled employment was coming increasingly to mean factory employment.

What happened to the boys for whom the cotton mills and shoe factories of Newburyport had no room? The narrowing of semiskilled opportunities in the sixties forced increasing numbers of the fathers of these youths to remain common laborers. This happened to some extent to the sons as well; the 1870 Census showed a rise in the concentration of sons in unskilled positions. It is striking, however, that this decade also saw a corresponding in-crease in mobility into the two higher occupational classes. In the case of the two younger groups in 1870, the increase in direct occupational inheritance was approximately equal to the increase in the skilled and non-manual category. For men in the 30-39 age bracket in 1870 the constriction of semiskilled opportunities during the Civil War decade resulted in a substantial rise in the proportion holding high status jobs, but virtually no increase at all in the unskilled category.

A certain number of laborers' sons gained a foothold in the white collar world after 1860—ten members of the group became clerks between 1860 and 1870, for example. But the skilled crafts were a more important source of upward mobility. The 1870 and 1880 figures show that it was uncommon for more than one in ten to cross the barrier dividing manual from nonmanual occupations, while two to three times as many youths characteristically found skilled employment. No single craft or group of crafts appears to have been unusually open to penetration from below; there was a broad scattering of upwardly mobile sons throughout the trades. The 1870 group, for example, included four blacksmiths, two carpenters, two machinists, two painters, two iron molders, a tailor, a baker, and a mason.

Two other aspects of the process of inter-generational mobility require comment—the role of ethnic differences and the influence of geographical mobility. It has already been demonstrated that the immigrant workman was markedly less successful than his native counterpart in climbing up the occupational ladder. Did the children of immigrant laborers face similar handicaps, or did ethnic barriers to mobility affect only the first generation immigrant? A comparison of the occupational distribution of native and foreign sons in 1850, 1860, 1870, and 1880 is presented in Table 6. The conclusion to be drawn from it is obvious: sons of Yankee laborers obtained high status

Table 6. Occupational distribution of sons of native and foreign-born laborers, 1850-1880

Occupational category	1850		1860		1870		1880	
	Native	Foreign	Native	Foreign	Native	Foreign	Native	Foreign
Number in sample	19	14	34	76	37	148	37	158
Unskilled	26%	71%	12%	8%	8%	27%	19%	27%
Semiskilled	53	21	53	88	38	55	38	50
Skilled	21	7	18	3	27	14	24	15
Nonmanual	0	0	18	1	27	5	19	8

employment in Newburyport much more easily than sons of foreign-born workmen in these years. The proportion of native youths in skilled and nonmanual positions was consistently higher than the proportion of foreign sons; the latter clustered heavily near the bottom of the occupational scale. But, unlike their fathers, immigrant children were not thought "incapacitated" for factory employment. The upper levels of the factory hierarchy were completely closed to them, but a high proportion found semiskilled positions in local factories.[22]

These ethnic differences in mobility opportunities narrowed somewhat in the post–Civil War years. The censuses of 1870 and 1880 showed gains for foreign sons in both the skilled and nonmanual categories. The popular belief that second-generation Americans labored under no special handicaps in the race for occupational status was excessively optimistic, but the evidence of Table 6 hints at the beginning of a trend toward some equalization of opportunities. It is interesting to note, however, that by 1880 none of these youths had advanced through the mobility channels so often stressed in impressionistic accounts of immigrant life—politics and religion. To become a priest required education; to become a ward boss required some education too, and a well-organized, politically conscious constituency. The Irish of Newburyport, and later immigrant groups as well, eventually attained these requisites, but only after long years of struggle.

Like their fathers, these youths tended to be transient members of the community, and migration seems to have influenced their occupational adjustment in much the same way. A certain number of working class youths who had already attained some occupational mobility in the community left Newburyport during these years, but the net effect of emigration was to improve the occupational distribution of the group as a whole by removing a disproportionately large number of the least successful. The persistence of these laborers' sons (Table 5) varied roughly by age: very young children and men above thirty tended to be relatively stable members of the community; boys in their teens and twenties were most likely to move on. The persistence rates of sons of native-born laborers were generally, but not uniformly, higher than those of immigrant children. None of these variations can be clearly attributed to changes in the occupational structure.

Fathers and Sons

This survey of the career patterns of Newburyport laborers and their sons in the 1850-1880 period suggests the following conclusions.*

1) Unskilled manual laborers characteristically remained common laborers; the odds that an unskilled laborer living in Newburyport would hold the same lowly position ten years later were at least two to one throughout this period. The sons of these laborers, by contrast, typically became semiskilled workmen; no more than one in four inherited the exact occupation of his father and remained in it.

2) Relatively few of the adult laborers studied worked their way up into a position in a skilled craft—approxi-

---

* It must be remembered, of course, that these conclusions refer not to the entire working class population of the community but to *unskilled* laborers and their sons. Recent mobility research suggests the likelihood that an investigation of the career patterns of *skilled* families would have revealed substantially greater movement into nonmanual occupations. Presumably it would also have disclosed evidence of downward occupational mobility, since skilled workmen (unlike common laborers) have status to lose.

mately one in ten. The sons of these men were considerably more successful in penetrating the skilled trades, at least after 1860; the 1870 and 1880 figures for sons in their twenties or older holding skilled jobs range from 17 to 37 percent.

3) The contrast between generations was less sharp at the top of the occupational scale. Entry into a non-manual occupation was almost as difficult for the son of a common laborer as for his father. Since working class families frequently found education for their children a luxury, this is not surprising. The possibility of purchasing a farm or opening a small business existed for both generations; approximately one laborer in ten was able to do this in the three decades studied.

4) The composition of the Newburyport working class was highly unstable. Large numbers of unskilled workmen drifted into the community, but only a minority remained for long. Migration was an important mechanism of occupational adjustment in that it was selective; the successful were less likely to leave than the unsuccessful.

5) Foreign-born workmen and their sons were handicapped in the occupational competition. The sons, however, experienced fewer obstacles to occupational mobility than their fathers; ethnic differences in inter-generational occupational mobility were narrowing somewhat by 1880.

6) Adult laborers employed in Newburyport in 1850 had somewhat greater prospects for occupational advance than those who arrived after 1850. In the case of the sons of these men, however, the trend was in the opposite direction. Some four fifths of the laborers' sons who entered the labor market during the 1850's found semiskilled positions; while the shrinking of semiskilled opportunities after 1860 forced some of these youths back into unskilled

jobs, an equally large group rose into skilled and non-manual callings.

Thus we can conclude that while these laborers and their sons experienced a good deal of occupational mobility, only in rare cases was it mobility very far up the social ladder. The occupational structure was fluid to some degree, but the barriers against moving more than one notch upward were fairly high. Success of the kind achieved by Stephen Fowle was attainable, but only the few were able to grasp it.

5 · *Property, Savings, and Status*

Occupation, of course, is not the sole determinant of social status; men make certain social advances without changing their occupations at all. Class is not unidimensional; as Weber notes, "only persons who are completely unskilled, without property and dependent on employment without regular occupation, are in a strictly identical class status."[1]

The social group with which this book deals consisted of men who did at one time hold a "strictly identical class status" in a nineteenth century New England city. By any criterion the unskilled manual laborers of Newburyport at mid-century stood at the bottom of the social ladder. But how permanent was their lowly status? An assessment of the extent of occupational mobility out of the unskilled laboring class has been presented. The other major determinant of class status suggested by Weber—possession of property—should now be considered. "Property mobility" is a dimension of social mobility which has received too little attention in the literature of social stratification. Movement from the propertyless segment of the working class to the strata of workmen possessed of a "stake in society" was a critically important process in the nineteenth century city and it requires systematic analysis.

Historically, the image of the laboring class as a propertyless permanent proletariat has been more than a figment of the Marxist imagination. Many of the classic European social surveys suggest that it was a sober reality in early industrial communities. Engels' estimate of *The*

Condition of the Working Class in England in 1844 was
something less than a dispassionate evaluation, but a
similar impression of the situation of at least a portion of
the working class emerges from the reports of English
statisticians of the day. One of the earliest of these investigations, an 1838 inquiry in Bristol, found that 17 out of
5981 manual laborers interviewed (0.3 percent) owned
their own homes, while only one in seven possessed a
savings account or belonged to a benefit society.[2] The
inquiries of Booth in London and Rowntree in York at the
turn of the century led to the conclusion that a large segment of the working class lived at the bare subsistence
level. In dismal detail Rowntree traced the "cycle of
poverty" which governed the life of the workmen of
York; few had savings of any size, and only eight laborers
in the entire city owned homes of their own.[3]

It was not at all clear in 1850 that the economic situation of the laborer in the New World was much better.
In Newburyport the common workman lacked real property or savings, and was repeatedly exposed to unemployment and destitution. A variety of evidence from other
American communities points to a similar conclusion.

Yet in the New World the security and respectability
insured by property ownership were considered within
the reach of even the lowliest laborer. A Newburyport
minister voiced the common faith when he preached that
in America "property must be in the hands of the many;
all should be well educated, all industrious, all have a
house and home."[4] Brought to the city, the Jeffersonian
ideal became the belief that the urban laborer might
enjoy a surrogate freehold farm in the form of a substantial bank account and title to his home.

That a great many laborers lived in miserable poverty at one point in time, it must be understood, did not necessarily contradict this hope. The emphasis was always that a common laborer could become prosperous through years of hard, honest work. Thus it was stressed that the "magic influence" of property-owning affected men of "the very humblest class" only after a suitable period of diligent endeavor on their part. Once sufficient learning had been gained in the school of adversity, a small lot might be purchased. The workman's first building would be a simple shanty, but soon "a happy transformation in the character of the dwelling" could be expected "whenever industry was combined with thrift and frugality." Timber would be replaced with brick, symbolizing the rise of "the family of the laborer . . . up the social scale."[5] This was the myth. Let us see whether it was grounded in reality in the Newburyport case.[6]

The Ownership of Real Property, 1850-1880

Between 1850 and 1880 the American economy underwent two major depressions and a number of minor recessions. This fact, coupled with what we know about Newburyport wage levels and about the incidence of unemployment at the bottom of the occupational scale, makes the findings of the present inquiry into working class property mobility rather surprising. Real estate was strikingly available to working class men who remained in Newburyport for any length of time.[7] From a third to a half of these workmen were able to report some property holdings after a decade of residence in the city; after 20 years the proportion of owners had risen to 63 percent in one group and 78 percent in another. That an ordinary workman in Newburyport might in time accumulate a property stake was not merely a possibility; it was a strong probability.

The typical size of these accumulations, by men who had once lived on the margin of subsistence, was similarly impressive. Table 7 provides detailed evidence. The range of reported holdings was fairly wide, but the median figure was $600 or more for each group at each census. Only an insignificant fraction of these propertied workmen held less than $300, while a large and rising proportion reported accumulations valued at $1000 or more. The 1880 figures suggest a slowing (and, in the case of the 1850 group, a reversal) of the trend toward greater property ownership, but this is largely a statistical artifact, caused by the shift from census replies to local tax valuations.

The proportion of property owners in the three groups increased more dramatically than the absolute number—which again points to the selective influence of working class migration patterns. Laboring families that failed to attain a property stake had less to tie them to the community, and they left Newburyport in disproportionately large numbers during these years. Four fifths of the local laborers possessed of property in 1850 still lived in the city in 1860, but less than a third of their propertyless counterparts; a strong positive correlation between property ownership and persistence in Newburyport was found for the other groups as well.

All of these accumulations, of course, did not represent the fruits of unskilled manual labor. The members of some of these families had achieved significant intra-generational or inter-generational occupational mobility. Discussion of the relationship between occupational mobility and

TABLE 7. Property holdings of laboring families[a]

Year	Number of families	Property owners		Percentage distribution by value			Median holding
		Number	Percent	Under $300	$300–999	$1000 or more	
				1850 Census group			
1850	175	18	11%	0%	72%	28%	$600
1860	71	23	32	0	70	30	800
1870	49	38	78	8	47	45	800
1880	34	18	53	0	56	44	950
				1860 Census group			
1860	256	28	11	4	86	11	700
1870	105	50	48	8	46	46	800
1880	70	44	63	5	52	43	800
				1870 Census group			
1870	256	74	29	5	53	42	700
1880	121	49	41	6	61	33	700

[a] It may be noticed that the group numbers here are somewhat larger than those in the occupational mobility tables in the preceding chapter. This is because the unit of study has shifted from the individual to the family. If a father in the 1850 group died in 1868, obviously no occupation would be listed for him in the Census of 1870. But if one of his employed sons continued to live with the family in 1870, the family would still be included in these property calculations.

property mobility will be deferred until the next chapter. Suffice it to say here that these two varieties of upward social movement were not as closely connected as might be expected, and that each deserves separate analysis.

The Use of the Mortgage

It is conceivable that these property estimates give a seriously distorted impression of the wealth of working class families in Newburyport. Both census and tax records ignore debts incurred in obtaining property; full value is recorded even if the land and buildings in question are heavily mortgaged. Did a reported holding of several hundred dollars by a laborer usually represent a net asset of that magnitude, or must these figures be greatly discounted for outstanding debt?

About half of the Newburyport laborers who accumulated real property in the 1850-1880 period financed their purchases by resorting to a mortgage.[8] Exactly two thirds of the 327 laboring families who resided in the city ten years or more came into possession of some property; between 1855 and 1879, 96 of these 217 owners borrowed money against their real estate. To the laborer, the function of the mortgage was simple: it allowed him to enter the class of property owners before he had accumulated enough savings to pay the full purchase price on a lot or house. In none of the cases examined could the mortgage be considered an essentially speculative instrument, a means of capitalizing on rising land values.[9] The sums borrowed were usually small; 80 percent were less than $700 (Table 8). They ordinarily were borrowed against the single plot of land and cheap house in which the laborer himself resided. These were utilitarian, not specu-

TABLE 8. Mortgages held by laborers, 1855-1879[a]

Value	Number	Percent
Under $300	46	36%
$300-699	57	45
$700-999	14	11
$1000-1499	5	4
$1500 and over	5	4
	127	100

[a] Ninety-six individuals from the sample contracted mortgages; the total number of mortgages studied was greater than ninety-six because several persons took out more than one mortgage.

lative, purchases; Newburyport real estate offered few attractions for anyone interested in fat future profits.

These small sums were borrowed for a relatively long term, at substantial interest. The going rate was about 7 percent per annum; as much as 10 percent was occasionally paid on very small short-term mortgages. When the other costs of the mortgage were calculated (charges for drawing up the abstract, recording the transaction, and so forth) the expense of borrowing a few hundred dollars for several years could amount to half the principal. The amortizing mortgage, so common today, was rare. Though interest was collected semiannually, the principal was paid in a lump sum at the end of the term. Forty percent of the mortgages analyzed were granted by the two local savings banks; the remainder were offered by private parties. Both institutional and private lenders seem to have charged laborers at the prevailing community rate. There was no evidence of the discriminatory use of credit facilities which has often handicapped ethnic minorities in the United States.

These findings on working class mortgages suggest an

important modification of the conclusion drawn above. Property mobility by ordinary laborers was very common in Newburyport in the 1850-1880 period, but census and tax records give a somewhat exaggerated impression of the speed with which about half of these workmen accumulated the sums they reported. The debts against their property were eventually paid off—only a handful of the mortgages analyzed were ever foreclosed—but it was often a slow and expensive task to discharge the burden.

The Laborer and the Savings Bank

The prying historian finds it a good deal easier to obtain information on real estate holdings than to discover anything about personal savings. Such information is supposed to be private. But it was possible to circumvent this taboo to some degree. Nothing will ever tell us how many dollars Newburyport workmen may have stowed away in mattresses or sea chests, of course. Evidence, however, makes it reasonable to infer that the great majority of laborers with substantial personal savings deposited them in savings banks. These fragments reveal much about the economic situation of the working class in nineteenth century Newburyport, and allow us to appraise the relationship between the laborer and a favorite American institution of self-improvement.

The prosaic savings banks of America have been spoken of in the kind of ecstatic superlatives usually reserved for the Constitution. "The establishment of savings banks ought to be celebrated as a great event in the world, no less than the introduction of the compass, or the invention of printing," proclaimed a distinguished economist. In the financial world, according to another enthusiast, the savings banks "reach down to the people as the ballot box does in the political world"; a third judged savings institutions second in effect only to "our common schools" as guardians of the American way of life.[10]

The savings banks of the United States received these accolades because they allegedly served to impress "the importance of the public peace and of the perpetual stability of good order and good government . . . upon the great mass of the community with that strong conviction which individual interest never fails to inspire."[11] It was clear to the prophet of the savings bank movement that the primary danger to "good order and good government" came from the lower class. Without an opportunity to share in the material prosperity of a country, the impoverished laborer was said to "regard the whole structure of society, which holds him in this condition, as an inhabitant of a conquered territory looks upon a citadel of the conquerors." He was therefore "naturally" and even "justifiably" an "enemy of the government claiming his allegiance," and a grave threat to the social order.[12] An explicit purpose of the savings bank was to avert class conflict by uplifting the lower class and making its members contended bourgeois.

The paternalistic objective of the pioneers of the American savings bank movement was to be reached by rigidly individualistic means. Workmen could be "helped" only to help themselves. It was "not by the alms of the wealthy" that "the good of the lower classes" was to be promoted, declared the organizers of one of the earliest of American savings institutions; charity only bred "idleness and hypocrisy." The genuine "benefactor to the poor" was he who encouraged them "in habits of industry, sobriety, and frugality."[13] All the traits dear to the savings

bank enthusiasts were summed up in the cardinal virtue, "enlightened self-interest," "the cornerstone of all
progress."[14]

Both Manchesterian individualism and paternalistic
condescension toward "the lower orders" were neatly
blended in an analogy of which savings bank advocates
were particularly fond. Savings institutions were "kinder-
garten schools, where the young, the helpless, and unin-
formed" could be taught "the advantages of economy and
thrift." The poor were dutifully to master "lessons in
thrift," and to be paid "a premium for accepting the
lessons."[15] Star pupils would pile up large bank balances;
lazy or stupid ones deserved the poverty that would be
their reward.

The savings bank movement began in Europe at the
close of the eighteenth century, in response to some of
the disturbances and dislocation accompanying the immense changes we refer to as the Industrial Revolution.
The problem of poverty was old, but it had taken on new
dimensions when men were uprooted from rural environ-
ments and plunged into the chaotic new urban centers.
The urban family became entirely dependent on a money
wage. Earning opportunities increased greatly, but the
flow of income to the workman became much more ir-
regular. Life in a competitive money economy imposed
the harsh necessity of using financial resources with calculated efficiency.[16] The European savings banks were
part of a complex of workingmen's protective associations
which grew up at this time, ranging from social clubs to
mutual benefit societies and trade associations. The particular function of the savings bank was to perform the
difficult educational task of inducing the workers of an
area to forego immediate consumption expenditures and

to husband their financial resources for use in times of trouble. They were based on the premise that the problem of working class poverty was not essentially a deficiency of total income, but only a failure to use income rationally.

The primary emphasis in European discussions of savings institutions was always on the security the workmen gained from having their savings in a safe place. As Patrick Colquhoun put it in his classic *Treatise on Indigence* (1806), poor men who had "a little in reserve" would regard savings banks as "guardian angels by whose wise regulations and kind regard to their welfare they are shielded from the dread of misery and want."[17]

When savings banks were transplanted in the New World, they were quickly given a different rationale. They were no longer viewed primarily as instruments providing security for men destined to remain in the working class, but rather as vehicles of upward mobility. Patrick Colquhoun was content to promise the working class patron of the savings bank protection against "misery and want"; Harvard's Francis Bowen advised the frugal American laborer that he could expect to accumulate enough wealth to retire as a carriage-owning gentleman.[18]

The American savings bank was to promote social mobility in the following manner. Because of tax exemptions and other legal privileges, savings banks supposedly offered the small depositor both security and high interest payments. This was to tempt even the ordinary workman to save something out of his wages. The commitment to save regularly would sharpen the individual's sense of "enlightened self-interest," and inspire him to search for new economic opportunities. As the laborer saw his dimes becoming dollars, "an anxiety to further improve his worldly condition arises; by careful management he avoids drawing upon his small deposits, and agreeably anticipates the day when the accretions of his capital will be sufficient to enable him to establish business for himself, and acquire a comfortable and easy subsistence."[19]

The crucial assumption was that savings accounts, once established, would expand steadily and rapidly. The savings banks were held to be magic "cisterns"; once money was trapped in them, it became capital, and capital had a happy tendency to multiply itself. This was the basis of the remarkable argument that any man with a bank account was a capitalist. According to the old European "systems of political economy, mankind were divided into two classes—the capitalist and the laborer." But in America, "through the agency of savings-banks, in these later years" political economy had to be written anew, for "the laborers have become the capitalists in this new world!"[20] The instant a workman set aside a few dollars in a bank he qualified for membership in the capitalist class, and the sustained growth of his surplus "capital" was assured. If, in fact, the savings banks of America achieved what the theory promised, superlatives were very much in order. The consequence of their efforts would be nothing less than that "all the members of the community, except a few, the most unfortunate, or the most vicious," would be "brought into the class of capitalists."[21]

Was there any truth in the theory of the savings bank enthusiasts? A vigorous debate on the subject was conducted in Massachusetts in the 1870's. Provoked by skeptical reformers on the staff of the newly created Bureau of Statistics of Labor, the dispute centered around the charge that the special legal privileges enjoyed by the savings banks were unjustified, and that in fact the banks exerted very little uplifting influence on the laboring class. It was asserted that Massachusetts savings institutions chiefly benefited the middle class, and that the bulk of deposits represented not earnings from wage labor but "profits upon labor." The parties to this debate produced a great volume of conflicting testimony, studded with statistics; yet no direct evidence on the central problem ever appeared.

The absence of direct evidence was due largely to the fact that the Massachusetts savings banks insisted on keeping individual accounts confidential. They were not legally obligated to release more than statistics of deposits broken down into very broad categories, and they held rigidly to this prerogative. To make use of these statistics, critics of the banks were forced to argue on the basis of arbitrary assumptions as to the size of deposit a "typical workman" might make. The Bureau of Statistics of Labor assumed that deposits of more than fifty dollars were not likely to be made by the normal wage laborer. Bank officers strenuously objected to this premise and to the conclusion that large savings accounts must therefore belong chiefly to members of the middle class. "The mere fact of a large deposit standing in a man's name is no index that he is not a laborer," urged a Fall River bank official. "We have many laborers with $1000 on deposit." Indeed, testified a Salem banker, very large accounts were most likely to belong to the kind of person "who removes snow from sidewalks, digs your grounds in the spring, or may assist in the cleaning of your house."[22]

Any attempt to adjudicate the Massachusetts controversy would begin with the question whether it was common or unusual for an ordinary laborer to have an account in a savings bank. It is impossible to make an exact judgment as to the total number of savings accounts held by laborers in Newburyport between 1850 and 1880. But something can be learned from the very limited information available.[23] There is no doubt that a majority of men in the relatively settled sector of the local laboring class made deposits at some point in their lives. Three hundred and twenty-seven laboring families lived in Newburyport at the Census of 1860; 410 were counted in 1870. One hundred and fifty-four of these opened accounts at the Institution for Savings between July 1866 and January 1876.[24] Since in many cases children kept their savings separate, these 154 families held a total of 209 accounts. Even if this ten-year period was exceptionally prosperous and even if laborers were less well represented on the rolls of the other savings bank in the city—there is no reason to believe that either was the case —it is evident that it was common for unskilled workmen to have savings accounts.

This is striking, but it goes only a small step toward validating the theory of the savings bank enthusiasts. That theory hinged on an assertion about the amount of savings the manual worker might accumulate. Savings banks were able to transform laborers into capitalists because deposited funds were thought to grow rapidly into very substantial sums, providing a capital stock on which to enter business. Did the accounts held by laborers at the Institution for Savings expand in the way prophesied by spokesmen of the savings bank movement?

Basic information about the size of deposits and time span of accounts has been made available for a sampling of working class depositors.[25] Only two of these accounts ever surpassed $1500; 80 percent of them remained under $1000; nearly half represented savings of less than $300.

These are impressive figures, given working class wage levels in the period, but the interest on accounts of this size clearly fell far short of providing the "comfortable and easy subsistence" supposedly within reach of the frugal laborer.

The size distribution of these accounts interestingly resembles the mortgage figures presented earlier (Table 8). If we recall that mortgages were generally repaid in a lump sum at the end of the term rather than in installments, we begin to see a chief function of these savings accounts: to accumulate funds with which to repay the mortgage on the laborer's home. This interpretation finds further support in Table 9, which provides some detailed

TABLE 9. Initial deposits, closing entries, and time spans of laborers' savings accounts over $700

Maximum balance	Initial deposit	Closing entry	Time open (years)
$1600	$ 80	$288	28
1501	145	698	16
1265	200	107	10
1236	167	435	23
1215	130	445	20
1050	374	16	28
1039	100	682	14
1035	76	1035	2
963	50	963	12
954	100	336	8
927	239	927	$\frac{1}{2}$
750	350	48	$2\frac{1}{2}$
723	300	642	14

information on the thirteen largest accounts in the sample. It appears that these accumulations were made slowly; the time span of the largest account was twenty-eight years, and the average length the eight accounts above $1000 were open was more than seventeen years. The fact that the closing entry was so often large amounts is consistent with the suggestion that the savings bank served as a place in which to gradually build up the funds needed for lump sum repayment of a mortgage.

The typical laborer who settled in Newburyport during this period did indeed patronize the savings banks. Manual workers did sometimes accumulate savings of a thousand dollars or more. If the Newburyport case is at all representative of conditions throughout the state, the critics of Massachusetts savings institutions were mistaken in their skepticism about the extent of working class saving.

The savings banks enthusiasts, however, had little understanding of the real situation. The "laborers with $1000 on deposit" who allegedly existed in great numbers in Massachusetts were hard to find in Newburyport. Despite the fact that our sample of thirty-nine contained a disproportionately large number of especially prosperous men from the group, only one fifth of the accounts ever reached $1000, and nearly half remained under $300. Nor did funds accumulate in these accounts at the dizzying speed predicted by the theorists of savings bank capitalism. The exceptional laborer who managed to build up a balance of $1000 did so through long years of effort; the sum usually represented his maximum achievement rather than a mere first step toward a new career as a merchant. And often a large savings account balance did not reflect a true surplus of total income over total expenditures, because the savings bank served as a secure place to hold what were, in effect, installments to pay off a mortgage.

The savings bank, therefore, may have facilitated capital accumulation and continuing mobility for depositors from higher social levels, but to the laborer it offered security. It encouraged mobility into the strata of workmen possessed of a "stake in society," only rarely mobility into the entrepreneurial class. The savings banks played an important role in the process of home ownership, and they made it easier to set aside small amounts for emergency use.[26] The thrifty and temperate laborer might reasonably hope, with luck, to accumulate a few hundred dollars on which to survive old age at a time when pension plans and social security were unknown.

Poverty and Progress

Few students of nineteenth century American communities have expressed much optimism about the economic situation of the urban working class during the 1850-1880 period. Wages for unskilled and semiskilled labor were never very high in the best of times, and unemployment was endemic to the economic system. These three decades were punctuated by national financial panic in 1857, a postwar slump, and a prolonged depression in the 1870's. A fairly characteristic judgment of working class opportunities for property mobility is Shlakman's verdict for Chicopee, Massachusetts: "Savings accumulated during the good years were eaten up in the frequent and severe depression periods." Another scholar reports that wages in Holyoke in this period were "little more than enough to live on."[27]

An equally pessimistic diagnosis of the economic prospects of the laboring class might easily have been returned by an observer of the Newburyport scene in 1850. And in many respects the lot of the laborer in 1880 seemed little better. Real earnings of unskilled workmen seem to have increased only slightly, if at all, in this period, and efforts to improve wages by collective action were still doomed to failure. When laborers employed to lay down additional track for the Newburyport City Railroad struck for a pay increase in 1871, they were fired and promptly replaced. Local mill hands attempted to resist a wage cut in 1875, and the strike was crushed just as easily.[28] Workmen fortunate enough to find steady employment had powerful incentives for docility; the specter of unemployment could never be far from their minds. As many as a thousand local residents had to seek public relief in bad years; expenditures of the Overseers of the Poor reached new heights in the seventies.[29] Working class families were still under heavy pressure to sacrifice the education of their children for the immediate benefits of an additional paycheck. An eleven-year-old girl was killed in a mill accident in 1871; her father, an unemployed hatter, explained that he had been forced to send the girl to work when he lost his job.[30] The School Committee report for 1880 revealed that average daily school attendance amounted to a mere 60 percent of Newburyport children in the five to fifteen age bracket; about 400 school-age children were enrolled in no school at all.[31]

Despite all this, however, a careful tracing of the economic position of hundreds of working class families in Newburyport in these three decades yielded surprising conclusions. A substantial segment of the Newburyport laboring class made notable economic progress during this period. Some workmen advanced themselves occupationally, but more striking is the fact that so many managed to accumulate significant amounts of property while still laborers. A brief review of the performance of the Newburyport economy in the 1850-1880 period will make it possible to understand how men earning so little could have saved so much.

Not long after 1850 the rapid growth of the city's population came to an end. The total figure stood at 13,357 in 1855, at 13,538 in 1880; in the intervening quarter of a century it fluctuated between 12,500 and 13,500. The heavy downward pressure on the local unskilled labor market at mid-century eased somewhat. Irish peasants and New England farm boys continued to flock into Newburyport, but the influx of newcomers was approximately balanced by the emigration of other residents. The ebb and flow of migration varied with the business cycle; years of peak population tended to coincide with times of prosperity, while in recessions emigrants tended to outnumber immigrants.[32]

The failure of the city to increase its total population was symptomatic of its failure to achieve sustained economic expansion in this period. Local boosters still professed grandiose expectations. The *Herald* boasted that Newburyport's geographical position insured its future as a great metropolis. Boston was handicapped by being situated on a muddy island. Lowell was much too far up the river to compete with a community so blessed by Nature. Newburyport had but to "avail herself of her situation at the outlet of the river valley in connection with the ocean to stand at the head of them all."[33] For all the rhetoric of the newspaper and the newly established Board of Trade (1870), however, the dramatic economic growth of the 1840's was not sustained. The cotton mills never fulfilled their early promise. Often closed and rarely able to pay dividends, they managed to survive down to 1880, but attracted no new investors. Shipbuilding and related maritime enterprises, after the brief Civil War boom, fell into steady decline; the local fishing industry and the coasting trade similarly declined. Two large shoe factories and half a dozen smaller ones were established in the city during the seventies. The value of shoes produced locally approached $1,000,000 in 1879 and was growing rapidly, but this was little more than enough to offset the decline in other branches of Newburyport industry. A simple index sums up the situation reasonably well: the average annual increase in the assessed value of property in Newburyport was $218,000 for the 1837-1853 period; 'the comparable annual increase for 1853-1880 was less than a third that.[34]

There were sharp fluctuations in the level of economic activity in Newburyport during these years, but the impact of these fluctuations upon the local laboring class was by no means uniform. At any point in this period the Newburyport population included hundreds of impoverished unskilled men who had recently drifted into the community. Only a minority of them found employment sufficiently steady to hold them there; the others, like Negroes and Puerto Ricans in present-day America, were the first to be laid off in a recession and the first to be forced on relief. They were also least likely to remain in the city very long. After the collapse of 1857 an estimated 1000 of them left Newburyport for "locations where work is more abundant."[35] The return of prosperity produced a periodic swelling of this "floating" class. Some 1120 "tramps" applied for lodgings at the local jail during the economic recovery of 1879, for example. Three hundred and eight-one of them gave their occupation as laborer, and 235 others called themselves mill operatives; both groups were presumably attracted by the reopening of the local cotton mills early that year.[36]

Seasonal and cyclical economic fluctuations often had a disastrous impact upon this segment of the working class. The ability of relatively settled members of the laboring class to withstand economic hardship, however, was much greater. Perhaps the savings of Chicopee workers were in fact "eaten up in the frequent and severe depression periods," but the property accumulated by the settled segment of the Newburyport working class was not. The evidence on property mobility for 1850-1860 and 1860-1870 clearly indicates this. There was some hint of a decline in property mobility in the figures for 1870-1880, the decade of the second most severe and prolonged depression in American history, but this finding is suspect because local tax records (notoriously conservative) had to be used for 1880 rather than census estimates.[37]

A better gauge of the impact of the depression of the middle and late seventies was provided by a random check of propertied laborers recorded on Newburyport Assessor's Valuation Lists for 1870, 1873, 1876, and 1880. This check showed that the depression had strikingly little negative effect on working class property holdings. One third of the fifty families in the sample actually increased their real estate holdings between 1873 and 1876, during the depths of the slump. In 1880 only three of the fifty were substantially poorer than they had been in 1870; twenty-six had increased their accumulation of taxable property. The depression may well have slowed the pace at which local workmen discharged the mortgages on their homes, but rarely did it reverse the gains already made. The very low rate of foreclosures on mortgages held by local workmen in this period is further testimony of the remarkable ability of settled working class families to weather hard times.

Three reasons explain the striking ability of these families to accumulate property on pittance wages and to preserve it through prolonged depressions. First, it must be remembered that the most impoverished laborers, the working class families hardest hit in a depression, were forced to go on the road; a study of laborers settled in a particular community deals with a selected minority who tended to be the last to be fired in hard times and the first to be rehired when the economy picked up.

A second point of great importance is that these settled laboring families were rarely dependent on the income of the chief wage earner alone. One member of the family might often be out of work, but it was highly unusual for all able-bodied family members to be out of work simultaneously. The Newburyport *Herald* gave an illuminating instance. Tim Harrington sent his wife and children to work; when they were employed he bought only the family flour out of his weekly wages and deposited the surplus in the savings bank.[38] Unemployment rarely cut off the entire income of such families and ate up their savings; it commonly blocked only a portion of their income, and temporarily prevented further accumulation.

This is not to suggest, however, that these multiple-income families could live comfortably and still put money in the bank. It cannot be emphasized too strongly that the real estate holdings and savings accounts of Newburyport laborers depended on ruthless underconsumption. Few of these families earned much above the minimum subsistence figure estimated by the Massachusetts Bureau of the Statistics of Labor, but they very often managed to consume much less than this "minimum" and to save the difference. A recreational luxury like drinking, for example, was out of the question. One property-owning laborer is known to have fallen prey to the demon rum in this period; Tim Quinn, the newspaper admonished, quickly drank up his estate and was eventually ordered out of the city as a vagabond.[39] The workman who wished to accumulate and maintain a property stake in the community had compelling reasons for sobriety; it was no coincidence that a Roman Catholic Temperance Society was formed in Newburyport at just the time that the Irish immigrants began their climb upward into the propertied sector of the working class.[40]

The degraded economic status of the unskilled laborer in Newburyport, it is clear, was not a permanent condition. The laboring family that settled in the city was usually able eventually to elevate itself into the class of property owners. Few, however, obtained very large holdings. These accumulations were built up gradually and painfully; real estate purchases often had to be mortgaged, bank accounts grew by small accretions. To become a property owner out of earnings from unskilled manual labor required immense sacrifices—sacrifices so great as almost to blur the dichotomy between "property" and "poverty." Money in the bank and a place to live without paying rent did provide security against extreme want, and did give a man a certain respectability. Entry into the propertied sector of the working class was thus an important form of social mobility. But it was mobility within narrow limits, mobility which tended to close off future opportunities rather than open them. Whatever the "magic influence" of property, possession of small amounts of it allowed the laborer neither to improve the material circumstances of his family very much nor to give his children the education which would have enabled them to climb into the white collar world.

6 · The Process of Mobility

The laborers of Newburyport have so far been observed from two angles of vision. Hundreds of unskilled workmen and their sons were viewed first in their occupational role; and then in terms of the frequency with which they managed to accumulate savings and to purchase real estate. It was necessary to isolate these two dimensions of social mobility and to consider each separately, but that simplifying device can now be abandoned in order to deal with some of the key relationships between advances in the occupational and property spheres. First, characteristic patterns of working class family mobility will be identified by surveying some representative cases from the 287 families studied. Then the critical question of whether upwardly mobile fathers customarily succeeded in passing on their gains to their children will be systematically explored. That will lead to an interpretative review of the major findings concerning working class social mobility in the 1850-1880 period.

Patterns of Family Mobility

A rough classification of Newburyport's laboring families into high mobility, intermediate mobility, and static categories will make it easier to discern typical patterns of family mobility. The high mobility category, which includes a sixth of the 287 families studied, encompasses every family at least one of whose members entered a nonmanual occupation during these three decades. Those families whose male members were all confined to unskilled and semiskilled jobs, and who never came into possession of as much as $300 in property during these years are classed static.[1] The intermediate mobility category covers the range of cases between these two poles.

High Mobility Families. Forty-seven of the 287 laboring families who resided in Newburyport a decade or more between 1850 and 1880 were highly mobile. Twenty-two of these cases involved the mobility of adult laborers into nonmanual occupations; in the other twenty-five it was the son of the original laborer who first crossed over into the middle class occupational universe.

The most important avenue of high mobility open to the older generation was, surprisingly, not small business but agriculture. A New England manufacturing city seems an unlikely setting for the fulfillment of Jeffersonian dreams, but sixteen of the twenty-two highly mobile fathers became farm owners, and a good many other laborers did some farming on the side.

Newburyport residents in this period were within reach of a large supply of arable land. Six miles long but only half a mile wide, the city hugged the banks of the Merrimack River; open fields formed its western border. A workman like Thomas Ronan was alert to the possibilities that lay at his doorstep. In 1855, having scraped together a few hundred dollars from his wages, Ronan bought a small house on the western edge of town, and moved his wife and eight children from their cramped working class dwelling on Beck Street. Ronan reported his occupation as "farmer" on the 1860 Census, though he was not yet assessed as the owner of farm equipment or livestock. In 1864 he paid taxes on $900 in real estate, $200 in livestock, and a $100 wagon. By 1867 he had acquired a second house and two more farm lots, and his real property holdings had reached $1600. The Census of 1870 listed Ronan as the owner of $2000 in real estate and $1500 in personal property.

Ronan became more affluent than most of his fellow laborers who became farm owners—Dan Creedon's $1400, William Eustis' $1800, Ichabod Little's $1300 were more typical estate values—but the pattern of his ascent was characteristic of the group. The key step was the setting aside of enough money to purchase a lot on the outskirts of the city. Once land had been acquired, the process of becoming a full-fledged farmer was often slow. Ronan claimed his new status very quickly; other laborers continued to live in rented dwellings for years, working as day laborers and farming their plots in their spare time. In many cases it was impossible to distinguish a laborer who owned farm property from a farmer; census and city directory occupational listings for such men were frequently inconsistent. The sixteen farmers placed in the high mobility class here represent a minimum estimate. Some two dozen others who still reported themselves as laborers on the Census of 1880 owned small amounts of arable land and livestock, and undoubtedly derived some part of their income from agriculture.

About two thirds of the common laborers in Newbury-port at this time were born in rural Ireland, while a good many others were migrants from the farms of Maine, New Hampshire, and Vermont. They were, in short, no strangers to the soil. It was significant that life in the industrial city did not invariably require a total break from the rural environment to which these men were accustomed. This was the case in Newburyport, and there is evidence that it was true to some degree in even the larger urban centers of the period.[2] A select minority from the laboring class succeeded in becoming full-fledged farmers, and many others became yeomen part-time.

To rank farm ownership and operation a nonmanual occupation is a sociological convention; actually the farmer performed heavy manual labor. The farm owner is classed with the businessman and the professional because he was a proprietor—because he commanded capital, made decisions as to what he would produce, and sold at least part of his product for a profit. The laborers who became farm owners in Newburyport appear to have customarily produced little more than enough to satisfy the wants of their family and to have rarely become significantly involved in farming for the market. Even the exceptionally prosperous Thomas Ronan estimated the value of his produce at only $550 on the Census of 1870; most of these men supplied no detailed crop information on the agricultural schedules of the census because they produced less than the $500 minimum specified by the Census Bureau.

The fact that farm work was little different from ordinary labor, and that farms held by mobile laborers were not operated as businesses suggests that the environment in which the children of these mobile laborers grew up was not particularly conducive to success in the middle class world. The career patterns of the sons of the sixteen farm owners confirm this interpretation. Only two youths from this group entered a white collar, professional, or business calling: one became a clerk, and eventually an independent grocer; another began his career as a school teacher. Several simply stayed home and labored on their fathers' farms; some of these presumably would someday become independent farmers by inheritance. The majority, however, gravitated to simple manual occupations, becoming fishermen, mill operatives, butchers, masons.

Farming was much more accessible to the older generation in our sample than the other nonmanual callings. None of these workmen was able to enter a profession, of course, but it is surprising that only six of the entire group ventured into small business. The security of the farm and the familiarity of its tasks drew most of these successful laborers, including those with the largest stocks of capital. The few business owners were very small operators: Freeman Greenough's investment as a "provisioner" was a mere $300; William O'Neal's house, the front room of which served as a tavern and liquor store, was valued at $1000. Whether from insufficiency of capital, incompetence, or bad luck, these small businessmen were much less prosperous than their brethren who purchased farms.

Business pursuits, on the other hand, gave the children of mobile laborers an environment somewhat more favorable to attainment of high status positions. The experience of the Freeman Greenough family suggests some of the possibilities. The Greenoughs came to the city from Maine sometime in the forties, and the father found work as a day laborer. Freeman and one of his sons were classified as laborers in the Census of 1850, while two more of his boys were mill operatives. A few years later, with his small savings, he opened a "provisions" shop at his place of residence. The business returned very little profit, judging from his tax assessments, but Greenough was able to keep it going until his death in 1881. Three of his sons left Newburyport while still youths, one of them with some employment experience as a clerk. A fourth, Joseph, began his career as a hostler. In 1870, at

34, he was still in a humble calling, a driver with no taxable property. His account at the Institution for Savings must already have contained a substantial capital reserve, however, for in the next decade his rise was meteoric. The 1873 assessments show him with five horses and two carriages, worth $900; in 1876 it was twelve horses, five carriages, four hacks, a stable, and a house, a total investment of $4800. By 1880 Joseph's livery stable was valued at $11,000; by 1883, $15,000. Joseph's oldest boy was registered in the Latin preparatory section of the high school in 1880; it is very likely that with this much education he entered a nonmanual calling after graduating. Freeman Greenough's fifth son, Henry, had a more erratic career. He was a mill operative as a youth, later a confectioner, then a clerk in a provisions shop. By 1870 he had returned to the mill, and in 1880 he was recorded as a hack driver, probably working for his successful brother. Two of Henry Greenough's sons, however, found white collar jobs.

In all, twenty-two Newburyport families were ranked in the high mobility category because of the intra-generational mobility of an unskilled manual laborer; another twenty-five families entered that category by virtue of the social advances of their children. The composition of these two groups present sharp contrasts. Three quarters of the older generation achieved high status by the purchase of a farm; none of the second generation high mobility cases moved into agriculture. Half of these mobile sons found white collar jobs, a category of occupation entered by none of the older generation of laborers. The other 50 percent of these sons, as opposed to one quarter of the fathers, became independent small businessmen. Many of these youths had brief experience as factory operatives, but not one made his ascent within the corporate hierarchy. The humble mill hand who struggles to become foreman and ends up chairman of the board, it was shown earlier, was rarely portrayed in the success literature of this period; he was a later creation. In this small way, at least, the mid-nineteenth century mobility ideology accurately mirrored social reality.

The businesses opened by the sons of Newburyport laborers were precarious ventures. They were neighborhood affairs, requiring only enough capital to buy a small inventory of goods and to pay the rent—five of these sons became retail grocers, three of them were ice dealers, two were fish sellers.[3] Low capital requirements allowed easy entry; members of this group typically worked in some manual job for a few years in order to accumulate savings on which to operate. Profits, not surprisingly, were minimal. Only Stephen Fowle and Joseph Greenough reported a rapid and sustained increase in wealth over the period. The threat of bankruptcy was not negligible. One youth opened a grocery with $500 in 1860 and lost everything in five years; he was forced to find work in a hat factory, where he was still employed in 1880. Had this study been carried past 1880, other instances of downward mobility would have been recorded; several of these tiny enterprises were no longer listed in the 1886 city directory. For fathers and sons alike, then, business ownership was not an unrealizable goal; neither, on the other hand, was it a guarantee of secure prosperity once attained.

A new development was the small white collar elite group—fourteen clerks, a bookkeeper, and a clerk lawyer —which had come into existence by 1880. Only two of the members of this group had ever worked in a manual occupation. Boys did not begin their careers as laborers or operatives and later edge their way up into white collar positions. The white collar and laboring worlds were clearly separated. One entered the white collar group only after having received considerable schooling, and one entered it directly. The immense growth of the white collar occupations, just beginning throughout America during this period, was to make the distinction between inter-generational and intra-generational mobility opportunities increasingly sharp; the type of mobility represented by these white collar workers was to become the chief means of social ascent.

Since the white collar worker was necessarily an educated man, the family which produced him had to be in a position to forgo the immediate economic benefits of child labor long enough to allow him to attend school longer than his working class peers, who customarily began work in their early teens. It is not surprising, therefore, that the fourteen families whose sons became clerks and professionals were markedly more prosperous than the families of sons who ventured into business for themselves. Four fifths of the fathers of the latter group remained propertyless unskilled laborers; fully two thirds of the fathers of the former group became property owners, and several were occupationally mobile as well. The case of John G. Buckley was representative. Indistinguishable from a hundred other destitute laborers in 1860, Buckley made a respected place for himself in Newburyport during the following two decades, though remaining a laborer. By 1880 Buckley had become the owner of four houses, worth $2200, and had been appointed a night watchman on the police force. (His younger brother Cornelius accumulated $2900 in real estate over the same period.) Sending his two sons to school was not an impossible drain on the John Buckley's resources: one attended a seminary and became a priest, the second took a position as a clerk after graduating from high school.

If white collar workers usually came from families which were able to give special advantages to them, other members of the family should have shared some of the gains. The career patterns of the brothers of these white collar youths fitted this expectation. The brothers of the laborers mobile into business callings usually found unskilled and semiskilled manual jobs; the siblings of the laborers mobile into white collar occupations tended to enter skilled or nonmanual occupations. A few took white collar jobs themselves, and about half chose skilled callings. Thus Pat Moylan's eldest son became a blacksmith, the other two sons obtained clerkships; John Carnes became a barber, James Carnes a clerk; Jeremiah McDonald became a clerk, his younger brother an office boy. The youngest children, as we might expect, were most likely to achieve the highest status; it was often the increment to family income produced by the employment of their elder brothers that paid for their education.

Intermediate Mobility Families. The category "intermediate mobility" designates families whose members remained entirely with the working class occupational world between 1850 and 1880, but who succeeded in elevating themselves *within* the working class during this period. The forty-seven families in the high mobility class accounted for all the dramatic interclass mobility achieved by unskilled manual laborers in Newburyport at this time. But the other 240 laboring families included in the survey cannot be indiscriminately characterized as static. Within the broad penumbra of the manual laboring class there were important variations in occupational status and in economic position. Two types of intermediate mobility were distinguished here. A family was placed in this category either if one of its members rose into a skilled occupation, or if it acquired a significant amount of property.

Only one fifth of the 145 families in the intermediate mobility class achieved occupational mobility into a skilled craft. Thirteen of the older generation of our sample entered skilled positions between 1850 and 1880. They included four carpenters, three masons, a painter, a tailor, a ropemaker, and an engineer. Wage levels in the skilled trades were well above the prevailing rate for unskilled labor; all but two of the thirteen came into possession of property worth $500 or more. New security of employment, the relative ease of home ownership and saving, and pride of craft all gave grounds for a feeling of status improvement.

In one important respect, however, the gains of these men were limited. An essential element of the superior status of the traditional artisan was that he was able to transmit craft status to his children. The son of the skilled tradesman was expected to serve an apprenticeship himself, and then to enter a craft, often that of his father. Only two of the twenty sons of these mobile laborers followed this course; fourteen became factory operatives or seamen, and another four became casual laborers. To the extent to which the ability to pass on social and economic advantages to one's children is a criterion of success, the success of these laborers was distinctly qualified.

The skilled trades were a somewhat more important avenue of mobility for the younger generation. In our analysis only sixteen families appear to boast a son in a skilled occupation, but the figure is misleading low. To classify families according to the attainments of their most successful member obscures the extent of intermediate mobility of this kind; many of the brothers of youths in white collar jobs held skilled positions themselves. The analysis in Chapter Four provides a better measure of the dimensions of mobility of this kind: laborers' sons who had learned a trade were still a fairly select minority in 1880, but skilled positions were definitely more accessible to them than to their fathers.

Much the largest portion of the intermediate mobility group consisted of families whose members remained in the low-skill, low-pay occupational universe throughout these decades, but who were able to accumulate significant property holdings.[4] The wealth of the 116 occupationally static families in the intermediate mobility category is indicated in Table 10. The variation was wide. A

TABLE 10. Maximum property holdings of occupationally static laboring families[a]

Size of holding	Number of families	Percentage of group
$300-599	27	23%
$600-899	37	32
$900-1199	22	19
$1200-1499	9	8
$1500 and over	21	18
Total	116	100

[a] Families are categorized here according to the maximum figure listed in census schedules and assessor's valuation books, 1850-1880.

small elite, twenty-one families, reached the $1500 mark; a few of these went well above that figure. Jeremiah Long, for instance, already owned a $700 house in 1850. Two of his sons were employed as mariners. Their wages plus the rent paid by four boarders gave Long an unusually large income. In 1856 he bought another house, increasing his real property holdings to $1300; in 1860 he paid taxes on property worth $1700; and by 1870 the Census listed him as the owner of $3000 in real estate and $2000 in personal property.

A more typical figure from the wealthier stratum of propertied laborers was Tim Marooney. Marooney had scraped together $400 by 1867, when he invested it in a shack on the edge of the city. With two cows, a few chickens, and no rent to pay, Marooney found it possible to save a substantial portion of his wages. By 1870 he paid taxes on $500 in personal property as well as $500 in real estate; during the seventies, with the aid of four mortgages, he built a second house on Railroad Street and a third one on Auburn Street. Marooney was worth $1900 in 1880. The family of James Barrett eventually arrived at about this economic level too, but its success came in the second generation. Barrett himself, a common laborer on four successive censuses, never acquired any taxable property. Both of his sons took semiskilled positions while in their early teens. One left Newburyport during the Civil War and never returned; the other was at various times a mill operative, a mariner, and a comb factory employee. The 1882 city directory listed the second as a day laborer like his father, yet by this time he had become the owner of two houses valued at $1800.

These twenty-one relatively wealthy families represented but a small fraction of the total laboring group, of course. The average property-owning laborer in Newburyport accumulated holdings of less than a thousand dollars. The modest progress of the Norton family was characteristic of the dozens of small property holders. The native-born father was a laborer in 1850 and 1860, then a watchman. He saved nothing during those years, so far as can be determined. Three of his four sons as teen-agers worked in the mills. One son moved away in the late sixties. A second became a teamster; he possessed no taxable property by 1880, but did hold an account at the Institution for Savings. The third Norton boy became an operative in a comb factory and was able to purchase a $600 house after two decades of employment there. The fourth, a fisherman, claimed $200 in personal property on the Census of 1870 and was a savings bank depositor; despite the fact that three of his young children were employed in 1880, however, as yet he owned no real estate. Not much of a success story, surely, but not a condition of absolute stagnation either. As the Nortons might have viewed it, one member of the family had definitely advanced into the ranks of the respectable, home-owning citizenry, while two others had taken at least a short step in that direction by setting aside some savings.

Static Families. Two thirds of the laboring families in Newburyport had advanced themselves at least as much as the Nortons by 1880. The remaining third, ninety-five families, were unable to rise out of the most depressed, impoverished segment of the manual laboring class. A man like John Martin, for instance, was a casual laborer in 1860; he later became a laborer at the local gas works, living with his family in a small building owned by the gas company. An Irish immigrant, Martin was illiterate, and his children saw more of the factory than they did of the schoolhouse. Martin's daughters worked in the cotton mills until marriage; one son became a fisherman, the second an operative in a rope factory. Dennis Sughrue was still an ordinary laborer in 1880; his fourteen-year-old boy was a mill hand, while his older son had graduated to the brickyard. Neither family payed any property taxes at all during this period. The Martins, the Sughrues, and the Lowrys had their names in the newspaper occasionally, when one of them was arrested for drunkenness; heavy drinking on a common laborer's wages was a nearly foolproof way of keeping one's family in dismal poverty. About this substantial segment of the Newburyport working class little more can be said. These men were failures according to the values of the competitive society in which they lived, and the early careers of their children suggested that the habit of failure could easily develop in this environment.

The statement that as many as a third of the laboring families resident in Newburyport at this time achieved neither occupational mobility nor property mobility, however, is in one respect highly misleading. Families which lived in the community for only ten years during the period studied were obviously less likely to accumulate property or climb in the occupational hierarchy than families more firmly rooted in Newburyport. Table 11, which classifies families according to length of residence in the city, shows this clearly. Over 40 percent of the families in Newburyport for ten years remained at the very bottom of the social ladder; only 5 percent of the laboring families who lived there throughout the 1850-1880 period are found in the static category. And, similarly, the proportion of families in the high mobility and intermediate mobility categories rose steadily with increased length of residence in the city. Table 11 provides a simple overview of the cumulative significance of sev-

TABLE 11. Mobility of laboring families according to length of residence

	Ten years	Twenty years	Thirty years
Number in sample	145	101	41
High mobility	8%	21%	32%
Intermediate mobility:			
Occupational skill	8	7	27
Property			
$1000 or more	16	19	12
$300–999	26	22	24
Static	43	32	5

eral social processes—selective geographical mobility, occupational mobility, and property mobility—which affected the status of the unskilled laboring families of Newburyport. It reinforces the broad conclusion that the great majority of families who settled in the community for very long were able to make at least a modest social advance.

From Generation to Generation: Social Mobility as a Cumulative Process

An important aspect of the social mobility patterns of working class families in nineteenth century Newburyport has only been touched on so far. Was social mobility usually a cumulative process? Was the son of an upwardly mobile laborer likely to emulate his father and continue to climb upward, or were his career prospects no better than those of a youth whose father remained a propertyless unskilled workman?

In Table 12 the occupational achievements of these working class youths are classified according to the highest occupation attained by their father in the 1850-1880 period, and the results are rather surprising. No consistent

TABLE 12. Occupational status attained by laborers' sons according to the highest occupation of their fathers

Son's occupation at the last census on which he was listed in the 1850-1880 period	Father's highest occupation in the 1850-1880 period			
	Unskilled	Semi-skilled	Skilled	Non-manual
Number in sample	234	38	23	24
Unskilled	26%	3%	9%	29%
Semiskilled	54	63	70	29
Skilled	13	24	17	8
Nonmanual	8	10	4	33

positive relationship between the occupational mobility of fathers and sons is revealed. The children of laborers mobile into a semiskilled occupation were more successful than the sons of static laborers in both the semiskilled and skilled callings, as we would expect. But workmen who climbed into a skilled trade were unable to transfer higher status to their children; their sons found skilled jobs less often than the sons of semiskilled men, and were the least successful of all the groups at penetrating the nonmanual occupations. And the sons of the small elite of laborers who rose into a nonmanual occupation during this period, paradoxically, clustered in unskilled laboring jobs more heavily than the sons of men still at the bottom of the occupational scale. The children of these highly mobile fathers, it is true, obtained nonmanual positions more often than did men in the other groups. But even so, only a third of them attained middle class occupational status, and this is a liberal estimate, since it includes youths working on a farm owned by their father as nonmanual employees. Table 12 provides no support for the belief that occupationally mobile men imparted exceptionally high mobility aspirations to their children, nor for the hypothesis that a mobile father was able to ease his sons' entry into a higher status occupation.

If the occupational mobility of working class fathers did little to further their children's career prospects, perhaps property mobility had a more positive effect. Common sense suggests that youths from the thrifty, respectable, home-owning segment of the working class would develop higher ambitions than the children of laborers living at the bare subsistence level, and that they would possess superior resources in the contest for better jobs. The evidence, however, does not confirm this plausible hypothesis. Property mobility and inter-generational occupational mobility were not necessarily complementary forms of social mobility; indeed, Table 13 indicates that

TABLE 13. Occupational status attained by laborers' sons according the property holdings of their fathers

Son's occupation at the last census on which he was listed in the 1850-1880 period	Father's maximum property holding in the 1850-1880 period		
	Less than $300	$300-899	$900 or more
Number in sample[a]	121	65	48
Unskilled	24%	22%	35%
Semiskilled	59	57	38
Skilled	7	18	21
Nonmanual	11	3	6

[a] The numbers here are smaller than on Table 12, because property data was analyzed only for families resident in Newburyport for a decade or more during the period.

in some instances they were mutually exclusive. The sons of property-owning workmen entered skilled manual callings more often than the sons of propertyless laborers, but they remained disproportionately concentrated in un-

skilled positions and, most surprising, somewhat underrepresented in nonmanual occupations.

This striking discovery recalls an aspect of working
class property mobility about which the prophets of the
mobility ideology were understandably silent. The ordinary workman of nineteenth century Newburyport could
rarely build up a savings account and purchase a home
without making severe sacrifices. To cut family consumption expenditures to the bone was one such sacrifice. To
withdraw the children from school and to put them to
work at the age of ten or twelve was another. As Table 13
shows, the sons of exceptionally prosperous laborers did
not enjoy generally superior career opportunities; the
sacrifice of their education and the constriction of their
occupational opportunities, in fact, was often a prime
cause of the family's property mobility.

This pattern was particularly characteristic of Irish
working class families in Newburyport. It was shown in
Chapter Four that immigrants and their children moved
upwards on the occupational scale with greater difficulty
than their Yankee counterparts. When we consider property mobility, however, the roles of the two groups are
reversed. In Table 14, which reveals ethnic differences in
family mobility patterns, the occupational advantages of
the native are again evident. But within the large group
of laboring families whose members remained in unskilled
and semiskilled jobs, the immigrants were notably more
successful in accumulating property. Of those who had
been in Newburyport for ten years nearly 60 percent of
the native families but less than 40 percent of the foreign
families failed to accumulate significant property holdings. Thirteen percent of the native families in residence
for thirty years but none of the foreign families in this

TABLE 14. Mobility of native-born and foreign-born laboring families by length of residence

	Ten years		Twenty years		Thirty years	
	Native	Foreign	Native	Foreign	Native	Foreign
Number in sample	36	109	27	74	16	25
High mobility	8%	8%	30%	18%	31%	32%
Intermediate mobility:						
Occupational skill	8	7	15	4	38	20
Property						
$1000 or more	8	18	4	24	6	16
$300-999	17	28	19	23	13	32
Static	58	38	33	31	13	0

group were completely immobile in both the property and occupational hierarchies. In each of the three groups close to 50 percent of the immigrant families obtained a property stake in the community while remaining near the bottom of the occupational ladder; the comparable figure for native families was only half that.

That Irish working class families were especially successful in accumulating property but especially unsuccessful in climbing out of the low-status manual occupations was hardly a coincidence. The immigrant laborer received wages no higher than those of the Yankee workman, but he had a greater determination to save and to own. Perhaps the land hunger displayed by the Irish laborers of Newburyport was a manifestation of older peasant values. In any case, it was a hunger which could be satisfied to a remarkable extent by even the lowliest laborer—but only at a price. The price was not only ruthless economy; equally necessary was the employment of every able-bodied member of the family at the earliest possible age. The cotton mill or the shoe factory was not to provide the teen-agers of the second generation with the education made increasingly necessary by a rapidly industrializing economy, as the exceptionally low mobility of Irish youths into nonmanual occupations so plainly reveals.

For the working class families of nineteenth century Newburyport, therefore, social mobility was not a cumulative process. The varying kinds of social advances made by laboring families were not complementary aspects of a smooth natural progression out of the working class occupational world. Property mobility did not usually facilitate inter-generational occupational mobility; often it was achieved by sacrificing the education of the younger generation. Nor did the movement of a laboring father into a higher-status occupation seem to improve the career prospects of his children very much. The upward advances of these ordinary laboring families remain impressive, but the facile assumption of progress from generation to generation must be abandoned.

The Meaning of Mobility: A Trial Balance

If nineteenth century Newburyport was to develop a permanent proletarian class, the families dealt with in this study should have formed it. These unskilled workmen began at the very bottom of the community occupational ladder in the 1850-1880 period. Their situation seemed anything but promising. They lacked both vocational skills and financial resources. Many were illiterate, and few had the means to see that their children received more than a primitive education. Most were relative strangers in the city, migrants from New England farms or Irish villages. Few inhabitants of Newburyport at mid-century were more likely candidates for membership in a permanently depressed caste.

That these working class families did not remain in a uniformly degraded social position throughout the 1850-1880 period is by now abundantly clear. If the Newburyport laboring class gave birth to no self-made millionaires during these years, the social advances registered by many of its members were nonetheless impressive. A brief review of the findings on geographical, occupational, and property mobility will clarify the significance of these social gains and provide a fresh perspective on social stratification in the nineteenth century city.

By 1880 the undifferentiated mass of poverty-stricken laboring families, the "lack-alls" who seemed at mid-century to be forming a permanent class, had separated into three layers. On top was a small but significant elite of laboring families who had gained a foothold in the lower fringes of the middle class occupational world. Below them was the large body of families who had attained property mobility while remaining in manual occupations, most often of the unskilled or semiskilled variety; these families constituted the stable, respectable, home-owning stratum of the Newburyport working class. At the very bottom of the social ladder was the impoverished, floating lower class, large in number but so transient as to be formless and powerless.

The composition of the Newburyport manual labor force in the latter half of the nineteenth century, we have seen, was extraordinarily volatile. A minority of the laboring families who came to the city in those years settled for as long as a decade. Most did not, and it was these floating families whose depressed position most resembled the classic European proletariat. Recurrently unemployed, often on relief, they rarely accumulated property or advanced themselves occupationally. Substantial numbers of these impoverished unskilled workmen, men who "had no interest in the country except the interest of breathing," were always to be found in Newburyport during this period, but this stratum had remarkably little continuity of membership.[5] Members of this floating group naturally had no capacity to act in concert against an employer or to assert themselves politically; stable organization based on a consciousness of common grievances was obviously impossible. The pressure to migrate operated selectively to remove the least successful from the community; a mere 5 percent of the laboring families present in Newburyport throughout this entire thirty-year period found both occupational mobility and property mobility beyond their grasp.

The floating laborers who made up this large, ever renewed transient class occupied the lowest social stratum in nineteenth century Newburyport. A notch above it was the settled, property-owning sector of the working class; above that was the lower middle class, the highest social level attained by members of any of these laboring families. To obtain middle class status required entry into a nonmanual occupation and the adoption of a new style of life; this was an uncommon feat for either unskilled laborers or their children. Five sixths of the laboring families resident in Newburyport for a decade or more during this period found the middle class occupational world completely closed to them. And among the remaining sixth, the high mobility families, were many which remained partially dependent on manual employment for their support. It is doubtful that many of the elite high mobility families developed the attitudes and behavior patterns associated with the middle class style of life. This seems particularly unlikely in the case of laborers who became the operators of small farms, whose sons rarely entered middle class occupations. Nor did a marginal business or a menial clerkship necessarily provide the economic security and inspire the commitment to education needed to insure the transmission of middle class status to the next generation. The importance of the small group of laborers and laborers' sons who purchased shops and farms or found white collar jobs should not be minimized: these men did provide proof to their less successful brethren that class barriers could be hurdled by men of talent, however lowly their origin. But it should be emphasized that many of these upwardly mobile workmen obtained only a precarious hold on middle class status, and that their social milieu often differed little from the milieu of the propertied sector of the working class.

By far the most common form of social advance for members of laboring families in Newburyport in this period was upward movement *within* the working class, mobility into the stratum between the lower middle class and the floating group of destitute unskilled families. A few men from these intermediate mobility families became skilled craftsmen; this was extremely rare for the older generation but less unusual as an inter-generational move. Most often, however, these families advanced themselves by accumulating significant amounts of property while remaining in unskilled or semiskilled occupations. Here were men who offered the market little more than two hands and a strong back, but who succeeded in becoming respectable home owners and savings bank depositors.

What was the social significance of these modest advances? Nineteenth century propagandists took a simple view. The property-owning laborer was "a capitalist." If there was a working class in America, as soon as "a man has saved something he ceases to belong to this class"; "the laborers have become the capitalists in this new world." Accumulated funds, however small, were capital, and the possession of capital determined the psychological orientation of the workman. It was the nature of capital to multiply itself; he who possessed capital necessarily hungered for further expansion of his holdings. To save and to invest was the first step in the process of mobility; investment inspired a risk-taking, speculative mentality conducive to further mobility. The distinction between the "petty capitalist" workman and the rich merchant was one of degree. To move from the former status to the latter was natural; it happened "every day." Similar assumptions lie behind the still-popular view that "the typical American worker" has been "an expectant entrepreneur."[6]

This was sheer fantasy. A mere handful of the property-owning laborers of Newburyport ventured into business for themselves. More surprising, the property mobility of a laboring man did not even heighten his children's prospects for mobility into a business or professional calling. Indeed, the working class family which abided by the injunction "spend less than you earn" could usually do so only by sacrificing the children's education for an extra paycheck, and thereby restricting their opportunities for inter-generational occupational mobility.

Furthermore, the use these laborers made of their savings testifies to their search for maximum security rather than for mobility out of the working class. An economically rational investor in nineteenth century Newburyport would not have let his precious stock of capital languish in a savings bank for long, and he certainly would not have tied it up in the kind of real estate purchased by these laborers. The social environment of the middle class American encouraged such investment for rising profits, but the working class social milieu did not. The earning capacity of the merchant, professional, or entrepreneur rose steadily as his career unfolded—the very term "career" connotes this. The middle class family head was ordinarily its sole source of support, and the family was able both to accumulate wealth and to improve its standard of living out of normal increments in the salary (or net profits) accruing to him over the years.

Ordinary workmen did not have "careers" in this sense. Their earning capacity did not increase with age; in unskilled and semiskilled occupations a forty-year-old man was paid no more than a boy of 17. Substantial saving by a working class family thus tended to be confined to the years when the children were old enough to bring in a supplementary income but too young to have married and established households of their own.

The tiny lots, the humble homes, and the painfully accumulated savings accounts were the fruits of those years. They gave a man dignity, and a slender margin of security against unpredictable, uncontrollable economic forces which could deprive him of his job at any time. Once the mortgage was finally discharged, home ownership reduced the family's necessary expenses by $60 to $100 a year, and a few hundred dollars in the savings bank meant some protection against illness, old age, or a sluggish labor market. A cynical observer would have noted the possibility that home ownership served also to confine the workman to the local labor market and to strengthen the hand of local employers, who were thus assured of a docile permanent work force, but few laborers of nineteenth century Newburyport were disposed to think in these terms.

Families belonging to the propertied stratum of the working class, in short, were socially mobile in the sense that they had climbed a rung higher on the social ladder, and had established themselves as decent, respectable, hard-working, churchgoing members of the community. They had not, however, set their feet upon an escalator which was to draw them up into the class of merchants, professionals, and entrepreneurs.[7]

The contrast between the literal claims of the rags-to-riches mythology and the actual social experience of these families thus appears glaring. A few dozen farmers, small shopkeepers, and clerks, a large body of home-owning families unable to escape a grinding regimen of manual labor: this was the the sum of the social mobility achieved by Newburyport's unskilled laborers by 1880. Could men like these have felt that the mobility ideology was at all relevant to their lives?

I think so. True, many of the optimistic assertions of popular writers and speakers were demonstrably false. Class differences in opportunities were deep and pervasive; a large majority of the unskilled laborers in Newburyport and a large majority of their sons remained in the working class throughout the 1850-1880 period. Not one rose from rags to genuine riches. Whoever seeks a Newburyport version of Andrew Carnegie must settle for Joseph Greenough, keeper of a livery stable worth $15,000, and Stephen Fowle, proprietor of a small newsstand. But we err if we take the mobility creed too literally. The rapt attention nineteenth century Americans gave Russell Conwell did not mean that his listeners literally believed that they soon would acquire riches equivalent to "an acre of diamonds." One ingredient of the appeal of mobility literature and oratory was that pleasant fantasies of sudden wealth and a vicarious sharing in the spectacular successes of other ordinary men provided a means of escaping the tedious realities of daily existence. Fantasies of this sort are not likely to flourish among men who have no hope at all of individual economic or social betterment. And indeed the laborers of Newburyport had abundant evidence that self-improvement was possible. To practice the virtues exalted by the mobility creed rarely brought middle class status to the laborer, or even to his children. But hard work and incessant economy did bring tangible rewards—money in the bank, a house to call his own, a new sense of security and dignity. "The man who owns the roof that is over his head and the earth under his dwelling can't help thinking that he's more of a man than though he had nothing, with poverty upon his back and want at home; and if he don't think so, other people will."[8]

The ordinary workmen of Newburyport, in short, could view America as a land of opportunity despite the fact that the class realities which governed their life chances confined most of them to the working class. These newcomers to urban life arrived with a low horizon of expectations, it seems likely. If it is true that "in the last analysis the status of the worker is not a physical but a mental one, and is affected as much by comparisons with past conditions and with the status of other groups in the community as by the facts in themselves," the typical unskilled laborer who settled in Newburyport could feel proud of his achievements and optimistic about the future.[9] Most of the social gains registered by laborers

and their sons during these years were decidedly modest—
a move one notch up the occupational scale, the acquisition of a small amount of property. Yet *in their eyes* these accomplishments must have loomed large. The contradiction between an ideology of limitless opportunity and the realities of working class existence is unlikely to have dismayed men whose aspirations and expectations were shaped in the Irish village or the New England subsistence farm. The "dream of success" certainly affected these laboring families, but the personal measure of success was modest. By this measure, the great majority of them had indeed "gotten ahead."[10]

7 · *Laborer and Community in 1880: Toward Social Stability*

"THE NEW QUESTION, which has been an old question for long years in Europe, is making itself heard loudly here in America," declared the Newburyport *Herald* in 1877. "It is the question of the status of the laborer."[1] The great railroad strike of that year electrified the nation, provoking warnings that the working class was acquiring "a Samson-like strength."[2] It might soon rise up like a European mob to pull the temple of civilization down in ruins. The terrible memory of civil war was still fresh. Could it be, pondered a character in a popular novel of the seventies, that "the labor question" would prove the "irrepressible conflict" for his generation?[3]

"The labor question" never exploded into an "irrepressible conflict" in the United States. The findings of this inquiry into working class social mobility in Newburyport should help to make clear why these dark fears proved groundless. No study of a single community, of course, can provide a comprehensive explanation of a central feature of the social order of a great nation, but the social experience of unskilled workmen in one city during the 1850-1880 period does suggest some clues to the larger problem.

The social structure of Newburyport in these years, if less fluid than middle class propagandists believed, did offer men at the bottom of the social ladder substantial opportunities to improve their lot. Only a small minority of these laborers and their children had attained middle class occupational status by 1880, but somewhat larger numbers had risen into more attractive manual positions, and the great majority of those who settled in Newburyport had accumulated some property stake in the community. A survey of the Newburyport social scene three decades after the initial shock of urbanization and industrialization will reveal some of the ways in which the social patterns that have been analyzed facilitated the integration of the working class into the community and helped to produce a new basis for social stability.

The Role of the Voluntary Association

After the rapid growth of the forties and early fifties, the population of Newburyport leveled off, hovering around the 13,000 mark between 1855 and 1880. A hasty observer might conclude from this that the community was sealed off from the larger society after 1855, and that the old social equilibrium was re-established as the newcomers of 1840-1855 came increasingly under the influence of the political and social elite of the old community. If so, Newburyport would appear radically different from Lawrence, Lynn, New Haven, and other rapidly growing cities of the age; it would be a stable, backwater "Yankee City" isolated from the main currents of American life.

The image of Newburyport as a static, self-contained community, enshrined in Warner's Yankee City series, is false. The total Newburyport population has been remarkably stable since 1855, but this does not mean that the composition of the city's population has been stable. Despite the seeming stagnation and isolation of Newburyport in the 1855-1880 period, the change in the composition of its population in these years was as rapid and drastic as that in most American cities of the age, and it decimated the leadership of old Newburyport. The exceptional volatility of the new working class of the community has already been described: a steady stream of Irish peasants and New England farm boys poured into the city during these years; most of them left in short order and were replaced by other "permanent transients." This rapid turnover in population was not confined to the working class, however. When the editors of the 1879 edition of the Newburyport city directory compared their list of Newburyport families with the first local directory, published thirty years earlier, the results were astonishing. Of the 2025 families recorded in 1849, only 360 were to be found in Newburyport in 1879. Within the span of a generation the community had experienced something very close to a complete turnover of its population.[4]

To invoke "the Puritan tradition" and the supposed continuity of traditional community leadership as an explanation of the increased stability of industrial Newburyport in the sixties and seventies, therefore, will not do. Indeed, the absence of such continuity and the need for new forms of community integration to accommodate a population largely made up of newcomers was the dominant fact about Newburyport social life in this period. A new social form, appropriate to a complex, diversified community with a highly fluid population, did crystallize in Newburyport during these years: an intricate network of overlapping voluntary associations, "the characteristic social unit of the modern city."[5]

The rapid proliferation of voluntary organizations was one of the most striking features of Newburyport social life in the three decades after 1850. These were not inventions of the latter half of the nineteenth century, of course. "Ordered social gatherings for specific purposes have not been uncommon at any time in New England," noted the *Herald* editor in 1874. But, as he went on to observe, the quantitative expansion of these in Newburyport in recent years seemed so great as to amount to a qualitative social change.[6] A number of charitable, religious, and social societies existed in Newburyport at mid-century, but they were not thought important enough to merit listing in the first city directory. Contrast the detailed registers published thirty years later, recording the officers and meeting places of several dozen organizations. In addition to scores of satellite associations affiliated with churches, there were five Odd Fellow Lodges, four Masonic Lodges, seven temperance societies, twelve charitable associations, and a galaxy of such organizations as the Y.M.C.A., the Knights of Honor, the Ancient Order of United Workmen, the Royal Arcanum, the Mutual Benefit Association, the Blue Ribbon Reform Club, and the Newburyport Rifle Club. The Newburyport Orchestral Club was formed in 1876, the Historical and Antiquarian Society in 1877, the Newburyport Yacht Club in 1878.

The formation, within a short span of years, of dozens of voluntary organizations was a response to a general social need brought about by the disruption of older institutions of community integration. The forest of associations which grew up in the changing cities of nineteenth century America was in certain ways the functional equivalent of the traditional household and the institutions which supported it. These associations were "the key to the social system of the nineteenth century city" because they, rather than the community itself and its formal political leaders, provided the focal point for social life.[7] The relatively monolithic power structure of preindustrial Newburyport and the sense of community loyalty which went with it was never re-created. The allegiances of Newburyport citizens were increasingly dispersed and particular; complaints about the absence of community solidarity tended to disappear toward the end of this period not because solidarity had been restored but because most citizens had lost the capacity to even envisage any "renewal of the spirit of former times."[8]

Neither the number and diversity of these voluntary associations, however, nor the fact that they pursued the particular purposes of their specialized memberships, should lead us to underestimate their stabilizing and cohesive influence. If the integration and social control provided by this network of voluntary organizations was looser than the old Federalist pattern, it was nonetheless important. The membership of each of these groups commonly overlapped with that of one or more of the others, and the leadership of all of them tended to be drawn from the middle and upper social levels and to consist of men with similar class interests and similar social philosophies.

To elaborate and document this sketchy analysis is a task that cannot be attempted here. One question about these voluntary associations, however, must be considered at greater length. Many of these organizations—the Yacht Club and the Historical Society are obvious examples—were patently not for the ordinary workingman. This suggests the possibility that the entire associational network which grew up in industrial Newburyport was a middle class phenomenon, and that it had little or no impact on the working class, just the social layer which had seemed most dangerously unintegrated and divorced from the community to anxious observers at mid-century. Was this the case, or did some of the major voluntary associations of this period embrace the ordinary workingman and knit him into community fabric?

It is exceedingly difficult to learn anything about the social life of the ordinary laborer in Newburyport a century ago. The membership rolls of local organizations have not survived, and no team of social investigators ever administered questionnaires to these men. Tiny fragments of relevant data occasionally appeared in the press. It is evident, for example, that the volunteer fire companies, vital social and recreational organizations in the nineteenth century cities, drew their membership from all classes. A onetime laborer like Luther Carter was head of the Naiad Queen Fire Association, Steamer Number 3, for some years. Both the Fearnot Hose Company and the Little Mac Hose Company had several participants from the ranks of unskilled labor. The Ancient Order of United Workmen and the Council of the Sovereigns of Industry were mentioned occasionally in the Newburyport press of the seventies, but neither organization lasted long enough to make any mark on the community.[9]

We should be forced to rest content with impressions derived from such tidbits of information but for the circumstance that so many of the laboring families of Newburyport at this time were Roman Catholic. Since we know that the membership of the Catholic Church in Newburyport in these years was overwhelmingly working class, to trace the activities of the church and the host of voluntary associations affiliated with it is to describe the associational life of a large fraction of the Newburyport working class.

The Church of the Working Class

The Catholic Church came to Newburyport with the new working class, and the story of its growing strength and its gradual and hesitant acceptance by the Protestant majority is also the story of the integration of the new working class into the community. To many troubled citizens of Newburyport at mid-century, the alien newcomers formed an isolated, atomized mass, detached from and hostile to the community. By 1880 great numbers of these workmen, now industrious, home-owning citizens, were identified as devout members of a church which had been "Americanized" and was clearly in Newburyport to stay. The Church of Immaculate Conception was welcomed by few Yankees, but by 1880 it was widely tolerated as a lesser evil. Whatever the religious reservations of the Protestant majority, the powerfully conservative social influence of Catholicism was coming to be appreciated. A Newburyport attorney summed up the new attitude crudely and effectively when he remarked: "When we pull down a Catholic church, we must put up a penitentiary."[10]

Both the Irish and their church encountered suspicion and some hostility in Newburyport in their first years there. Little can be learned about the activities of the Newburyport Catholic community in the 1850's. Special religious events—communion ceremonies, Easter services—occasionally received mention in the local press, but rarely anything more. No Irish or Catholic groups participated in the massive Fourth of July celebration in 1854. The newcomers were distinctly outsiders. When they offended some tenet of Yankee morality it was a matter for public concern; otherwise they were ignored. Not until it sponsored a public lecture by the famous Irish-American orator Thomas d'Arcy McGee was the Independent Benevolent Society, "a society of . . . foreign residents, who associate for intellectual and moral improvement and for pecuniary aid and assistance in sickness and distress," referred to in the local paper.[11]

This lonely item appeared in 1856. Contrast with it an ordinary newsnote from the 1870's. The local priest, Father A. J. Teeling, was leaving the city for a visit to Europe; the Catholic community held a farewell gathering for him and presented him with a gift of $1000. The roster of sponsoring organizations read as follows: The Men's Sodality, The Holy Name, The Married Ladies' Sodality, The Young Ladies' Sodality, The Rosary, The Church Choir, The Catholic Battalion, The Holy Angels' Sodality, The Society of the Infant Jesus, and The Ancient Order of Hibernians! Music was provided by the Catholic Band.[12] The energies of this multitude of Irish associations were conspicuously demonstrated in the great Saint Patrick's Day parades of the seventies; the sympathetic reporting these received in the press suggests something of the new status of the Irish in the community. As many as a thousand sons of Erin usually turned out for the proceedings. Men of the Father Lennon Benevolent Society appeared resplendent in hats with green ostrich plumes, sashes trimmed with a silver fringe, white belts, and dark suits. Gaudily uniformed Hibernians displayed a large and costly green silk banner depicting Saint Patrick banishing the snakes, as well as a gigantic American flag. The Catholic Church could claim the allegiance of a quarter of the Newburyport population by 1880; no wonder that the mayor and the City Council saw fit to march with the priest at the head of the Saint Patrick's Day processions. Nor did the determination to build parochial schools arouse violent opposition; the 1880 Catholic Fair to raise funds for that purpose was attended

by the Mayor, the aldermen, the School Committee
members, and several Protestant leaders, including a
Congregational minister.[13]

The subsidence of Know-Nothing fears and the growing
acceptance of the Catholic population was partly a result
of the Civil War. The crisis of the Union heightened
common loyalties and dissolved many of the suspicions of
the fifties. The war seemed no respecter of persons; local
men fought and died "independent of rank, of office, of
social position." The problem of how to "weld all the
conflicting and discordant elements" of the community
into "one compact body" had once appeared almost in-
soluble, declaimed the Memorial Day orator. "No
prophet's voice could foretell" that the war would act as a
"mighty furnace" in which these "discordant elements
were melted and moulded into one organic whole."[14] The
Irish proved eager recruits and able soldiers. One of them
later boasted that his countrymen were Americans twice
over—"by their oath under the law, and by their sword in
the war."[15]

If local Irishmen were proving themselves true Americans on the battlefield, their church was proving itself
American in its devotion to property and free competition. The Catholicism the immigrant brought to the New
World was a fatalistic peasant religion which sharply con-
flicted with the optimistic, expansionist assumptions of
American social thought of the age. Clerics who could
write that "in more than 99 cases in a 100 we shall have
reason to rejoice if the son turns out as well as the father"
were challenging the essence of the ideology of mobility,
as were the Italian Catholics whose view of worldly success was that well-to-do Protestants "were under the
most especial protection of the devil, who fattened them

in this world that they might burn better in the next."[16] The clash between these opposing world views was undoubtedly one source of the Know-Nothing protest in the fifties. But the speed with which the Catholic world view accommodated itself to American conditions was impressive. In Newburyport Catholicism was well on its way to being "Americanized" within a generation of its establishment.

Reverend Henry Lennon, the local parish priest from 1848 to 1871, and his successor, Reverend A. J. Teeling, were builders. They were dedicated to accumulating property as well as to saving souls, and they saw clearly that a thrifty, hard-working, well-educated congregation would contribute to that end. As early as 1853 Father Lennon won the praise of the managers of the Free Evening School for his support: "Father Lennon is always ready to assist in a good work, and especially in those matters that tend to elevate his own people, for whose advancement in this city his labors are untiring."[17] A dramatic action taken by the priest in the financial crisis of 1857 showed his control over his flock working to the advantage of the community. According to local legend, still repeated twenty years later, the decisive factor in halting a disastrous run on the savings bank was Father Lennon's advice to his congregation to leave their deposits untouched. The Church of the Immaculate Conception was mortgaged for $8000 at that time, and the priest is supposed to have announced: "You call for your money from the savings bank; the bank forecloses the mortgage on us; I call for the money from you and pay it over and the bank has the money and you have paid at once, with hardship, a debt which spread over some years, would have been easy to bear."[18]

The struggle to build church facilities out of the slender earnings of an almost exclusively working class congregation was exceptionally difficult in the 1850's. As savings began to mount in the sixties and seventies, and as a small group of Catholic businessmen and professionals emerged, larger sums poured into church coffers. In 1874 alone $17,000 was devoted to improving the Green Street structure and to acquiring additional real estate. Between 1871 and 1879 Newburyport Catholics gave an estimated $65,000 for the maintenance, improvement, and expansion of church property.[19]

The financial sacrifices made by Newburyport Catholics were impressive testimony to their religious dedication. A list of donors of $50 or more to a special fund drive in 1879 included some two dozen ordinary laborers from the mobility sample.[20] These were enormous sums to come from men earning little more than a dollar a day, of course, and they suggest a necessary qualification to the broadly correct conclusion that "it is difficult to distinguish the Irish drive to advance the cause of the Church from the drive for social status."[21] True, the church prospered as its communicants prospered. True, the Catholic workman derived status from his identification with the largest and most rapidly growing church in the community. But the fact remains that the church was a heavy drain on resources which, from the point of view of worldly success, might have been put to more productive uses. It has already been demonstrated that the Irish working class families of Newburyport, though more successful at accumulating property than their native counterparts, were markedly less mobile in the occupational sphere. The financial sacrifices the Irish made to further their religion may have had an effect similar to that of their drive for home ownership. Both promoted maximum concentration on immediate accumulation, and discouraged such long-term investments as higher education or even apprenticeship for one's children. A perceptive observer of the Irish community in New York concludes that the development of solid middle class dynasties among Irish Catholics was inhibited by the fact that "a good part of the surplus that might have gone into family property has gone to building the church."[22] For the Catholic workmen of Newburyport the point is slightly different, for these men accumulated more family property than Yankees of similar occupational status and gave heavily to the church as well. It was rather that both the land hunger and the religious devotion of the working class Catholic led him to seek property at the cost of education and the forms of mobility which required education.

Some of the Newburyport Irish, of course, did manage to climb out of the working class. The emergence of a small elite of Catholic businessmen and professionals in the sixties and seventies, some of them recruited from the ranks of labor, was of great significance. This group of successful men of property shared the prudent conservatism of the local priesthood. While the great majority of the Newburyport Catholic population was working class, the leadership of the elaborate network of church-related social organizations came largely from the business class. The key figures in the Father Lennon Benevolent Society in 1871, for example, were mostly businessmen.[23] Through their control of the voluntary associations, respectable and successful men such as these acted both as models for their ethnic group, and as mediators between it and the larger community. The career of John Quill, prominent in several of these societies, illustrates the point well. Quill opened a grocery near the waterfront in the early fifties, and carried on a thriving business until his death in 1880. He served as a financial counselor and general adviser to a good many of his countrymen; the records of the Institution for Savings show that illiterate Irish depositors usually brought either the priest or John Quill to sign the account book for them. The *Herald* noted Quill's passing with an editorial praising his beneficial influence on the local Irish and concluding: "He was very well educated, and a worthy and honest man, who had the respect of all who knew him."[24]

The respect won by "worthy and honest" Catholic men of property like John Quill, Patrick Henry, and Hugh McGlew did not, of course, signify a complete reversal in the attitudes of the Protestant majority toward Catholicism. A speech given in Newburyport in 1880 denounced all Catholics as "political and ecclesiastical tools of the Roman priesthood," and declared that the power of the Church in America was a clear violation of the Monroe Doctrine.[25] The *Herald* editor brooded over the fact that Catholics, only a quarter of the population of New England, accounted for three quarters of the births; a correspondent offered the consolation that infant mortality was exceptionally high among the impoverished Catholic masses.[26] The newspaper took a perverse pleasure in the prospect that the successor to the dying Pius IX would likely be reactionary: "The more reactionary the result of the election, the better for the cause of progress and civilization. There is nothing better for the right and the truth than the baldest and boldest advocacy of the wrong and the false."[27]

Despite the gains which had been made since the fifties,

in 1880 Newburyport was still a divided community, and it appeared likely to remain so. The division, however, was not the simple class division of "have-alls" and "lack-alls" that loomed on the horizon at mid-century. Religious and ethnic differences had outweighed class considerations. The large Irish, Roman Catholic component of the working class was securely attached to a church and a church-related associational structure dominated by a priest and a business elite firmly committed to the prevailing American ideology of enterprise and success. The Catholics of Newburyport, a fourth of the population in 1880 and destined to increase further with continuing immigration, were set off from the rest of the community in many ways. The elaborate organizational structure which had grown up by then was designed to meet all the social needs of the Catholic population, and it provided a series of "structural fences . . . contrived to keep the ethnic individual articulated to the church and the community while keeping him from straying too far out" into the community social system.[28] The parochial schools established in Newburyport in 1882 were the capstone of this system.

The integration of the Catholic population into the larger community, therefore, was partial, and the attitude of the community was accordingly a blend of hostility and approval. The Catholic Church was "aggressive, temporizing, and deceitful," but it was by no means "an unmitigated evil."[29] Religious objections and mistrust of Catholic separatism competed with appreciation of the church as an instrument of discipline and control over "the dangerous classes."[30] A deeply ambivalent editorial on the problem summed up the sentiment which had come to prevail by 1880: "There is not a reasonable person in the town, who employs a Catholic girl in his family, who would not prefer one devoted to her religion, constant at church . . . When they deny their religion they seldom accept ours, but that class furnish the night walkers, the drunkards and the criminals."[31]

The Politics of Consensus

A European visitor observing the campaign of 1880 in Newburyport might well have been astonished at the violence of the political rhetoric. "Free trade makes cheap labor," pontificated the local Republican leader, "cheap labor is degraded labor; degraded labor makes tramps; tramps make criminals; criminals make Democrats." Poll "the respectable part of this community," he continued, "and you will find a Republican vote. Then poll the slums, penitentiaries, and cock-pits and you will get a solid Democratic vote."[32] A workingman replied in kind: "I was born in poverty and . . . have never known anything else. My radicalism and my democracy have been starved into me by long months of privation, by long hours of miserably paid work . . . My feelings are bitter and my words are fierce on the subject of the non-producing class which lives on the earnings of productive labor in insolent superiority and keeps it in silent slavery."[33]

Fierce words, however, were the stock-in-trade of the political orator; it would be folly to consider them proof of the depth and sharpness of actual political conflict in the community in which they were uttered. A case for the opposite assumption might even be made—that the extraordinary verbal violence of American politics in the post–Civil War period grew out of and served to conceal the relative absence of genuine issues, and that political contests were as much as anything else an elaborate game.

In Newburyport, at least, despite these rhetorical portents of class war, the chief characteristic of the local political setting in 1880 was the failure of the two parties to become sharply polarized along class lines and the extent of interparty consensus on such matters as the rights of property and the virtues of free competition.

The character of politics in Newburyport, of course, was partly determined by the fact that the local party organizations were branches of the two national parties. Party principles and objectives were defined at the national level, and local politicos naturally worked within the framework of issues established by national leaders. The most conspicuous feature of the national political struggles of this period was the relative absence of party conflict over essentials of economic and social policy. Recent historians have characterized the entire American political tradition in terms of a "Lockean" consensus; "the range of vision embraced by the primary contestants in the major parties" of America, Hofstadter contends, has always been "bounded by the horizons of property and enterprise."[34] Certainly American party battles from the Civil War to the Populist Revolt seem to bear out this view.

The national political consensus in this period must be taken as a given here. But the Newburyport example does suggest some of the social roots of consensus politics in one small community, and it may make somewhat more comprehensible the attachment of the American working class to slogans and policies which were then meeting sharp opposition from their European counterparts. At the heart of the American consensus was the ideology of mobility; Horatio Alger was a primary symbol of the American political tradition. In Newburyport, at least,

one reason why these ideas held sway in the latter half
of the nineteenth century was that they bore a certain
resemblance to social reality. Even at the very bottom
of the class ladder there were abundant opportunities for
modest self-advancement, and the workmen who failed to
climb at least one notch upwards rarely remained in the
community for very long. The desperate economic grievances and the rigid social barriers which fed the class-
based parties and the ideological politics of the Old
World were missing from the Newburyport scene: this
was a chief determinant of the character of local politics.[35]

Newburyport was no longer a one-party town. The
party balance had become very delicate; the shift of a
small bloc of voters was often enough to swing a local
election. Campaigns accordingly were hotly contested.
The chief issues dividing the national parties of this era
were civil service and the tariff, while local political conflict centered around the perennial problem of the tax
rate and the question of "rum or no rum."[36] None of these,
obviously, were the stuff of which "irrepressible conflicts"
are made.

There were, it is true, broad class and ethnic differences
between the two parties. In 1880 the *Herald* located the
center of gravity of the Democratic party in the solid
South and in "the dangerous classes" of the Northern
cities; it identified the Republican party with the "great
truth" that "the future of the Union must be entrusted to
Puritan hands and must be guided by Puritan influence."[37]
There was a grain of truth in these stereotypes as they
applied to the Newburyport scene: the predominantly
working class Irish were indeed securely in the Democratic fold, and the Yankee businessmen of the community were mostly Republicans.[38] But these were only

general tendencies. A shred of precise evidence about the political preferences of the most impoverished members of the community at one point in this period is available, and it fails to confirm the stereotype of the Democratic party as the party of the lower class. Of the 300 Newburyport citizens who declared themselves too poor to pay their poll tax in 1880 and allowed the party organizations to put up the money for them, roughly half chose to accept Republican favors.[39] And it can hardly be said that the Democratic party of Newburyport at this time was in the hands of "the dangerous classes"; a long list of Democratic ward officials in 1880 included no ordinary workmen at all.[40]

Only in the heat of a campaign, in any event, could the "dangerous classes" of the community be considered even remotely dangerous. The truth which subsequent decades would confirm was already clear by 1880: that in a community in which opportunities for individual self-advancement were widespread, the growing political power of the working class presented no fundamental threat to the established order.[41] The rise of the once feared Irish to political power, still in its early stages in 1880, illustrates the point well. Hugh McGlew and Thomas Cuseck, both prosperous Irish-American businessmen, served on the City Council during the seventies. In 1884 Albert E. Moylan, a laborer's son but himself a clerk, was elected to the Council; the ascent of the second generation had begun. A handful of the newcomers won appointment to the police force in the seventies; the stereotype of the Irish cop was soon to be born.[42] The local party organizations were still almost exclusively in the hands of the natives—only one minor ward official in 1880 had an obviously Irish name—but this too would change before long.[43] By the turn of the century the descendants of Newburyport's laborers had captured the local Democratic organization; in 1903 James F. Carnes, the son of an unskilled workman, became the city's first Irish-American mayor.[44]

Thus the political arena too was open to ambitious men of talent. And the Irish-Americans who rose to political prominence were precisely those who had risen dramatically in the occupational and property spheres—businessmen and professionals, leaders in a variety of ethnic and religious associations. The shift in the ethnic composition of the local government, therefore, brought little change in either the class affiliations of Newburyport's rulers or the main outlines of public policy. James Carnes began his career as a clerk, and was a successful businessman before he became mayor. Another case history demonstrates the same point. Jeremiah Cashman remained a common laborer throughout the period 1850-1880, but he managed to accumulate about $1000 in real estate, which two of his nine children used after his death to establish the firm of Cashman Brothers, "Stevedore and teamster and dealer in stone, sand and ballast. Excavating in all its branches."[45] Michael Cashman took over the business eventually, and became one of the richest coal and oil dealers in Essex County; only after this kind of success did he venture into politics and win election as mayor of Newburyport.[46]

As a group, the Irish of Newburyport had gotten ahead in the ways that mattered most to them. If even the second generation remained heavily concentrated in working class occupations, mobility of a kind had been within reach of the Irish from their first years in Newburyport. Through toil and sacrifice they had been able to buy homes, build their church, and obtain a slender margin of economic security. It must have seemed fitting that the politicians who rose from their ranks were successful businessmen, men whose careers appeared to embody most fully the promise of American life.[47]

A New Jerusalem

"Progress is the law of nature," the men of Newburyport knew. Their own experience proved it. They had been steadily "casting off the incumbrances of the past and . . . living nearer to God—that is, more in accordance with His natural intellectual and moral laws, which are better known now than in the days of our fathers."[48] The editors of the Herald drew on Saint-Simon for the wisdom that "the Golden Age, which a blind tradition has placed in the Past, is before us"; they found evidence of the moral superiority of nineteenth century civilization in the fact that "Jonathan Edwards saw no evil in lotteries, which now even the law forbids!"[49]

By 1880 Social Darwinism was presumably sweeping the land, but pessimistic social lessons drawn from the doctrine of the survival of the fittest were not very often voiced in Newburyport. The conception of society as an open race, of course, had been a cliché in the community well before Darwin, Spencer, and Sumner were heard from. But this idea could be given a variety of emotional shadings, and varying policy implications could be drawn from it. Rather than flourishing with new scientific support, the strict Malthusian emphasis on the struggle for existence was less common in Newburyport in the post–Civil War years than it had been at mid-century. Laissez-faire was still in vogue, but there was growing optimism that an open race was a race in which there were few losers. The fierce injunctions that workmen must stop frittering away their wages on idle luxuries, so common at mid-century, tended to be replaced by a new consumption ethic. "Every new comfort that is generally adopted by the working class" was seen to benefit "the whole society." A high level of expenditures by workmen was said to generate purchasing power which kept the economy running at full capacity.[50]

General prosperity for the working class was regarded as a political as well as an economic necessity. The property mobility of Newburyport workmen promoted confidence that "the doctrine that 'property is theft' can obtain with only a small minority in a country . . . such as ours. Too many own some property; and a shanty or a rod of land, a horse and cart, preserve the owner from theories which would rob him of his little all." So long as the ordinary man had a realistic hope of "getting property at some time," he would remain within the orbit of consensus politics.[51]

Newburyport residents in 1880 were still persuaded of the uniqueness of American social arrangements, which they regarded as the prime cause of the progress they gloried in. They saw a stark contrast between the Old World and the New: "The European is born to a condition in life; he is one of a class from the cradle to the grave."[52] From this perspective the violent social struggles of Europe appeared as contests between the people and the forces of feudal reaction, with the people seeking essentially those democratic social and political institutions already enjoyed by Americans. These assumptions led the sober Republican Newburyport *Herald* to adopt some rather striking political postures. The International Association of Workmen was defended against "the slanders" of its enemies.[53] (One wonders what the burghers of Newburyport would have made of Bakunin and Marx had they appeared to expound their views before the Newburyport Atheneum!) The Commune of Paris was staunchly supported as a "brave struggle" for the rights of man.[54]

The major American newspapers took quite a different view of the Commune, which led the *Herald* to complain that the cause of freedom "does not receive the justice which is due from the American press. It might be expected that people struggling for Republican liberty would receive encouraging words from the newspapers of a republic, that their mistakes and weaknesses would be considered with some allowance, and not denounced as bitterly as they are by the most arbitrary monarchs and the haughtiest aristocrats."[55] Most modern historical writing suffered from the same bias, argued another editorial. The original French Revolution, "the greatest step ever taken for liberty and human progress," had yet to be properly analyzed in a history written "from the democratic point of view."[56] A review of a volume of local history insisted that the evolution of the community could best be understod in terms of the revolutionary democratic principles of the French Revolution: "The obscure annals of the most remote parish of a remote New England town are initimately connected with, and bring irresistibly to mind one of the greatest movements in modern history and one of the most immemorial of events."[57]

Opinions like these followed logically enough from the premises of the mobility ideology; enthusiasm for the democratic revolutions of Europe had, in fact, been traditional in America. This enthusiasm, however, rapidly waned after the Civil War. The labor question had not yet become a central political issue, but rumblings were being heard; some Americans were beginning to identify their situation with that of the European upper classes, and many others were at least attaining a heightened appreciation of social peace. One scholar dates the reversal of "the historic American attitude" toward revolution at the time of the Commune.[58] This reversal can be charted in newspapers published in the large cities, where the economic advance and social assimilation of the massive working class appeared slow and uneven; it did not manifest itself in Newburyport. It is likely that the unusual survival of the older optimistic sentiments in Newburyport was connected with the community's notable success and absorbing the lower class into its economic, social, and political structure. The resident of a stable small community might well feel more tolerant of social upheaval than the New Yorker; he had less reason to doubt the ability of the American social order to withstand the strains of urbanization and industrialization, less reason to fear that class conflict might erupt into violence in his own city.

Not even the great railroad strike of 1877, which struck terror in the breasts of so many Americans, did much to undermine the confidence of Newburyport's citizens, at least if newspaper editorials and letter columns provide any basis for judgment. No one positively approved the principle of striking. "Who are the men who strike?" asked the *Herald*. "Are they the kind of men who move the world? Are they the men who in the end achieve success for themselves?" No. The strikers were the petty and weak who cared only for the size of their paychecks, men not properly "inspired by their work."[59] At the first news of mob violence in Pennsylvania, the paper permitted itself this hysterical outburst: "Underneath the intelligence and the industry, the self-restraint, and the religion and morality of the American people, there is the same ignorance and brutality, the same criminal class that is found in the Old World. It is a startling revelation . . . There is underneath a vast lava bed of seething lawlessness and crime ready to break out whenever opportunity offers."[60]

Once the first shock had worn off, however, the *Herald's* faith that the New World was still different from the Old quickly reasserted itself. The amazing thing about the strike, said an editorial a few days later, was the moderation and respect for property displayed by the workers. In a few isolated instances a small criminal element had been able to distort peaceful protest into bloody anarchy. But the laborers themselves—though guilty of not being "inspired by their work"—were not the villains of the piece. The men may have had "good cause for complaint"; perhaps a more progressive inheritance law was needed to prevent excessive concentration of wealth in the hands of the Vanderbilts. The controlling motive of the strikers was merely to obtain property of their own and hence to become "capitalists," in accord with the great American ideal. This was the clue to the central paradox of the strike: "The people said they had no bread, but we didn't hear of one bread shop or grocery store being robbed; they said they had no money, but no banking house was plundered; they said they had been wronged by their employers, but not a railroad king was shot and not a railroad manager had his house burned. In most places, the railroad men protected property, and only the incomings from the slums destroyed."[61]

Such civilized behavior on the part of workmen was

quite natural where the social rigidities and the unearned
privileges of the Old World did not exist. Certain difficulties, conceded the *Herald*, had been created in the
large cities by the immigration of European workers in-
fected with socialist ideas. (Bismarck was alleged to be
solving the social problems of Germany by systematically
exporting radicals to the United States.) Although there
were actually "no classes in the U. S. in the sense in
which they exist in Europe," this was not immediately
apparent to the newcomer whose preconceptions were
formed in a feudal society; these Europeans observed that
there were very rich men in America and equated them
with the upper class of the Old World, not realizing that
wealth and prestige here were always earned, not inherited.[62] But this was only a problem of adjustment, believed the men of Newburyport. Their social system had
successfully absorbed the influx of an Irish proletariat,
and it would meet the challenge posed by later immigrants equally well. European hatreds would "melt before
the kindly sunlight" of American free institutions, "where
all may meet on one common plane."[63] A second wave of
immigration was just reaching Newburyport in 1880, and
the *Herald* reported happily, "The large number of French
Canadians at the South end are acquiring a good reputa-
tion for quietness and sobriety."[64]

Newburyport was no more a community of believers,
at least in the theological sense. Some twenty men of the
cloth addressed a different God from twenty pulpits each
Sunday morning; none spoke with the commanding
authority of their predecessors. But the men of Newburyport shared a common secular faith, an abiding belief in
the American social system and the progress it seemed
to guarantee. The sermons which defined the new faith

appeared everywhere—in speeches, memoirs, popular novels, and editorials. America was "above" Europe as Europe was "above" Asia. This was "the law of progress." Europeans were welcome to come to the New World to share in its blessings, but "let them keep their popes and potentates on the other side of the water; their classes and castes belong not to us or to our age." Men from all the lower civilizations might "come to this, our higher home," might "climb up into our observatory, which shall bring you nearer the stars and the eternal heavens than the old countries ever dreamed of." America would happily absorb the newcomers so long as they met one condition—that they understood the principles of a uniquely open society and left undisturbed its sacred foundations: "Put not thy unhallowed touch upon the pinnacles of the holy temple which God, not we, have reared in the new world—new for a new people and a better; new for a new age and a higher; new for a new religion and a purer; and new for a new Jerusalem, which is from God out of heaven."[65]

8 · Newburyport and the Larger Society

One small nineteenth century community has been discussed at length in the preceding pages. The Census of 1850 found 62 cities of more than 10,000 in the United States, and by the end of the century the number stood at 440.[1] Can a study of social mobility patterns in one of these cities tell us anything of interest about the others? Is it possible, on the basis of the Newburyport example, to draw any broader conclusions about the social structure of nineteenth century America? Unless it can be shown that Newburyport was, in some important respects, representative of the larger society of which it was a part, this book will be of purely antiquarian interest. Newburyport, it will be argued here, was indeed a reasonably representative community with respect to the problems dealt with in this study. The Newburyport findings, therefore, do enlarge our knowledge of the American past. And knowledge of the past, in this instance, illuminates an issue of contemporary relevance—the question of whether it is more difficult to rise from the bottom of the social ladder in the United States today than it was in the America of Horatio Alger.

The Question of Representativeness

Because Newburyport was once the site of W. Lloyd Warner's famous inquiry into "the life of a modern community," a variety of claims and counterclaims as to the community's representativeness have already been made.

This controversy has created a forest of misconceptions which must be cleared away before we can speculate profitably about the larger implications of research conducted in Newburyport.

Warner's Yankee City study, reported in five bulky volumes, probably still ranks as the most intensive (and expensive) social survey ever carried out in a small American city. Regrettably, however, nowhere in these books was there any systematic consideration of the problem of generalizing the findings of the study to other American communities. Warner simply proceeded from the unexamined assumption that Newburyport and the small towns he later studied with similar techniques were "representative American communities," and that what was true of them was true of American society as a whole. A latent function of the pseudonyms he applied to these cities was to lend an aura of typicality: "Yankee City" is manifestly a place of more universal significance than Newburyport, Massachusetts; "Jonesville" is more truly American than Morris, Illinois.[2]

Warner's facile equation of Newburyport and Morris with America has drawn the fire of many critics, and it has been pointed out that from Warner's own description it appears that Yankee City was a very special kind of community, deviant from the American norm in several fundamental respects. The Yankee City project originated as an offshoot of Elton Mayo's famous study of industrial relations at Western Electric's Hawthorne plant, on the outskirts of Chicago. Warner, a young anthropologist, was asked to carry out a community study which would pursue some of the questions raised by the Hawthorne findings. Chicago was too large to study as "a total community," Warner quickly decided, while the smaller industrial cities in the Chicago area (Cicero, Gary, and so forth) were unsatisfactory because "they had a social organization which was highly disfunctional, if not in partial disintegration." He sought a small community, something in the range of 10,000 to 20,000, and "above all a well-integrated community." Ideally, it should be self-contained, as insulated as possible from "disruptive" influences emanating from large cities undergoing "rapid social change." Its population should be "predominantly old American," and it should have "developed over a long period of time under the domination of a single group with a coherent tradition." Newburyport appeared to him to be such a city, one whose "Puritan tradition" remained "unshattered," one whose "social superstructure . . . remained very much what it had been at the end of the War of 1812."[3]

To discover so isolated and static a community in modern America, it might be expected, would require some industrious searching, but critics of the Yankee City series have generally taken for granted that Newburyport was in fact the unchanging "old New England town" Warner found it to be, and have concentrated their attack on Warner's assumption that such a community could be considered a miniature replica of the larger society. C. Wright Mills and others have argued that little can be learned about the dynamics of social stratification in urban, industrial America from the study of so obviously deviant a case.[4] Florence Kluckhohn raises the possibility that the dominant modern American values of expansion, achievement, and mobility have not equally penetrated every community in the United States, and suggests that certain small towns display a "substitute cultural orientation." Static, self-contained Yankee City, which possessed "a quite rigid status system in which upward movement is exceedingly difficult," is her prime example.[5] The fact that Newburyport is the backward-looking, hierarchical old Yankee town of the novels of John P. Marquand has similarly helped to foster the impression that Newburyport was in fact one of the least "typical" American communities Warner could possibly have chosen.[6]

This is a plausible line of argument, and it would be convincing if the portrait of Newburyport supplied in the Yankee City series was reasonably accurate. But in fact the Yankee City whose "social superstructure . . . remained very much what it had been at the end of the War of 1812" was largely a creation of Lloyd Warner's imagination.[7] Every investigator admittedly sees the community he studies from a particular, limiting perspective; a degree of subjectivity is perhaps inescapable in treating a complex social object. But, whatever the bounds of legitimate subjectivity, in the Yankee City series Warner far exceeded them.

Readers of this study of nineteenth century Newburyport will have great difficulty in recognizing Warner's portrait by the sitter. As late as the 1930's, according to Warner, the "Puritan tradition" of Yankee City remained "unshattered," for the community's population was happily still "predominantly old American." But in point of fact the population of Newburyport ceased to be predominantly old American more than half a century before the Yankee City team began its labors! The effects of mass immigration, the high birth rate of the newcomers, and the heavy migration of old residents from the community produced a radical change in the composition of the Newburyport population in the 1850-1880 period. Immigrants and their children constituted almost half of the city's population in 1885, and a majority of the remaining "Yankees" were not from old Newburyport families. Little more than a tenth of the family names recorded in the city directory for 1879 were to be found in the first Newburyport directory thirty years before. The economic and social transformation the community underwent midway in the nineteenth century effectively shattered the social superstructure of preindustrial Newburyport. If the Federalist ethos lingered on in a few old families, the dominant values in this city of mobile newcomers were progress, expansion, and mobility, and the actual opportunity structure of the community was open enough to sustain these values.

These remarks about Warner's portrait of Newburyport point to an interesting—if somewhat paradoxical—conclusion: since the city in fact was much less static, deviant, and isolated from the larger society than the mythical Yankee City, it is possible that Warner's assumption that Newburyport was "a representative American community" has more to be said for it than critics have usually allowed. It is obvious that in certain ways every community, like every individual, is *sui generis*; it is equally obvious, however, that cities that are part of a particular social order are exposed to common influences and display some common characteristics. Though Newburyport cannot be assumed to "represent" *the* nineteenth century American city, it is the one city of the period for which detailed information about mobility opportunities open to ordinary workmen is available. This book deals with what is admittedly but a single case, but to make full use of this single case it is legitimate to speculate about the likelihood that similar mobility patterns prevailed in other nineteenth century American com-

munities. Some general considerations and a few suggestive fragments of evidence pertaining to specific cities
provide a foundation for such speculation.

The most surprising comparison is provided by Curti's
intensive study of Trempealeau County, Wisconsin, in the
1850-1880 period. *The Making of an American Community,* strictly speaking, does not deal with a community, but rather an entire rural county, whose total
population in 1880 was little more than that of Newburyport. Curti presents a close analysis of the geographical
mobility, occupational mobility, and property mobility
of both the agricultural and nonagricultural population
of this booming county in the first decades of its settlement, and argues that the striking mobility he discovered
supports a number of hypotheses derived from Frederick
Jackson Turner. Since there were very few unskilled
workmen living in Trempealeau County in these years, a
detailed comparison of the findings of the two studies is
not possible, but on the whole the Newburyport and
Trempealeau County data provide little support for the
stark contrast so often drawn between the fluid social
order of the frontier and the rigid, class-ridden society
of the Eastern city.[8]

As we would expect, the rate of population turnover
on the frontier was very high; in none of the occupational
and ethnic groups studied did as many as half the members remain in the county a decade, and the average persistence rate for the entire sample was 25 percent for
1860-1870 and 29 percent for 1870-1880. But if the population of Trempealeau County was extremely volatile in
these years, it was only slightly more volatile than the
population of supposedly static Newburyport. Similarly,
the property mobility of the inhabitants of this frontier

community (including a handful of unskilled laborers who settled there in these years) was remarkable, but so too was the property mobility of Newburyport's laborers. In only one respect were the prospects of laborers on the frontier—if the few unskilled men in Curti's sample provide a basis for judgment—distinctly more favorable. While business and white collar occupations were generally closed to them, many attained occupational mobility of a kind by purchasing and operating farms. Even in Newburyport farming was a vehicle of occupational mobility for laborers, but it was naturally more important in a rural county. It is significant that property mobility seems to have been accompanied by improved occupational status more often in Trempealeau County than in Newburyport, but it does not alter the general conclusion that for men at the bottom of the class ladder mobility opportunities in one newly industrialized city and one newly opened frontier county in the 1850-1880 period did not differ radically.

It is reasonable to anticipate that the level of opportunities in other American communities undergoing urbanization and industrialization in these years resembled the Newburyport pattern to at least some degree. No historical investigations comparable to the Curti inquiry and the present study have as yet been carried out in any of these cities, but some fragments of relevant data point to this conclusion. It is very clear, for example, that the marked volatility of the Newburyport population was not at all unusual, and it is likely that the selective character of the working class migration cycle revealed by the Newburyport evidence was common to other American cities of the age. The rate of population turnover in Rochester, New York, for 1849-1859 was even higher than in Newburyport, we know, and other studies indicate the extreme instability of the manual labor force in such communities as Biddeford, Maine, and Lowell, Holyoke, and Chicopee, Massachusetts.[9] In Massachusetts, then the leading industrial state in the country, the State Census of 1885 showed that little more than a third of the state's population had been born in their city of current residence; even when native-born Americans alone were taken into account, the figure was less than 50 percent.[10] Thus one striking characteristic of working class life in Newburyport—the fact that so many workmen were transients, drifting from city to city according to the dictates of the labor market—was a local reflection of a national phenomenon of major importance.

Nor does it seem likely that the remarkable property mobility achieved by the settled segment of the Newburyport laboring class was peculiar to this small community. It is difficult to believe that, on the whole, conditions in Newburyport were uniquely conducive to working class prosperity. Quite the contrary. After the boom of the 1840's the local economy was notably sluggish by comparison with cities like Portsmouth, New Bedford, Lynn, and New Haven. From the point of view of economic growth Newburyport represents anything but a favorable case, and any variations from the Newburyport pattern of working class property mobility turned up by future investigators may well lead to a more optimistic view of the lot of the workman in nineteenth century America. True, many scholars have ventured rather pessimistic judgments about working class savings and home ownership in particular cities, but since none of these writers have actually traced individuals, it would be well to be skeptical of their conclusions. The opinion that working class savings in Chicopee were small enough to melt away during periods of recession, for example, has been advanced on the basis of accurate knowledge of wage levels and dubious guesses as to "minimum" family budgets. The Newburyport evidence casts considerable doubt on such estimates of minimum consumption standards, and fragments of data from Lawrence and Holyoke in this period reinforce these doubts.[11]

It is likely, too, that the patterns of occupational mobility for unskilled laborers and their sons in other nineteenth century industrial cities did not often differ radically from those described here. For the immigrant sector of the working class, at least, relevant evidence exists in the form of a Bureau of the Census monograph analyzing the occupational distribution of the nation's immigrant groups from 1850 to 1950. The fact that the unit of analysis was not individuals but groups whose composition was changing—the "born in Ireland" group for 1850 includes only a fraction of the "born in Ireland" group of 1880—precludes a detailed comparison with the Newburyport findings, but these national data tell a broadly similar story.[12] In Newburyport and in the United States generally the Irish immigrants entered the labor market at the bottom and climbed slowly; if a substantial minority of them advanced within the working class occupational world, only a select elite rose into nonmanual positions. The sons of these men found greater opportunities in business and white collar callings, but they too remained disproportionately concentrated in manual occupations; characteristically, though, the son of an Irish immigrant became a semiskilled factory operative rather than an unskilled day laborer, and significant numbers of them entered the skilled trades.

The Newburyport evidence suggests that much the same pattern held for unskilled migrants from rural America, with the difference that the native-born laborer, somewhat less successful than the immigrant at accumulating property, tended to rise a little more rapidly in the occupational sphere. Whether or not these ethnic differences in types of social mobility were the rule in other American cities is a question which merits investigation. A recent analysis of data from the Census of 1930 has shown that in Detroit, Los Angeles, Chicago, and Philadelphia foreign-born residents were more likely to own their own homes than the sons of immigrants, who in turn had higher home ownership rates than the sons of native-born parents. This fits with the Newburyport findings, and suggests the interesting possibility that in these major twentieth century cities too some immigrant groups may have invested in real estate at the cost of other forms of social mobility.[13]

It may seem outrageous to suggest that a study of the experiences of manual laborers in Newburyport can reveal anything of interest about the working class of Boston or New York. In their comprehensive survey, *Social Mobility in Industrial Society*, Lipset and Bendix confidently assert that "in a small city like Newburyport . . . which has not increased in population for a century, the chances for a lower-class individual to rise must necessarily be less than in a large city in which new positions of higher status are constantly being created."[14] This judgment, however, rests on questionable premises. It is not at all clear that the process of urban growth in the nineteenth century produced a disproportionately greater expansion of high status positions in large cities than in smaller ones. Nor can one assume a simple relationship between the stability or instability of a city's total population and the fluidity of its occupational structure. Even in a community with a declining population, exceptionally high emigration of high status individuals could create a vacuum drawing large numbers of lower class persons up the occupational scale.

Some empirical evidence which suggests the inadequacy of the Lipset and Bendix formulation is supplied in Table 15, which compares the Newburyport findings

TABLE 15. Occupational status attained by unskilled laborers over ten-year periods, selected cities, 1850-1950[a]

	Unskilled	Semi-skilled	Skilled	Non-manual	Number in sample
Newburyport					
1850-1860	64%	16%	15%	5%	55
1860-1870	74	12	8	5	74
1870-1880	79	6	10	5	102
Norristown					
1910-1920	70	14	6	10	825
1920-1930	70	12	10	8	925
1930-1940	52	30	10	8	1180
1940-1950	51	26	12	12	1065
Chicago, Los Angeles, New Haven, Philadelphia, St. Paul, San Francisco					
1940-1950	65	26		9	—

[a] The Norristown data were drawn from local city directories by Sidney Goldstein; see *Patterns of Mobility, 1910-1950: The Norristown Study* (Philadelphia, 1958), pp. 169, 175, 178, 185. The figures for the six major cities are from Gladys L. Palmer, *Labor Mobility in Six Cities: A Report on the Survey of Patterns and Factors in Labor Mobility, 1940-1950* (New York, 1954), p. 115. Semiskilled, skilled, and service workers are combined in one category in the Palmer report, unfortunately, but the unskilled and nonmanual estimates are acceptable for comparative analysis. The number of unskilled laborers in the sample is not reported, but the survey as a whole is based on some 13,000 work history schedules collected in the six cities.

concerning the career patterns of ordinary laborers with
the results of mobility inquiries dealing with Norristown,
Pennsylvania, between 1910 and 1950, and with six
major American cities in the 1940-1950 decade. The Norristown population in 1910 was more than twice that of
Newburyport, and it continued to grow rapidly for another quarter of a century. The chances for a man from
the unskilled labor class to ascend the occupational scale
should therefore have been greater in Norristown than
in supposedly static Newburyport, and they should have
been greater still in Chicago, Los Angeles, and the other
burgeoning metropolises studied in the 1940-1950 period.
This expectation is not borne out by the evidence. The
mobility patterns of common laborers in these cities of
radically different size and growth patterns display an
impressive resemblance. Movement into a nonmanual
occupation was somewhat rarer in Newburyport than in
the other communities, it is true, but this probably indicates a trend toward greater opportunities in twentieth
century American cities regardless of size and rate of
growth. If size and rate of growth were as important as
Lipset and Bendix claim, the six large cities should have
shown higher rates of mobility than Norristown, while in
fact their rates were slightly lower.[15] A further difficulty
with the Lipset-Bendix theory is that as the Norristown
population leveled off (1930-1950), mobility from the
bottom of the occupational ladder did not decline correspondingly; instead there was a marked increase in
movement into semiskilled positions, and a slight increase
in movement into skilled and nonmanual callings. Several
studies of the occupational mobility of sons of common
laborers in a variety of twentieth century cities will be
reviewed below; these point to similar conclusions.

The evidence is admittedly fragmentary, and it is obvious that information about mobility patterns in certain large cities in recent decades provides but a slender basis for speculation about the large cities of the nineteenth century. Nevertheless, these suggestive similarities in the rates of occupational advance of unskilled laborers and their sons in a variety of American cities are sufficient to call into question the assumption that differences in community size and rate of population growth result in very drastic intercity differences in the structure of opportunities. They suggest instead that the patterns of working class mobility found in Newburyport in the latter half of the nineteenth century were the result of forces which were operating in much the same way in cities throughout the entire society.

It is worth observing that, even if it could be shown that with respect to working class mobility opportunities the differences between the great metropolitan centers and Newburyport were differences of kind rather than simply of scale, Newburyport was perhaps more representative of the nineteenth century American city than New York. In 1850 only a seventh of the American urban population lived in cities as large as 250,000 and two thirds lived in cities of less than 50,000. Several giant cities grew up in the next five decades, but their growth was not at the expense of the small and medium-sized communities of the land. The importance of the glamorous big city in the social history of nineteenth century America should not be exaggerated; New York, Chicago, Philadelphia, Boston, and the others were part of the urban landscape, but only one part.[16]

If the mobility prospects of working class families in the great metropolitan centers of the nineteenth century did diverge much from the Newburyport norm, it is likely that they differed not in being more favorable, as Lipset and Bendix hold, but in being less favorable. The moderate occupational advances and the impressive property accumulations of Newburyport's laborers were in part a result of the fact that pressures to migrate from the community operated selectively on men at this social level; the working class family which failed to advance itself significantly simply did not stay in Newburyport very long. Little is known about the stability of the working class populations of the large cities of this period, but it seems unlikely that after arriving in Boston or New York a completely destitute laboring family would ever return to a small community like Newburyport. For this reason, a city like Boston soon developed an "unskilled, resourceless, perennially unemployed Irish proletariat."[17] Unlike the smaller community, the metropolis provided a haven for the demoralized and destitute, and they probably clustered there in disproportionately large numbers. In the big city slums, therefore, it is quite possible that a somewhat smaller proportion of laboring families became savings bank depositors and home owners. Nevertheless, it is doubtful that the difference was as dramatic as might be thought. The workmen of the large cities too climbed the occupational ladder in time, and left the slums for better neighborhoods; an exhaustive analysis of building permits issued in three of Boston's "streetcar suburbs" in the last quarter of the nineteenth century supplies some valuable hints on the gradual operation of this process in one major city.[18] Nineteenth century Boston indeed had its proletariat, but on the whole the composition of this group was constantly changing.

The greatest variations from the social patterns described in this book are likely to be found not in the great cities but in the small towns. Even in 1900 the United

States still contained quiet villages and market towns in which the factory and the immigrant were unknown. The myth of Yankee City should be a vivid reminder of the dangers of inferring an absence of economic and social change from a superficial index like population stability; nevertheless it is true that there were American towns in this period which remained relatively static and traditional. Precisely what this means as to social mobility opportunities is unknown, since such a community has yet to be studied thoroughly. Many of these may have lacked a substantial working class and have been virtually unstratified; in preindustrial Newburyport and some other old New England towns, however, class lines appear to have been sharp and movement out of the lower class difficult. Further research will be necessary before we can speak about the openness of the class structure in communities of this type.

To emphasize that this study of one small New England city provides some insights into the position of the working class in other American communities of the period is not to claim that Newburyport was representative of the United States in any statistical sense.[19] The point is rather that this was a community undergoing a process of transformation that eventually affected all American cities and towns to one or another degree, and that it is likely that there were important uniformities in the social consequences of urbanization and industrialization in each of these communities.

Social Mobility Trends in the United States: A Refutation of the Blocked Mobility Hypothesis

Has the American class structure become increasingly rigid during the past century? Is it harder for a poor man in present-day America to "pull himself up by his boot-straps" than it once was? The paucity of historical knowledge about social mobility in the United States had made it impossible to deal with these questions satisfactorily. If, however, it can be assumed that the opportunity level in nineteenth century Newburyport is a rough index of the openness of the national class structure at the time, the present study provides a new starting point for gauging mobility trends in America.

The scarcity of hard evidence about social mobility trends in the United States has not meant a scarcity of dogmatic assertions about the question. The prevailing orthodoxy, at least until very recently, has been the view that the American class system has been becoming "less open and mobility increasingly difficult for those at the bottom of the social heap." "The evidence from Yankee City and other places in the United States," Lloyd Warner declared in 1947, strongly indicated that both manual laborers and their children then enjoyed fewer opportunities to rise than was common in the nineteenth century; on the expanding frontier and in the idyllic craft structure of the nineteenth century city social mobility had been "certain," but the spread of the factory system had degraded the worker and had blocked the "ladder to the stars."[20]

The contrast between the boundless opportunities of the past and the constricted horizons of the present has a long ancestry in the history of American social thought. Early in the century of limitless opportunity, indeed, artisans threatened by the economic changes of the Jacksonian era sounded this note; after the Civil War the complaint that the "traditional" high level of mobility was declining sharply became a commonplace of social protest. In 1885 a sensitive observer gave vivid expression to this sentiment: "The man at the bottom of the ladder leading up to the social heavens may yet dream that there is a ladder let down to him; but the angels are not seen very often ascending and descending; one after another, it would seem, some unseen yet hostile powers arc breaking out the middle rungs of the ladder."[21]

What was a slogan in the nineteenth century became an influential social theory in the twentieth century, a theory which is not without its defenders today. The blocked mobility hypothesis received a compelling if tentative statement in Robert and Helen Lynd's brilliant studies of Muncie, Indiana. While *Middletown* (1929) and *Middletown in Transition* (1937) attempted to deal with every major aspect of community life, the dominant concern of these volumes was to delineate the social consequences of industrialization in a city "as representative as possible of contemporary American life," and a central conclusion was that "a fundamental alteration in the vaunted American ladder of opportunity" had taken place. The dream of mobility had been rooted in "past reality," the Lynds affirmed, but in the industrial present "the chance for the mass of the population to 'go up in the world' to affluence and independence" was "shrinking noticeably."[22]

Important as the Middletown inquiry was, however, it was the city of Newburyport which served as the test case for the most comprehensive and influential formulation of the blocked mobility hypothesis. Volume IV of the Yankee City series, *The Social System of the Modern Factory*, is an interpretation of "the industrial history" of Newburyport which aims at answering "fundamental questions about the nature of our industrial society." In the evolution of this small city Warner saw evidence that the "traditional" open class structure of the United States was becoming increasingly rigid; the "blue print of tomorrow" drawn up in Yankee City included the likelihood that America would soon see "revolutionary outbreaks expressing frustrated aspirations."[23]

The Social System of the Modern Factory has been sharply criticized before, but the Lynd-Warner view of the social consequences of industrialization has enjoyed great popularity.[24] Now that detailed information on social mobility patterns in one nineteenth century American city is available—and that city the very community in which the Warner study was carried out—a thorough critical assessment of the blocked mobility hypothesis is possible. We will see, from an analysis of the chief methodological failings of the Warner and Lynd field studies of social stratification and from a survey of evidence on social mobility in American communities during the past century, that we can finally lay to rest the notion that social mobility is becoming "increasingly difficult" for Americans at the bottom of the social ladder.[25]

The Social System of the Modern Factory began as an effort to account for the strike which closed all the shoe factories of Newburyport in 1933 and eventually resulted in management recognition of the shoe workers' union. Warner portrayed the strike as a dramatic success, and argued that such a radical departure from the community's tradition of social peace and labor quiescence required elaborate explanation. The field interviews, Warner admitted, revealed that Newburyport citizens tended to think of the strike as a struggle over economic grievances provoked by the depression: "Each man, owner and worker and townsman, spoke his own brand

of economic determinism." But Warner found these answers superficial; there had been depressions, wage cuts
and the rest in the city before, he observed, yet this was
the first "successful" strike. There had to be some "secret"
as to "why the Yankee City workers struck and . . . why
men in other cities strike." That secret, Warner decided,
lay "beyond the words and deeds of the strike"; it could
only be ferreted out by probing deeply into the evolution
of the community's productive system.[26]

There follows, accordingly, an excursion into "The Industrial History of Yankee City," and a hasty sketch of
changes from colonial days to the twentieth century. This
begins with a hymn to the Golden Age of the craftsman,
when every youngster became an apprentice and every
apprentice a master. Then, according to Warner, the local
youth was gradually trained in the complex skills of his
calling, and eventually became "an inextricable member
of the honorable fraternity of those who made, and who
knew how to make, shoes." In this system, presumably,
"workers and managers were indissolubly interwoven into
a common enterprise, with a common set of values."[27] To
strike was unthinkable. The workman held a respected
place in the community, and there was little social distance between him and the men for whom he worked.
Economic power was concentrated at the local level, and
the age-graded skill hierarchy of the craft assured maximum social mobility opportunities.

One day, however, the serpent "mechanization" entered
this Eden: "The machine took the virtue and respect from
the worker, at the same time breaking the skill hierarchy
which dominated his occupation. There was no longer a
period for young men to learn to respect those in the age
grade above them and in so doing to become self-respect-

ing workers. The 'ladder to the stars' was gone and with it much of the structure of the 'American Dream.'"[28] The shoe industry, Warner argued, underwent a technological revolution which shattered the craft order and destroyed local economic autonomy. The sudden decision of New-buryport laborers that a union was necessary to defend their rights was an inescapable consequence of this revolution. The growth of giant factories controlled by absentee owners opened up a vast social gulf between worker and manager. The steady encroachment of the machine rendered all manual skills useless; there resulted a sharp "break in the skill hierarchy." The status of all laboring jobs became equally degraded, and opportunities to rise into supervisory and managerial posts were eliminated. The "secret" behind the upsurge of union support in 1933 was thus a series of fundamental changes in the character of the productive system which separated the shoe workers from the community, blocked the mobility opportunities they had once enjoyed, and inspired a new sense of labor solidarity and class consciousness.

This portrait of a community in crisis, of course, represents a striking reversal of the image of Newburyport presented in earlier volumes of the Yankee City series. The reader may wonder if there were *two* Yankee Cities; the research for *The Social System of the Modern Factory* might almost have been conducted in another community. The placid New England town Warner selected for investigation because of the extraordinary continuity and stability of its traditional social structure suddenly became the site of a study in social disorganization and class conflict.[29]

Warner's new interest in historical change and his determination to present a dynamic analysis of the impact of larger social forces on Yankee City was commendable. The main thesis of this influential book, however, was unsubstantiated. Warner's account of the evolution of Newburyport from "the simple folk economy of the earliest community" to the 1930's was a serious distortion of the city's actual history, and a classic example of the old American habit of judging the present against a standard supplied by a romantic view of the past. The sweeping conclusions about the American class structure he drew from this case study are not in accord with the Newburyport evidence, nor do they square with the findings of other recent mobility studies.

As an attempt to explain the shoe strike of 1933, *The Social System of the Modern Factory* can be quickly dismissed. This strike did not in fact represent as radical a departure from community traditions as Warner believed. "Everyone in management and labor agreed that the strike could not have happened" in the good old days, Warner reports, but strikes had taken place in Newburyport—in 1858, in 1875, and a good many times since.[30] The strike of 1933 was distinctive only in that it was more successful than previous strikes, and not much more successful at that. As Oscar Handlin has pointed out, the union asked for a closed shop and a 10 percent wage increase; it actually won simple recognition and no raise. And within three years the union had lost out in one of the two factories still open. The events of 1933, therefore, were not unprecedented, and massive changes in the community need not be invoked to explain them.[31]

Even if this be doubted, the explanation of the strike offered in this volume is wholly unsatisfactory, because the causes to which Warner attributed the supposedly drastic changes of the 1930's were fully operative in New-

buryport several decades before the events they presumably explain. Once upon a time the Newburyport
economy was organized along craft lines; labor was
content, social mobility was "certain," to strike was unthinkable. Warner is exceedingly vague as to the actual
dates of this idyllic craft age, but he alleges that memories
of it were alive in the minds of the strikers of 1933, and
one chart makes it appear that craft and apprenticeship
relations prevailed in local shoe production until "approximately World War I."[32] The vagueness is not accidental,
for the craft order portrayed in this volume is but a Never
Never land conjured up by the author. Not a shred of
evidence pertaining to Newburyport itself is cited in
support of this account; none could be. The situation of
the workman in the "simple folk community" of old never
bore much resemblance to this rosy image, as the brief
sketch of Federalist Newburyport in Chapter Two should
indicate. And in any event the craft order had virtually
disappeared in Newburyport and similar industrial cities
long before the nineteenth century drew to a close without
producing a powerful union movement, much less "revolutionary outbreaks expressing frustrated aspirations."

Well before 1880 the Newburyport economy was dominated by large textile and shoe firms. Production was
highly mechanized in both industries. The factory labor
force found no inviting "ladder to the stars" before them;
in the substantial sample of workers and their sons studied
for the 1850-1880 period not a single instance of mobility
into the ranks of management or even into a foremanship
position was discovered! Nor does Warner's stress on the
importance of absentee ownership of the factories find any
confirmation in the history of the community. All of the
textile mills and some of the shoe factories were controlled

by absentee owners in this early period; this was a common pattern in many American industries from the very beginning of industrialization.[33] And, more important, labor-management relations in those firms still in local hands were not in fact characterized by the happy solidarity Warner attributed to them, local mythology to the contrary notwithstanding. Whether the Yankee Protestant mill owner lived on High Street or in Boston could have mattered little to his Irish Catholic employees, whose willingness or unwillingness to strike was governed by more tangible and impersonal considerations.

The acceptance *The Social System of the Modern Factory* has won in some quarters, and the prevalence of the ahistorical style of social research the book exemplifies, made this lengthy critical analysis necessary. These criticisms, however, do not apply to more sophisticated formulations of the argument that the effect of industrialization is to degrade the status of the skilled workman and to narrow the range of mobility opportunities open to men on the lower rungs of the social ladder. In the Middletown volumes, for example, the Lynds built their argument on solid historical foundations, presenting a well-documented sketch of the craft order as it functioned in Muncie in 1890 and showing convincingly that in the glass industry so important to the local economy technological changes had destroyed the old craft hierarchy by 1925. While the Lynds successfully demonstrated that the status of the glass factory operative of 1925 was markedly inferior to that of the glass blower of 1890, however, they were seriously in error in believing that they had proved that the mobility opportunities of the ordinary workman were "shrinking noticeably" as mechanized production spread.[34]

This judgment depended upon a false assumption about the sources of the new factory labor force, an assumption which ignored the interrelated processes of migration and occupational adjustment we saw operating in Newburyport in the 1850-1880 period. The Lynds presented no evidence which indicated that either the glass blowers of the 1890's or their children held semiskilled factory jobs in significant numbers in 1925, and there are excellent reasons to doubt that they did. The population of Muncie grew at a rapid pace between 1890 and 1925, and a great many of the newcomers were ill-educated, unskilled men from rural Indiana, Kentucky, and other near-by states, men to whom factory employment meant improved rather than declining status.[35] Few of the happy craftsmen of 1890 actually entered the factory; many of the skilled trades were flourishing in 1925 and still flourish today, and even the ill-fated glass blowers appear to have been rather gradually displaced, so that in most instances they probably retired before their skills were completely without value. It is doubtful that the sons of these victims of technological change typically became semiskilled factory operatives either; a detailed study of inter-generational mobility in near-by Indianapolis at about the same time reveals that sons of skilled workmen had excellent prospects of either finding skilled work themselves or entering the rapidly expanding nonmanual occupations. Of the sons of craftsmen in the Indianapolis sample for 1910, for example, 49 percent were themselves in skilled callings and almost a quarter had crossed over into nonmanual positions.[36]

Had the Lynds been more alert to these processes, had they investigated the social origins of the machine tenders of 1925 and traced the career patterns of the children of skilled craftsmen, they would have better understood the relative lack of militant class consciousness and the optimistic faith in individual opportunity which was one of their principal findings. In Muncie as in Newburyport, it seems clear, the new factories were not crowded with *déclassé* artisans; the factory labor force was made of men who had little status to lose—migrants from rural America or the Old World. For these elements of the population factory employment meant new earning opportunities and the prospect of accumulating a modicum of property, not a fall from paradise.[37]

These glaring flaws in two important field studies of social stratification in American communities suggest, at a minimum, that the proposition that social mobility is becoming "increasingly difficult for those at the bottom of the social heap" has yet to be established.[38] The findings of the present study, however, when coupled with scattered evidence concerning social mobility in several twentieth century American cities, permit a more definite verdict: to rise from the bottom of the social scale has not become increasingly difficult in modern America; if anything it appears to have become somewhat less difficult.

The available evidence on intra-generational occupational mobility for unskilled laborers is regrettably not very plentiful. The only inquiries closely comparable to the Newburyport study deal with mobility in Norristown from 1910 to 1950 and in six large cities between 1940 and 1950 (see Table 15). The career patterns of common workmen in these cities, however, displayed a striking resemblance, and the small differences which did exist all indicated slightly superior opportunities in the twentieth century community. Only one laborer in twenty from the Newburyport sample rose into a nonmanual position, while the figure for Norristown, Chicago, Los Angeles, and the others was approximately one in ten. The tremendous expansion of menial white collar and sales positions which has produced these new opportunities in the nonmanual occupations has also tended to blur income and status differentials between manual and nonmanual callings, of course, so that upward mobility into a routine white collar job means less of a status advance than it did a century ago.[39] This is an important qualification, but it remains the case that the rise from an unskilled laboring position to virtually any nonmanual occupation represents significant upward mobility. Mobility of this kind is not being blocked; it appears to be on the increase in the modern American city.

Much more is known about the occupational attainments of the sons of unskilled laborers in the United States, and it is possible to conclude with some confidence that in the past century there has been a mild trend toward greater upward mobility. The available evidence is summarized in Table 16. The occupational categories used in the various studies varied slightly, and there were differences in sampling techniques which could produce artificial variations. The consistency of the findings, given these facts, is impressive.

Of the sons of unskilled laborers employed in nineteenth century Newburyport seven out of ten held unskilled or semiskilled jobs themselves and one was in a nonmanual position of some kind; of the sons of unskilled laborers working in Norristown in 1952, five out of ten held unskilled or semiskilled positions, while three were in nonmanual callings. The data from San Jose, Indianapolis, New Haven, and the other communities listed on Table 16, covering the years 1900-1956, indicate that this

TABLE 16. Occupational status attained by sons of unskilled laborers, selected samples, 1860-1956[a]

	Unskilled	Semiskilled	Total of unskilled and semiskilled	Skilled	Nonmanual	Number in sample
Newburyport 1860-1880	22%	49%	71%	19%	10%	245
San Jose, California ca. 1900	60	4	64	16	20	70
Indianapolis 1910	36	20	56	28	16	1195
New Haven 1931	—	—	72	13	15	153
San Jose 1933-34	42	17	59	14	28	242
Indianapolis 1940	30	32	62	16	21	675
National sample 1945	38	20	58	17	25	41
Chicago, Los Angeles, San Francisco, Philadelphia 1950	20	34	54	27	20	—
Norristown 1952	14	34	48	24	28	86
National sample 1956	25	28	53	28	20	87

[a] The Newburyport figures represent the distribution of occupations held by laborers' sons aged 20 or over in 1860, 1870, or 1880. The age limitation was essential to avoid an overrepresentation of boys holding their first jobs. Most of the other studies reported made some attempt to eliminate very young males, but the varying age limits of the samples remain an inescapable source of variation between the studies. The San Jose figures were calculated from Percy E. Davidson and H. Dewey Anderson, *Occupational Mobility in an American Community* (Stanford, 1937), pp. 20, 29. The ca. 1900 estimate for San Jose is not very reliable since it depends on a retrospective estimate (in 1933-34) by respondents

contrast reflects a genuine trend. It may be objected that the first column of the table, which shows the extent of direct inheritance of unskilled manual positions in these several cities, does not reveal any such clear trend. Neither does the second column, which measures movement into semiskilled occupations. But this should come as no surprise, for the Newburyport evidence showed that the unskilled and semiskilled occupations constituted a common occupational universe; while there were status differences between these two job categories, they were small and movement between the two was very easy. The same held true in other American communities, Table 16 shows clearly; the concentration of laborers' sons in unskilled jobs and in semiskilled jobs fluctuated widely from city to city, but the concentration of sons in the *low-skill occupational universe* (column three) varied relatively

---

of the regular occupation of their fathers and grandfathers. Unskilled and semiskilled occupations, unfortunately, were not distinguished in the New Haven survey; John W. McConnell, *The Evolution of Social Classes* (Washington, 1942), p. 216. The Indianapolis figures are for all of Marion County, Indiana, which includes some suburban and rural fringes around Indianapolis as well as the city itself. They were calculated from the detailed mobility tables included in Natalie Rogoff's *Recent Trends in Occupational Mobility* (Glencoe, Ill., 1953). The 1945 sample of the adult white population of the U. S. is reported in Richard Centers, "Occupational Mobility of Urban Occupational Strata," *American Sociological Review*, 13 (1948): 197-203. The 1950 data for Chicago, Los Angeles, San Francisco, and Philadelphia were gathered in the Occupational Mobility Survey carried out under the auspices of the Committee on Labor Market Research of the Social Science Research Council, seven university research centers, and the U.S. Bureau of the Census, and was published in Stanley Lieberson, *Ethnic Patterns in American Cities* (Glencoe, Ill., 1963), pp. 186-187; the number in the sample was not reported. The Norristown figures, based on data from the Norristown Household Survey, are for adult whites; see Sidney Goldstein, ed., *The Norristown Study*, p. 109. The 1956 national sample was selected by the Survey Research Center of the University of Michigan; reported in S. M. Miller, "Comparative Social Mobility: A Trend Report and Bibliography," *Current Sociology*, 9 (1960), p. 78.

little. The unskilled and semiskilled total is a better indicator of mobility trends than either separately, and it shows a modest but definite improvement in the prospects of youths of lowly birth. More than two thirds of them remained in low status callings in Newburyport; a figure this high was reported in only one of the nine twentieth century studies,[40] and the lowest concentration of sons in unskilled and semiskilled work was found in the three post–World War II inquiries.

The converse of this decline in the tendency of youths from unskilled working class families to remain in the low-skill occupational universe, of course, was their growing representation in the skilled and nonmanual occupations. The skilled column of Table 16 actually presents a rather confused picture; the variation in skilled opportunities from community to community was sizable, and it is difficult to see any clear trend, though the fact that three of the four highest figures were from the postwar studies should be a valuable reminder that the disappearance of the glass blower and the shoemaker of old must not be confused with a disappearance of the skilled crafts themselves.[41]

The evidence of a modest trend toward increased mobility from the bottom of the occupational scale into business, professional, and white collar callings is fairly persuasive. A few of the figures seem surprising, but it is surely significant that the six studies covering the 1933-1956 period show two to three times as many laborers' sons in nonmanual positions as the figures for Newburyport in the latter half of the nineteenth century and for Indianapolis in 1910. In recent decades white collar and professional occupations have made up an ever increasing segment of the American occupational structure, and during the same period the American educational system has become markedly more democratic. The fruits of these two developments are graphically displayed here, in the rising proportion of laborers' sons who no longer face the necessity of making a living with their hands. Whatever the effects of mechanization, the closing of the frontier, the narrowing of class differences in fertility, and a host of other factors which have inspired gloomy prophecies of an increasingly rigid class structure in the United States, their combined effect has evidently been insufficient to offset the forces making for improved mobility opportunities for men at the bottom of the occupational ladder.[42]

Occupational mobility, of course, is not the only significant form of social mobility—simply the form which has received most scholarly attention. To the ordinary workmen of nineteenth century Newburyport social advance through the accumulation of property was an extremely important, and far more accessible, goal. Are there any signs that opportunities for property mobility by men of lowly status are being blocked in twentieth century America? Much of the needed research has yet to be done, but it is doubtful indeed that a serious case could be made for the blocked mobility argument in the property sphere. While it is not at all clear that the distribution of income in the United States has become markedly more equal in recent decades, it is incontestable that in every occupational class absolute levels of real income have risen dramatically. The extraordinary devotion to home ownership displayed by the Irish working class families of Newburyport has not been uniformly shown by American workmen in subsequent decades, but other forms of investment—the automobile, for example—have become increasingly important. The two Middletown volumes are rich with data concerning these changes in the working class style of life, and a few later studies supply evidence on property mobility in the post–World War II period. Chinoy's suggestive report, *Automobile Workers and the American Dream*, shows in convincing detail how, for factory workers lacking any reasonable prospects of upward occupational mobility, "the constant accumulation of personal possessions" has provided substitute gratifications which allow them to retain a belief that they are "getting ahead."[43]

Whether our index of the openness of the class structure be the extent of intra-generational occupational mobility, of inter-generational occupational mobility, or property mobility, therefore, it is difficult to resist the conclusion that chances to rise from the very bottom of the social ladder in the United States have not declined visibly since the nineteenth century; they seem, in fact, to have increased moderately in recent decades.

To say this is not to say that opportunities are boundless in present-day America, that ours is a society in which every "deserving" man holds a status in accord with his "true merit." Opportunities are neither boundless nor are they equal in the United States today, as an abundance of sociological research into class differences testifies.[44] The mere fact of being born into a middle class or a working class home still profoundly influences the life chances of every American—his prospects of obtaining a college education, finding a good job, living in decent housing, even his prospects of enjoying mental and physical health and living to an advanced age. The plight of lower class Negroes is only the most glaring reminder of a larger problem too often forgotten in an age of affluence: tens of millions of Americans still live in a milieu which thwarts the development of their full human potentialities.[45]

All this is true, but we can obtain some true perspective on the preesnt only when we shed the rose-tinted spectacles through which the American past has characteristically been viewed. In the United States today the climb upward from the bottom rungs of the social ladder is not often rapid or easy, but *it never was*, if the experiences of the working class families of nineteenth century Newburyport are at all representative. Few of these men and few of their children rose very far on the social scale; most of the upward occupational shifts they made left them manual workmen still, and their property mobility, though strikingly widespread, rarely involved the accumulation of anything approaching real wealth. This was not the ladder to the stars that Horatio Alger portrayed and that later writers wistfully assumed to have been a reality in the days of Abraham Lincoln and Andrew Carnegie. It was, however, social advancement of a kind immensely meaningful to men whose horizons of expectations were not those of an Alger hero. Low-level social mobility of this sort does not seem to be more difficult for the American working class family today, and in certain respects it has become less difficult than it was a century ago.

If a more realistic evaluation of the past thus provides a less lurid perspective on the tendencies of the present, it need inspire no complacency. The romantic nostalgia which has led many Americans to believe that opportunity is "noticeably shrinking" is surely not the only basis for dissatisfaction with the status quo. The petty success stories enacted in nineteenth century Newburyport still occur daily. Whether the presence of opportunity of this kind is a sufficient test of the good society, however, may be doubted.

APPENDIX

Further reflections on the Yankee City series: the pitfalls of ahistorical social science

In recent years the historical profession has been exposed to invigorating new winds from a variety of related disciplines. Sociologists and social anthropologists have been particularly eager to suggest ways in which their brethren in the most traditional and least theoretical of the social sciences might broaden their horizons and deepen their insights into man's behavior in the past. Two newly established journals, *Comparative Studies in History and Social Theory* and *History and Theory*, and a number of recent books testify that this advice has not gone entirely unheard.[1]

This is all to the good. Surely E. H. Carr is correct when he remarks "the more sociological history becomes, and the more historical sociology becomes, the better for both."[2] The difficulty, however, is that the mutually enriching dialogue between history and sociology that Carr calls for has barely begun; so far, communication between these disciplines has largely been in the form of a monologue, with history on the receiving end. If historians have much to learn from their colleagues in sociology and social anthropology, the converse must be equally insisted upon. Ahistorical social science is as often narrow and superficial as sociologically primitive history, and it is certainly no less common.[3]

The critical examination of Lloyd Warner's Yankee City series which follows is an effort to make clear some of the pitfalls of this type of social science. The Yankee City volumes were widely praised at the time of their original publication, and they served to establish Warner for a time as the most influential American student of social stratification. It is true that the techniques of social analysis pioneered in the New-buryport study have come under severe attack in recent years, so much so, indeed, that a moratorium on criticism of Warner and "the Warner school" may perhaps seem called for.[4] The wish to put an end to an old and often sterile controversy is understandable, but I believe that some of the issues raised by the Yankee City study remain alive and important. The critical literature generated by the Yankee City volumes has focused too narrowly on matters of technique. Sociological commentators have not generally been disposed to link Warner's errors to the ahistorical methodological presuppositions which guided the Yankee City research. Indeed, similar assumptions still influence contemporary social research. An important school in social anthropology has proudly proclaimed "the irrelevance of history for an understanding of social organization";[5] though few sociologists profess so radical a view, in practice many of them appear to find history irrelevant.

What follows is in no sense a full and balanced appraisal of the five Yankee City volumes or of Lloyd Warner's contributions to an understanding of American society. Such an appraisal would pay Warner the tribute he deserves as a pioneer in his field—for having gathered a wealth of interesting data about a subject which had been too little studied, and for having inspired an enormous amount of further research and controversy. It would applaud certain of Warner's insights which have proved fruitful. It would note that Warner had the gift for social portraiture of a lesser social novelist; portions of the Yankee City volumes display some of the virtues of the novels of John P. Marquand, a writer who also dealt with Newburyport. Such an assessment would be more appreciative, in short, and perhaps it is long overdue. That, however, is a different task than the one undertaken here, and a larger one. These critical observations focus on what Warner failed to see about the community he studied so intensively in the 1930's and particularly on what he failed to see because of his misconceptions about the community's history. Some of the chief ways in which the Yankee City series presented a distorted image of Newburyport have been disclosed in the preceding chapters; the discussion which follows attempts to isolate the methodological assumptions responsible for these distortions.

The Uses of the Past

The Yankee City project was carried out on a scale that can only be described as prodigious. It still ranks as the most intensive, exhaustive, and expensive survey ever made of a small American city. The five published volumes consist of more than 1700 pages, with 208 tables, charts, and maps. The field work extended over a period of several years, and required the labor of some thirty research assistants. The amount of data collected was staggering. Warner at one point refers to "the millions of social facts" which were recorded; the study is replete with comments like this: "All of the types of social structures and each of the thousands of families, thousands of cliques, and hundreds of associations were, member by member, interrelated in our research."[6] "Social personality cards" were compiled for all 17,000 members of the community, and thousands of hours of interviews were conducted with local citizens. Aerial photographs were made of Newburyport and environs; detailed questionnaires were administered at gas stations and lunch stands along the highway to discover what transients had stopped in the city and why; the plots of plays performed by students and various social organizations were collected and subjected to content analysis (which yielded the illuminating conclusion that they all "clearly conformed to the standards of the local group"). An observer was stationed at the movie house to "see who attended the pictures and with whom they attended," and newsstands were closely scrutinized to see how actual purchases conformed to professed reading preferences. (One breathes a sigh of sympathy at the image of a haunted "upper upper" of Warner's Newburyport seeking furtively to pick up his monthly *Esquire* under the cool stare of a Radcliffe graduate student in sociology.) Death itself brought the citizen no more than partial respite from surveillance: "All the names of those persons buried in the several cemeteries were gathered and compilations were made of the members of several ethnic groups."[7]

Virtually every aspect of Newburyport life was probed by the Yankee City team—every aspect but one. Early in the first volume of the series the authors casually commented: "To be sure that we were not ethnocentrically biased in our judgment, we decided to use no previous summaries of data collected by anyone else (maps, handbooks, histories, etc.) until we had formed our own opinion of the city."[8] This was a remarkable and revealing utterance. To consult the historical record would be to fall victim to the biases and preconceptions of the historian, a man necessarily "unscientific," "culture-bound," "ethnocentric."

How, then, were Warner and his associates to form their "own opinion" about the Newburyport past? At times Warner was inclined to speak as if the past was simply irrelevant. A disciple of Durkheim and Radcliffe-Brown, he shared their distaste for the historical school in anthropological thought; the merely "ethnological or temporal aspects of social behavior" were of much less interest to him than "the scientific problems of explanation of the facts by classification and their interpretation by the formulation of laws and principles."[9] "The facts," in this context, meant the facts visible in the present.

It was quite impossible, however, for the Yankee City researchers to avoid making assumptions about what Newburyport had been like prior to their arrival on the scene; some

of these assumptions about this "static, old New England
town" have been reviewed in Chapter Eight. These, Warner
argued, were scientifically derived from direct observation of the image of the past held by present members of
the community. This seemed a plausible procedure for men
determined to "use the techniques and ideas which have been
developed by social anthropologists in primitive society in
order to obtain a more accurate understanding of an American
community."[10] Warner came to Newburyport after three years
of observing a tribe of Australian aborigines, a people without
a written history. In a community without written records,
the dead exist only in the minds and deeds of the living; there
history survives only as tradition, ritual, myth, "remembered
experiences . . . newly felt and understood by the living members of the collectivity."[11]

Rarely is the student of a primitive community able to find
sources which allow him to penetrate beneath this tissue of
myths; much of the past is irrevocably lost. The modern social
investigator, however, need not remain entirely at the mercy
of such subjective data. He may ask not only "what is remembered of things past?" but also "what was the actual past?"[12]
The historical record available to him, it need hardly be said,
is not pure, disembodied Truth; even the simple factual information it contains was gathered by men whose interests
and passions colored their perceptions, men who were "culture-bound." The point which must be underscored, though,
is that this record may be read in a way which allows us to
discriminate, at least to some degree, between the mythic past
and the actual past.

Warner eventually came to an awareness of this distinction.
The last of the Yankee City volumes, published long after the
others (1959), includes a lengthy and perceptive analysis of
the image of the Newburyport past presented in the pageants
staged during the tercentenary celebration of 1935. By utilizing historical sources Warner was able to detect and interpret
some interesting discrepancies between the real past and the

"history" portrayed in the pageants, which was what community leaders "now *wished* it . . . were and what they wished it were not. They ignored this or that difficult period of time or unpleasant occurrence or embarrassing group of men and women; they left out awkward political passions; they selected small items out of large time contexts, seizing them to express today's values."[13]

Regrettably, however, a similar indictment must be returned against the first four volumes of Warner's own study. "Where truth ends and idealization begins cannot be learned," the author of *The Social System of the Modern Factory* tells us.[14] This was not a limitation imposed by the absence of historical evidence; it was the result of Warner's own methodological commitments. In this instance and in many others Warner's interpretations rested on assumptions about the past which were demonstrably false. Warner's unwillingness to consult the historical record and his complete dependence on materials susceptible to anthropological analysis—the acts and opinions of living members of the community—served to obliterate the distinction between the actual past and current myths about the past. Thus the irony that the determination of the Yankee City investigators to escape the ethnocentric biases of culture-bound history led them to accept uncritically the community's legends about itself—surely the most ethnocentric of all possible views!

The ahistorical methodological predilections of Warner and his associates were responsible for a number of their glaring misconceptions about the nature of the community—such as the myth of Yankee dominance discussed above. Furthermore, these predilections contributed to the most serious conceptual flaws of the study. The key concepts of the work—class and ethnicity—were both based entirely on the opinion of Warner's local respondents, and were defined so as to render difficult any systematic study of the relationship between subjective opinion and objective social reality. An "ethnic," for example, was said to be a Newburyport resident who considered himself or was considered by others to be an ethnic and who participated in the activities of an ethnic association; any citizen who did not fulfill these two criteria, amazingly, Warner classified a "Yankee." We see here how a community in which immigrants and their children and grandchildren were an overwhelming majority could become, in Warner's mind, a city whose population was "predominantly old American."[15] Even greater difficulties inhere in Warner's ahistorical conception of the Newburyport class structure, as will be shown below.

Not only did the Yankee City investigators display an uncritical acceptance of the opinions of informants living in the community at the time; they tended to accept the opinion of informants from a particular social group with very special biases—Yankee City's "upper uppers." This was a group which fascinated Warner; he devoted an inordinate amount of space to them despite the fact that they constituted less than 2 percent of the Newburyport population. The upper uppers were the few dozen prominent old Yankee families who presumably had enjoyed high status in the community for more than a century. In fact Warner overestimated the continuity and rootedness of even this tiny elite, as they themselves were wont to do; though each of this vivid "composite drawings" of upper uppers depicted a family which had resided in the community for several generations, Warner's own questionnaires showed that at the time of the study fewer than 60 percent of the members of this group had actually been born in or near Newburyport, and that almost a quarter of them had been born outside of New England entirely.[16] These were the Yankee City families whose sense of infinitely subtle prestige distinctions was translated into Warner's famous theory that the community was stratified into six discrete prestige classes; this was the "single group with a coherent tradition" whose eagerness to equate Newburyport history with their own history led Warner to believe that the community's "social superstructure . . . remained very much what it had been at the end of the War of 1812" and to attribute the apparent stability of the Newburyport social order to the fictitious dominance of the Yankee.[17]

Class and Mobility in Yankee City

The concept of class was far and away the most important analytical tool utilized in the Yankee City series; the cardinal objective of these books was to describe the social stratification system of a New England city, and to analyze the behavior of local citizens in terms of social class categories. The core of Warner's first volume was a 380-page discussion of the composition of the six distinct classes he found in Newburyport, and his subsequent studies of the economic, political, religious, and associational life of the community were built upon this foundation. The conceptual apparatus developed to study social class in Newburyport was later refined and applied to several other American communities by Warner and his disciples; the stratification theory born in Yankee City became the earmark of "the Warner school."[18]

Warner defined class as "two or more orders of people who are believed to be, and are accordingly ranked by the members of the community, in socially superior and inferior positions"; the essence of class was thus social prestige. Warner rejected the view that "the most vital and far-reaching value systems which motivate Americans are to be ultimately traced to an economic order."[19]

This "simple economic hypothesis" he dismissed without further elaboration and evaluation. In what perhaps was an evasive attack on the Marxian theory of social stratification, Warner insisted on a democracy of causation. Class was social prestige, and prestige was "a multi-factored phenomenon"; an individual's class status was influenced by his "education, occupation, wealth, family, intimate friends, clubs, and fraternities . . . manners, speech, and general outward behavior." To this already long list Warner later added the social rating of the neighborhood and the character of the home in which a person resides.[20]

The task of delineating the class structure of even a small community would be overwhelming if the investigator had to measure and properly weight all of these components of status in thousands of cases. Warner's practical solution to this difficulty was seemingly straightforward. Rather than gathering data about all of the separate elements which enter into social prestige, Warner's team directly asked the inhabitants of Newburyport which of their fellow citizens they considered "inferior" and which "superior"; on the basis of such "direct observation" the investigators "worked out empirically . . . the existence of six stratified social classes."[21]

The apparent simplicity and objectivity of this technique quickly dissolves under close scrutiny. To poll every member of the community would have taken many years; Warner satisfied himself with "a fairly large sample of the total population," and merely inferred the rank of other citizens.[22] Just how large was "fairly large"? How was the sample constructed? How were disagreements between raters as to the status of an individual dealt with? Some of these questions of technique were eventually clarified by Warner in a later publication, *Social Class in America: A Manual of Procedure for the Measurement of Social Status*, but he was never able to demonstrate that what he presented as the communal consensus about the nature of the Newburyport class system was in fact anything more than the consensus of a small group of raters drawn disproportionately from the upper class. Indeed, at various points in the first Yankee City volume Warner let slip hints which suggest that working class inhabitants of the city perceived fewer than six discrete classes, and that they defined these in simple economic terms.[23]

By far the most important substantive flaw in Warner's stratification theory stemmed from this ahistorical and subjective concept of class; it was this which made him unable to come to grips with the problem of social mobility. Consider a striking passage which appears early in the first volume of the series. After relating how he and his colleagues empirically "discovered" the existence of the six distinct classes in Newburyport, Warner admits that "naturally there were many borderline cases. A class system, unlike a caste or other clearly and formally marked rank-order, is one in which movement up and down is constantly taking place in the lives of many people." He cites some examples, then remarks: "It was a problem in these and similar cases from other classes where such people should be placed. In order to make a complete study," he says casually, "it was necessary to locate all of them in one of the six classes, and this we did to the best of our ability on the basis of the entire range of phenomena covered by our data."[24] There were "many borderline cases"; social mobility was "constantly taking place." How many cases? How much social mobility, and of what kind? Surely these are important questions if we wish to understand the operation of a stratification system, yet Warner never provides us with the data with which to answer them.

Not that he ignored the subject of social mobility; these five volumes were rich with rhetoric about the American Dream, struggling immigrant boys, and the rest. Some 250 of Warner's pages, for instance, were devoted to various "composite drawings"; the central theme of these sketches was the mobility striving of persons from below, and the efforts of the social elite to exclude the climbers. While these sketches of "fictive persons" provided some insights into the process of social mobility in the community, they supplied no hard evidence at all. One grave limitation of the composite drawings is that they were constructed without regard for scientific canons of verifiability, in a manner which allowed the biases of the authors to operate unchecked. Even more important is the fact that they were presented without supporting quantitative data of any kind, so that it is impossible to know if the behavior described was in any way typical. Not even in the volume which attributed the shoe strike of 1933 to the frustrated mobility aspirations of the shoe workers was there a shred of evidence about the actual career patterns of individual laborers. Warner, it appears, was deeply interested in social mobility and wrote about it at length; he failed to take even the most elementary steps toward measuring it.

This was surely a remarkable omission in a massive research project which devoted several years to gathering "millions of social facts" about the social structure of one small community. What accounts for it? At least part of the answer lies in the fact that Warner's ahistorical method of conceptualizing and observing social class rendered the systematic study of social mobility virtually impossible. To define class as prestige rank, and to measure prestige by polling citizens leads all too easily to a static and superficial vision of the social structure. The investigator is limited to no more than a single snapshot of the present; the historical dimension is abandoned entirely. Changes in the status of individuals or in the shape of class structure itself can only be conjectured, for it is impossible to deduce social patterns of the past from a poll in the present. Intra-generational mobility, therefore, could not be measured at all with Warner's techniques, without a follow-up study conducted many years after the first one. By rejecting objective criteria of class, occupation or income, for example, Warner closed off the possibility of determining what the status of his Newburyport respondents had been ten or twenty years before the Yankee City research was carried out.

Inter-generational mobility, it is true, might have been studied to a limited degree within the confines of Warner's approach. "Social personality cards" indicated the prestige rank of every adult male in Newburyport at the time of the study; in some instances the fathers of local men were also resident in the city, and in those cases inter-generational mobility could have been computed by comparing the class status of fathers and sons. Warner announced in his first volume that this was actually done, but the findings were never reported.[25] It is possible, considering the rate of population turnover in the 1850-1880 period, that the population of Newburyport was still so volatile that such a comparison would have turned up disappointingly few cases in which both generations were represented in the city.

At only one point in the Yankee City series—in Volume III, *The Social Systems of American Ethnic Groups*—did Warner attempt to supply quantitative data about social mobility. While he made no effort to measure the mobility of the supposedly dominant Yankees of the community, the changing status of Newburyport's immigrants seemed too important a matter to overlook. Here were people who (presumably) had entered the class system at the bottom, yet many were found in the higher classes when the study was conducted. Something had to be said about the process by which they had elevated themselves in the status structure. This presented a difficult problem because Warner's basic technique for dividing the community into prestige classes could not be applied retrospectively to historical data. At the outset of his chapter on "The Ethnic Groups in the Class System" Warner complained that "old documents offer little material" useful for mobility analysis, but he was less than candid, for the trouble was not the documents, but the sterile definition of class Warner brought to the documents.[26] In fact, no conceivable body of historical materials could have supplied the kind of data needed to place citizens into six prestige classes.

After a futile effort to "assess the time factor in the process of social mobility" by reclassifying the 1933 data into "ethnic generations," Warner reluctantly turned his attention to two facets of ethnic mobility about which historical data was available: occupational mobility and residential mobility.[27] This could have proved a fruitful shift, but Warner was too predisposed against objective indexes of status to use them properly. "Class" was really social prestige, he believed, and it was prestige which most interested him. Perhaps this is why what should have been an enlightening analysis of the occupational and residential advances of Newburyport's immigrants was carried out in so careless a manner as to render it almost worthless.

Warner's entire discussion of ethnic residential mobility was based on the unexamined premise that the relative social standing of the various neighborhoods of Newburyport had not changed at all between 1850 and 1933. Deriving an order of six "zones" of the city from responses to the Yankee City inquiry, Warner constructed a "residential status index," which he then applied to data from city directories for 1850, 1864, 1873, 1883, and so forth.[28] No effort was made to justify the assumption that this index truly reflected the city's ecological pattern eighty years earlier, even though some of the relevant evidence—reports indicating the distribution of poverty by neighborhood, for example—could easily have been uncovered in newspapers from the period. It appears from his silence that Warner was not even aware that this was a problem; hence he left unexamined the doubtful premise on which the whole chapter rested.

A more serious flaw marred Warner's treatment of both residential mobility and occupational mobility: he advanced quantitative measures of the changing status of various ethnic groups over time without understanding that the composition of these groups was steadily changing. An illustration will suggest the importance of the distortions which were produced by this simple error. Warner's "occupational status index," based on a ranking of occupational categories roughly similar to that utilized in the present study, was used to trace the occupational distribution of residents with obviously foreign names from old Newburyport city directories. The "average occupational status" of each ethnic group was obtained by attaching the following arbitrary values to the various occupations: unskilled labor, 1; skilled factory work, 2; skilled craft work, 2.5; management-aid, 3; management, 4; professions, 6. The nineteenth century figures for the Irish read like this:

1850: 1.62; 1864: 1.76; 1873: 1.74; 1883: 1.76; 1893: 1.84. What does this tell us about the occupational mobility of the Irish in nineteenth century Newburyport? Warner believed he had proved that the Irish had achieved "moderate mobility" between 1850 and 1864, that they had made no gains at all for the next two decades, and that the period from the Civil War to the end of the century might be summed up in the phrase "mobility slight."[29]

These conclusions are markedly more pessimistic than the evidence presented in this book would seem to warrant. The disparity between the two studies is not primarily due to the fact that they drew their data from different sources, though it is true that the census schedules proved more complete and more accurate than the city directories used by the Yankee City researchers.[30] The basic cause of the disagreement is that, while the careers of individuals were traced in this book, Warner believed it reasonable to treat "the Irish" as an entity. That this was a procedure fraught with error should be clear from the data about population turnover presented previously. To compute overall occupational status indexes for all Irish names in the community in 1864 and in 1883 was of dubious value, because in fact a majority of the Irishmen living in Newburyport in 1864 had left the city by 1883, and the bulk of the 1883 group consisted of newcomers to the community. The similarity of the two indexes shows that in 1864 Newburyport citizens of Irish descent were mostly unskilled or semi-skilled laborers, and that this generalization still held true twenty years later. But this is no proof at all of the proposition that most of the individual Irishmen living in Newburyport during these two decades were fixed rigidly in their place.[31]

Warner's impatience with objective measures of class, his reluctance to consult the historical record, his inability to deal with social mobility satisfactorily, and his blindness to changes in the composition of the Newburyport population and the character of community institutions were all logically related. They stemmed from the basic delusion that the ahistorical, functionalist assumptions of the equilibrium school of social anthropology provided appropriate guidelines for studying a complex modern community. It is by no means clear that these suppositions are valid even for primitive societies; Leach's recent study, *Political Systems of Highland Burma*, makes a strong case for a dynamic, historically oriented approach to the primitive community. And, whatever the merits of Leach's recommendations for the study of primitive peoples, the distortions of the Yankee City volumes should suggest that the student of modern society is not free to take his history or leave it alone. Interpretation of the present requires assumptions about the past. The actual choice is between explicit history, based on a careful examination of the sources, and implicit history, rooted in ideological preconceptions and uncritical acceptance of local mythology.

NOTES

INTRODUCTION

1. See particularly F. W. Taussig and C. S. Joslyn, *American Business Leaders* (New York, 1932); C. Wright Mills, "The American Business Elite: A Collective Portrait," *The Tasks of Economic History*, suppl. V of the *Journal of Economic History* (Dec. 1945), pp. 20-44; Frances W. Gregory and Irene D. Neu, "The American Industrial Elite in the 1870's," in William Miller, ed., *Men in Business: Essays in the History of Entrepreneurship* (Cambridge, 1952), pp. 193-211; William Miller, "American Historians and the American Business Elite," *Journal of Economic History*, 9 (1949): 184-200; Mabel Newcomer, *The Big Business Executive* (New York, 1955). Chapter four of Seymour Lipset and Reinhard Bendix, *Social Mobility in Industrial Society* (Berkeley, 1959), analyzes this literature in detail and reports the findings of another empirical study of the question.

2. The case for "writing history from the bottom up" is well stated by Caroline Ware and Constance M. Green in C. F. Ware, ed., *The Cultural Approach to History* (New York, 1940), pp. 273-286.

3. The five Yankee City volumes were published as follows: vol. I, W. Lloyd Warner and Paul S. Lunt, *The Social Life of a Modern Community* (New Haven, 1941); vol. II, W. Lloyd Warner and Paul S. Lunt, *The Status System of a Modern Community* (New Haven, 1942); vol. III, W. Lloyd Warner and Leo Srole, *The Social Systems of American Ethnic Groups* (New Haven, 1945); vol. IV, W. Lloyd Warner and J. O. Low, *The Social System of the Modern Factory* (New Haven, 1947); vol. V, W. Lloyd Warner, *The Living and the Dead: A Study of the Symbolic Life of Americans* (New Haven, 1959).

4. William Foote Whyte, *Street Corner Society: The Social Structure of an Italian Slum* (Chicago, 1943).

5. Massachusetts Bureau of the Statistics of Labor, *Third Annual Report* (Boston, 1872), p. 343.

6. Oscar Handlin, to whom I am indebted for the original suggestion to look into the manuscript schedules, made extensive use of them in *Boston's Immigrants: A Study in Acculturation* (rev. ed.,

Cambridge, Mass., 1959). Much of F. L. Owsley's *Plain Folk of the Old South* (Baton Rouge, 1949) is similarly based on data from original census schedules. The chief objective of both of these volumes was quite different from that of the present study; neither author, accordingly, traced individuals from census to census. The only work closely comparable to this one in its use of census materials is Merle E. Curti, *The Making of an American Community: a Case Study of Democracy in a Frontier County* (Stanford, 1959), a history of Trempealeau County, Wisconsin, in the period 1850-1880.

Manuscript census schedules, unhappily, are essentially confined to the 1850-1880 period. The first six United States Censuses (1790-1840) aimed at little more than a simple enumeration of the population. Individual inhabitants of a community were not listed by name, and there was no effort to compile the economic and social data which make the later censuses so valuable a source for the historian. Most of the 1890 schedules, including all of those for Massachusetts, were destroyed by fire. The 1900 and subsequent censuses are presently classified "confidential" by law; thus only aggregated data, on which it is impossible to trace individuals, are available to the historian. Manuscript schedules for the communities of Essex County for the years 1850, 1860, and 1870 are available at the Essex Institute, Salem, Mass. Duplicates of these, plus the schedules for 1880, may be found in the Massachusetts State Archives, Boston.

1. LABORER AND COMMUNITY AT MID-CENTURY

1. Adna F. Weber, *The Growth of Cities in the Nineteenth Century: A Study in Statistics* (New York, 1899), p. 1.

2. For the early history of Newburyport, see the excellent recent study by Bejamin W. Labaree, *Patriots and Partisans: The Merchants of Newburyport, 1764-1815* (Cambridge, Mass., 1962), and the two thick volumes by John J. Currier, *History of Newburyport, Mass., 1764-1905* (Newburyport, 1906). The economic history of New England in these years is treated in Samuel Eliot Morison, *Maritime History of Massachusetts, 1783-1860* (Boston, 1921), and Edward C. Kirkland, *Men, Cities and Transportation: A Study in New England History, 1820-1900* (Cambridge, Mass., 1948), 2 vols.

3. Caleb Cushing, *The History and Present State of the Town of Newburyport* (Newburyport, 1826), p. 112.

4. Newburyport *Herald*, Jan. 22, 1856.

5. Percy Wells Bidwell, "Population Growth in Southern New

England, 1810-1860," *Quarterly Publications of the American Statistical Association*, 15 (1917): 828.

6. Much of this background material is drawn from articles written by Walter M. Whitehill, Barbara M. Solomon, and Robert G. Albion for the special centennial issue of the Essex Institute *Historical Collections*, 95 (1959): 67-198. See also Claude M. Fuess, *The Story of Essex County* (4 vols., New York, 1935).

7. Caroline Ware, *The Early New England Cotton Manufacture: A Study in Industrial Beginnings* (Cambridge, 1931), p. 82.

8. Cushing, *History of Newburyport*, p. 82.

9. William T. Davis, "Newburyport," in D. Hamilton Hurd, ed., *History of Essex County, Massachusetts, With Biographical Sketches of Many of its Pioneers and Prominent Men* (Philadelphia, 1888), II, 1774.

10. "Justitia," *Strictures on Montgomery on the Cotton Manufactures of Great Britain and the United States* (Newburyport, 1841), pp. 17-18. John P. Coolidge identifies James as the writer in *Mill and Mansion: A Study of Architecture and Society in Lowell, Massachusetts, 1820-1865* (New York, 1942), pp. 203-204n.

11. Compiled from the original manuscript schedules of the U.S. Census of 1850.

12. Evelyn H. Knowlton, *Pepperell's Progress: History of a Cotton Textile Company, 1844-1945* (Cambridge, Mass., 1948), p. 32; J. D. Parsons, *Newburyport: Its Industries* (Newburyport, 1887); Newburyport *Daily Evening Union*, April 5, 1853.

13. "The Diary of John Lord," IV, 658; entry for Feb. 16, 1846. This ten-volume diary by a Newburyport carpenter, covering the period 1837-1878, is the property of the Newburyport Public Library.

14. Cushing, *History of Newburyport*, p. 75; Joshua Coffin, *A Sketch of the History of Newbury, Newburyport, and West Newbury from 1635 to 1845* (Boston, 1845), p. vi.

15. *Union*, July 31, 1851; "Lord Diary," IV, 668 (April 30, 1847).

16. Mrs. E. Vale Smith, *History of Newburyport: From the Earliest Settlement to the Present Time* (Newburyport, 1854), p. 228.

17. *Union*, June 6, 1851.

18. On population see George W. Chase, *Abstract of the Census of Massachusetts, 1860, from the Eighth U.S. Census* (Boston, 1863), p. 202; Barbara M. Solomon, "The Growth of the Population in Essex County, 1850-1860," Essex Institute *Historical Collections* 95 (1959): 82-103. Mrs. Solomon is evidently unaware of the 1851 shift in the Newburyport-Newbury boundary. She cites

the decline of the Newbury population from 4426 in 1850 to 1444 in 1860 as indicative of the decline of the agricultural town in Essex County, and asserts that "manifestly in this instance . . . the agricultural productivity was declining." This is not the case. The boundary shift meant simply that 3000 persons classed as Newbury residents in 1850 were added to the Newburyport total in 1860. Cf. *Union*, April 15, 1851; "Lord Diary," V, 1034 (June 5, 1852). Lord speaks of "a census just taken" which placed the Newburyport population, after the boundary change, at 12,866. Currier, *History of Newburyport*, I, 161, cites a document in the State Archives indicating that Newburyport gained 2842 persons from Newbury as a result of the annexation.

19. Joseph H. Bragdon, *A Report on the Proceedings on the Occasion of the Reception of the Sons of Newburyport Resident Abroad* (Newburyport, 1854), p. 74; *Union*, July 31, 1851.

20. Wooster Smith, ed., *The Directory of Newburyport* (Newburyport, 1849).

21. *Union*, April 12, 1853.

22. *Union*, May 31, 1852.

23. The most obvious choice for a study of this kind was the textile operatives of the city, but this would have been less rewarding. The cotton mills were the most conspicuous feature of the Newburyport economy at mid-century, but their place in the community stratification system is easily exaggerated. The schedules of the Seventh Census show that only 106 of the 2450 males over fifteen years of age employed in Newburyport in 1850 were mill operatives; only 75 others worked in the textile factories as skilled craftsmen or foremen. The great majority of textile employees were women and young children, whose earnings supplemented those of the laborer. Since the occupation of the father established the family's position in the community social structure, the student of social stratification should focus his research on an occupational group composed largely of adult males. A further reason for selecting the common laborers of Newburyport rather than the factory operatives was that a few excellent studies of factory workers in nineteenth century communities have already been made, but none of ordinary day laborers. See, for example, Vera Shlakman, *Economic History of a Factory Town: A Study of Chicopee, Massachusetts* (Northampton, 1936); Constance M. Green, *Holyoke, Massachusetts* (New Haven, 1939); Hannah G. Josephson, *The Golden Threads: New England's Mill Girls and Magnates* (New York, 1949); Coolidge, *Mill and Mansion*.

24. Handlin, *Boston's Immigrants*, p. 60.

25. Vale Smith, *History of Newburyport*, pp. 286-287; *Herald*, June 20, 1850; *City Treasurer's Annual Statement of Receipts, Expenditures, Etc. of the City of Newburyport for the Year Ending Nov. 30, 1852* (Newburyport, 1853), pp. 24-29; *City Treasurer's Annual Statement for 1859*, pp. 29-32.

26. These characteristics are analyzed in Lord Beveridge's classic discussion of the economics of casual labor. See William H. Beveridge, *Unemployment: a Problem of Industry* (London, 1909), chaps. V and IX. Cf. J. R. Hicks, *The Theory of Wages* (London, 1932), pp. 47-48, 63-69; Lloyd H. Fisher, *The Harvest Labor Market in California* (Cambridge, Mass., 1953), pp. 7-9.

27. For example, James D. Burns, *Three Years Among the Working Classes in the United States During the War* (London, 1865); John F. McGuire, *The Irish in America* (London, 1868). A standard exposition of this view by an American is John Aiken, *Labor and Wages at Home and Abroad* (Lowell, 1849).

28. Boston *Pilot*, May 25, 1850, March 18, 1854; Handlin, *Boston's Immigrants*, chap. iii.

29. *Herald*, June 25, 1847.

30. *Herald*, April 6, 1858.

31. Letter to Thoreau, Sept. 8, 1843; printed in *The Atlantic*, 69 (1892): 592-593.

32. Massachusetts Bureau of the Statistics of Labor, *Fourth Annual Report* (Boston, 1873), pp. 90-108.

33. *Herald*, Feb. 16, 1856, Feb. 21, 1856, March 14, 1856, March 26, 1858.

34. *Union*, Dec. 21, 1850.

35. *Herald*, Jan. 8, 1850.

36. From a volume marked "Minutes of the Overseers of the Poor," in the Newburyport Public Library. The figures on public relief are drawn from the annual reports of the Secretary of the Commonwealth, *Abstract of the Returns of the Overseers of the Poor in Massachusetts* (Boston, 1837-1853; title varies slightly).

37. "First Annual Report of the Ladies General Charitable Society of Newburyport and Vicinity," *Union*, Nov. 5, 1850, Nov. 12, 1850; *Herald*, Feb. 21, 1856, March 26, 1858.

38. A full 365 days of work at $1.33 would bring in only $485. Studies conducted by the Massachusetts Bureau of the Statistics of Labor in the 1870's revealed that the common laborer was employed an average of some 240 days per year; it appears unlikely, from the fragmentary data available, that Newburyport laborers in the 1850's were employed much more steadily than this. A 240-day work year at $1.33 per day would yield $320.

39. Bureau of Labor, *Sixth Annual Report*, pp. 365-370; Handlin, *Boston's Immigrants*, pp. 60-62.

40. *Union*, Dec. 21, 1850; *Herald*, Nov. 21, 1857.

41. *Annual Report of the School Committee of the City of Newburyport for the Year 1859* (Newburyport, 1859), p. 15; *Report of the School Committee for 1869*, p. 12.

42. *Report of the School Committee for 1855*, p. 11; *Report of the School Committee for 1864*, pp. 17-19.

43. *Herald*, March 11, 1850; Robert H. Lord, John E. Sexton, and Edward T. Harrington, *History of the Archdiocese of Boston* (New York, 1944), II, 574-585.

44. Bureau of Labor, *Sixth Annual Report*, p. 321.

45. An English observer of American labor conditions reported finding this motto prominently displayed in the library of a progressively managed Connecticut textile mill. Daniel Pidgeon, *Old World Questions and New World Answers* (London, 1884), pp. 228-229.

46. "Third Annual Report of the Ladies General Charitable Society," *Union*, Nov. 12, 1852.

47. *Abstract of the Returns of the Overseers of the Poor for 1851*, p. 1.

48. *Pilot*, May 27, 1854; Robert W. Kelso, *The History of Public Poor Relief in Massachusetts, 1620-1920* (Boston, 1922), pp. 135-136.

49. *Saturday Evening Union and Essex North Record*, Dec. 19, 1855; *Union*, Nov. 12, 1852.

50. Solomon, "The Growth of Population in Essex County," pp. 87-91.

51. Marcus Lee Hansen, *The Atlantic Migration, 1607-1860: A History of the Continuing Settlement of the United States* (Cambridge, Mass., 1940), pp. 180-183; Lord, *History of the Archdiocese of Boston*, II, 118.

52. Quoted in George Potter, *To the Golden Door: The Story of the Irish in Ireland and America* (Boston, 1960), p. 51.

53. Quoted in Florence Gibson, *The Attitudes of the New York Irish Towards State and National Affairs, 1848-1892* (New York, 1951), p. 50.

54. Vale Smith, *History of Newburyport*, p. 236. See the *Union* for Nov. 6, 1849, May 31, 1851, June 5, 1851, April 26, 1852.

55. See the *Herald* for Oct. 6, 1849, Jan. 11, 1850, Jan. 24, 1850, March 8, 1856, March 16, 1858, March 26, 1856. Cf. the *Union* for Aug. 14, 1849, April 16, 1851. See also the *Union and Essex North Record* for April 29, 1854 and Nov. 3, 1855. For

similar difficulties of the Irish in another Massachusetts mill town in the 1850's see Green, *Holyoke*, pp. 49-50.

56. Computed from manuscript census schedules. In his intensive study of a Wisconsin farming county in the period 1850-1880 Curti found a number of farm owners who reported their occupations as "laborer" on the census schedules; *The Making of an American Community*, p. 145.

57. Bureau of Labor, *Sixth Annual Report*, p. 336; *Union*, Dec. 21, 1850; *Herald*, May 5, 1856.

58. See, for example, the advertisements in the *Herald*, Aug. 6, 1857.

59. The map on which these generalizations are based was constructed from a list of laborers drawn from manuscript census schedules, addresses taken from city directories for 1849 and 1851, and a detailed map, "Plan of Newburyport, Mass., from an Actual Survey" (Philadelphia, 1851); copy available in Newburyport Public Library. For comments on working class housing see the *Union* for Dec. 6, 1851, and March 3, 1852.

60. "Seventh Annual Report of the Ladies Charitable Society," *Herald*, Nov. 15, 1856; "Eighth Annual Report," *Herald*, Nov. 21, 1857; *Union*, March 15, 1853; *Herald*, Oct. 27, 1857.

2. THE PROBLEM OF SOCIAL CONTROL

1. *Herald*, Oct. 7, 1856. Emphasis added.

2. Wendell Phillips, *The Labor Question* (Boston, 1884), p. 19. Cf. Oscar and Mary F. Handlin, *Commonwealth; A Study of the Role of Government in the American Economy: Massachusetts, 1774-1861* (New York, 1947), chap. viii.

3. Henry Adams, *History of the United States of America during the First Administration of Thomas Jefferson* (New York, 1889), I, 108.

4. Oscar Handlin, "The Social System," in Lloyd Rodwin, ed., *The Future Metropolis* (New York, 1961), pp. 17-41.

5. William Gouge, *Of Domestical Duties: Eight Treatises* (London, 1622), quoted in Michael Walzer, "The Revolution of the Saints" (unpubl. diss., Harvard University, 1961), chap. v., p. 52.

6. Massachusetts statute quoted in Arthur W. Calhoun, *A Social History of the American Family* (New York, 1960), I, 73.

7. Quoted in Calhoun, *History of the American Family*, I, 72-73.

8. Quoted in Edmund Morgan, *The Puritan Family* (Boston, 1944), pp. 85-86. Cf. Kelso, *History of Public Poor Relief in Massachusetts*, pp. 30-31.

9. Morgan, *The Puritan Family*, p. 85.

10. Perry Miller, *The New England Mind: From Colony to Province* (Cambridge, 1953), Book I.

11. Cf. Wallace T. MacCaffrey, *Exeter, 1540-1640: The Making of an English Country Town* (Cambridge, 1958), and Robert and Helen Lynd, *Middletown: A Study in American Culture* (New York, 1929).

12. Labaree's *Patriots and Partisans* provides the most detailed account of the Newburyport class structure in this period; his Table I, pp. 4-5, indicates the occupations of 699 Newburyport males in 1773. For a vivid portrait of upper class social life in Newburyport in these years see the diary John Quincy Adams kept while serving his apprenticeship in the law office of Theophilus Parsons; published as *Life in a New England Town: 1787-1788* (Boston, 1903). For other information on the merchant aristocracy, see Morison, *Maritime History of Massachusetts*, pp. 153, 164-167; John P. Marquand, *Timothy Dexter Revisited* (Boston, 1960); Vale Smith, *History of Newburyport*, pp. 171-174, 349; Sara Emery, *Reminiscences of a Nonagenarian* (Newburyport, 1879), p. 239. For some fragments on the lower class, see Emery, *Reminiscences*, pp. 190, 335.

13. Marquand, *Timothy Dexter*, p. 89; Adams, *Life in a New England Town*, pp. 39-40n; Labaree, *Patriots and Partisans*.

14. Samuel Knapp, *Life of Lord Timothy Dexter* (Boston, 1848), pp. 22-23.

15. Minnie Atkinson, *A History of the First Religious Society in Newburyport, Massachusetts* (Newburyport, 1933), p. 45.

16. Reverend John Prince of Salem, quoted in Norman Jacobson, "Class and Ideology in the American Revolution," in Reinhard Bendix and Seymour M. Lipset, ed., *Class, Status and Power: A Reader in Social Stratification* (Glencoe, Ill., 1953), p. 552.

17. Adams, *History of the United States*, I, 76.

18. John J. Currier, *History of Newbury, Massachusetts, 1635-1902* (Boston, 1902), pp. 116-119.

19. Vale Smith, *History of Newburyport*, p. 21. See Atkinson, *History of the First Religious Society*, pp. 56-57, for a description of a local tithing man in the first decade of the nineteenth century.

20. Currier, *History of Newburyport*, I, 27; Vale Smith, *History of Newburyport*, pp. 149-150, 402. The quotation is from a Federalist tract, *Remarks on the Jacobiniad* (1798), quoted in Jacobson, "Class and Ideology in the American Revolution," p. 551.

21. James D. Phillips, *Salem and the Indies: the Story of the Great Commercial Era of the City* (Boston, 1947), p. 360.

22. Printed as an appendix in Theophilus Parsons, *Memoir of Theophilus Parsons* (Boston, 1859), pp. 359-402. The quotation is from p. 364.

23. Labaree, *Patriots and Partisans*, pp. 13, 104, 133.

24. Vale Smith, *History of Newburyport*, pp. 155-156.

25. Coffin, *A Sketch of the History of Newburyport*, p. 255.

26. Parsons, "Essex Result," p. 367.

27. Labaree, *Patriots and Partisans*, pp. 14-15, 52-54. Cf. Labaree's fuller discussion in "Local History: Contributions and Techniques in the Study of Two Colonial Cities," *Bulletin of the American Association for State and Local History*, 2 (1959): 225-234. Labaree stresses that many Newburyport merchants had once been shipmasters and that they "spoke with a quarterdeck authority which by the traditions and laws of the sea few citizens dared to challenge in this maritime community." This is a plausible interpretation, but my analysis suggests that the main elements of the institutional framework which promoted deference voting in Newburyport were not peculiar to seafaring communities.

Cf. Robert E. Brown, *Middle-Class Democracy and the Revolution in Massachusetts, 1691-1780* (Ithaca, 1955). "Democracy" for Brown is a purely formal concept, and he thus finds that early Massachusetts was markedly more democratic than previous writers have believed. By ignoring, as Brown does, the way in which social institutions determine whether or not a ballot is meaningful, one might also produce a study of middle class democracy under many a totalitarian regime. Suffrage is universal in many totalitarian states, and a high percentage of the electorate actually exercises the franchise. For a sociologically sophisticated treatment of elite rule in early New Haven, see Robert A. Dahl, *Who Governs? Democracy and Power in an American City* (New Haven, 1961), pp. 11-24. Charles S. Grant, *Democracy in the Connecticut Frontier Town of Kent* (New York, 1961) contains data which support the view taken here, though the author's interpretation of these data is not fully in accord with mine.

28. Cf. Carl Bridenbaugh, *Cities in Revolt: Urban Life in America, 1743-1776* (New York, 1955); Richard C. Wade, *The Urban Frontier: The Rise of Western Cities, 1790-1830* (Cambridge, 1959); Grant, *Democracy in Kent;* Phillips, *Salem and the Indies;* Dahl, *Who Governs?*

29. Reverend John Allyn, "Election Day Sermon," May 29, 1805; quoted in Jacobson, "Class and Ideology in the American Revolution," p. 552.

30. *Herald,* Oct. 7, 1856.

31. Davis, "Newburyport," p. 1774; "Justitia," *Strictures on Montgomery,* pp. 17-18.

32. My argument here follows Karl Polanyi, *The Great Transformation: The Economic and Social Origins of Our Time* (Boston, 1957); cf. Wilbert E. Moore and Arnold S. Feldman, ed., *Labor Commitment and Social Change in Developing Areas* (New York, 1960), chap. iii.

33. Hicks, *The Theory of Wages,* p. 47.

34. *Herald,* Jan. 19, 1858, Nov. 15, 1856. See also the evidence cited above, Chap. I, n. 55.

35. *Union,* Oct. 18, 1853, Oct. 31, 1851.

36. Bragdon, *Reception of the Sons of Newburyport,* p. 41.

37. Cushing, *History of Newburyport,* pp. 44-59; Currier, *History of Newburyport,* I, 258-308; *Herald,* Oct. 7, 1856. Only later was it to become clear that the existence of a great many churches, if well organized and linked together by other voluntary associations (the Y.M.C.A., for example), did not mean religious anarchy. Cf. the discussion of voluntary associations in Chap. 7 below.

38. *Union,* March 17, 1853; Davis, "Newburyport," pp. 1795-1801.

39. "Lord Diary," VI, 1152-1153 (Dec. 6, 1854).

40. *Union,* April 5, 1851, Feb. 10, 1853.

41. Letter to the editor, by E. V. S. (Mrs. E. Vale Smith?), June 25, 1851 *Union.*

42. "Seventh Annual Report of Ladies Charitable Society," *Herald,* Nov. 15, 1856; "Eighth Annual Report," *Herald,* Nov. 21, 1857.

43. Kelso, *History of Public Poor Relief,* pp. 135-136; *Pilot,* May 27, 1854; *Abstract of the Returns of the Overseers of the Poor for 1855; Abstract of the Returns of the Overseers of the Poor for 1859.*

44. *Report of the School Committee for 1843-1844,* p. 17.

45. *Report of the School Committee for 1865,* pp. 3-4. *Report of the School Committee for 1864,* pp. 23-25; cf. *1858,* pp. 7, 15-17, *1860,* p. 10, *1863,* pp. 12-13.

46. *Report of the School Committee for 1859,* p. 16; *1869,* p. 12.

47. *Union,* March 11, 1851, April 6, 1853; *Report of the School Committee for 1861,* pp. 11-12; *1869,* p. 11.

48. *Union,* Sept. 1, 1852. Cf. Dahl, *Who Governs?* chap. iii.

49. *Union,* June 9, 1851. Similarly low levels of political participation by working class groups have been noted in many

studies of voting behavior; for a comprehensive survey of this evidence see Seymour Martin Lipset, *Political Man: The Social Bases of Politics* (Garden City, 1960), chap. vi. Systematic investigation of class differences in voting behavior in Newburyport during this period, unfortunately, cannot be conducted with any precision because the class composition of the six wards of the city was too heterogeneous. There were no overwhelmingly working class or overwhelmingly middle class wards in Newburyport; as a result, only crude generalizations of the kind quoted in the text can be made.

50. See the *Union* for Aug. 8, 1849, April 15, 1850, Jan. 4, 1851, March 9, 1852, June 24, 1853.

51. "Lord Diary," VI, 1245 (Dec. 8, 1856).

52. *Herald*, Dec. 10, 1856.

53. *Union and Essex North Record*, Nov. 3, 1855.

54. *The Addresses and Proceedings at the Laying of the Corner Stone of the New Town Hall in Newburyport, July 4, 1850* (Newburyport, 1850), p. 17. Emphasis added.

55. *Herald*, Jan. 15, 1851; *Union*, May 19, 1853; *Herald*, Feb. 10, 1851.

3. THE PROMISE OF MOBILITY

1. *Union*, Sept. 20, 1852.

2. Louis Wirth, preface to Karl Mannheim, *Ideology and Utopia; an Introduction to the Sociology of Knowledge* (London, 1936), p. xxi. Mannheim himself employed the concept of ideology in a sweeping effort to "grasp in its totality the structure of the intellectual world belonging to a social group in a given historical situation" (p. 58). What I call the ideology of mobility, of course, was only one element of the total reigning ideology in Newburyport at mid-century.

3. Cf. Robert Merton's lucid formulation of the argument in "Social Structure and Anomie," *Social Theory and Social Structure: Toward the Codification of Theory and Research* (Glencoe, Ill., 1949), pp. 125-150.

4. Intellectual and literary historians have devoted considerable attention to success literature, the rags-to-riches myth, and so forth. A recent study of broad scope is Irvin G. Wylie, *The Self-Made Man in America: The Myth of Rags to Riches* (New Brunswick, N.J., 1954). See also Kenneth S. Lynn, *The Dream of Success: A Study of the Modern American Imagination* (Boston, 1955); Richard D. Mosier, *Making the American Mind* (New York, 1947). R. Richard Wohl's "The 'Rags to Riches' Story: an Episode

of Secular Idealism," in Bendix and Lipset, *Class, Status and Power*, pp. 388-395, contains some tantalizingly brief observations on the social functions served by the mobility ideology. Two excellent reports treat working class mobility attitudes in the present: Ely Chinoy, *Automobile Workers and the American Dream* (Garden City, N.Y., 1955); Bennett M. Berger, *Working Class Suburb: A Study of Auto Workers in Suburbia* (Berkeley, 1960).

5. The earliest American utterance of this sort was probably that of Virginia's Peter Arundle in 1622: "Yea I say that any honest laborious man may in a shorte time become riche in this Country." Quoted in Richard D. Morris, *Government and Labor in Early America* (New York, 1946), p. 45. Wyllie, *The Self-Made Man*, pp. 10-13, briefly treats this background; he concludes that the main elements of the mobility creed were not formulated in the United States until the Jacksonian period.

6. Cf. Rychard Fink's introduction to Horatio Alger, Jr., *Ragged Dick and Mark the Match Boy* (New York, 1962), pp. 5-33; Louis B. Wright: "Franklin's Legacy to the Gilded Age," *The Virginia Quarterly Review*, 22 (1946): 268-279.

7. Merrill D. Peterson, *The Jefferson Image in the American Mind* (New York, 1962), pp. 24-25.

8. Nathan Appleton, *Introduction of the Power Loom and the Origin of Lowell* (Lowell, 1858), p. 15. See also Charles L. Sanford, "The Intellectual Origins and New Worldiness of American Industry," *The Journal of Economic History*, 18 (1958): 1-16; Coolidge, *Mill and Mansion*, pp. 13-14, 165n, 171-172n.

9. Samuel Batchelder, *Introduction and Early Progress of the Cotton Manufacture in the United States* (Boston, 1863), p. 89.

10. Charles Cowley, *A Handbook of Business in Lowell, With a History of the City* (Lowell, 1856), pp. 162-163.

11. See the *Union* for Aug. 16, 1852, May 19, 1853, and Oct. 27, 1851; the *Herald* for March 7, 1859 and Sept. 12, 1862. The analysis of the Newburyport version of the mobility ideology which appears here is drawn largely from material printed in local newspapers, though nonlocal sources have occasionally been utilized where they provide a succinct formulation of a belief commonly held in Newburyport. The special biases of particular local editors and publishers would have to be taken into account in a study focused on attitudes toward controversial political issues of the day—abolitionism, for example—but the ideas dealt with here were shared by all the vocal elements of the community. For a few years in the early 1850's Newburyport had a Democratic daily as well as the Whig *Herald*, but these politically antagonistic

papers expressed the same assumptions about the nature of the American social system. This is not to assert that the local press reflected the world view of every inhabitant of the city. The newspapers were organs of middle class opinion; the relationship between middle class beliefs and the realities of working class life in this period will be discussed at length in subsequent chapters.

12. *Herald*, April 16, 1856.
13. John Aiken, *Labor and Wages at Home and Abroad* (Lowell, 1849), p. 21.
14. Francis Bowen, *The Principles of Political Economy, Applied to the Condition, the Resources, and the Institutions of the American People* (Boston, 1856), pp. 124-125. Cf. the *Pilot* for May 20, 1854.
15. *Union*, Aug. 23, 1853.
16. *Herald*, April 16, 1856.
17. *Union*, Oct. 31, 1853.
18. Bowen, *Principles of Political Economy*, p. 122.
19. *Herald*, July 4, 1877.
20. Bureau of Labor, *Thirteenth Annual Report*, p. 217.
21. *Herald*, Jan. 4, 1860.
22. *Herald*, Aug. 24, 1848.
23. *Herald*, Dec. 5, 1856.
24. *Herald*, July 3, 1856.
25. *Herald*, Nov. 8, 1848.
26. *Herald*, March 1, 1856; *Union*, Oct. 20, 1851.
27. *Herald*, Jan. 24, 1850; June 7, 1850.
28. *Saturday Evening Union and Weekly Visitor*, Nov. 11, 1854; *Union*, Jan. 12, 1852.
29. *Herald*, May 10, 1856.
30. *Union*, Aug. 29 and 30, 1851.
31. *Herald*, March 13, 1858.
32. *Herald*, Jan. 9, 1850; Jan. 24, 1845.
33. *Herald*, Feb. 7, 1850; July 21, 1849.
34. *Herald*, May 10, 1856.
35. Bowen, *Principles of Political Economy*, pp. 109-110.
36. Aiken, *Labor and Wages*, p. 16.
37. Willard Phillips, *A Manual of Political Economy* (Boston, 1828), p. 151.
38. *Herald*, May 10, 1856.
39. A. Forbes and J. W. Greene, *The Rich Men of Massachusetts* (Boston, 1851), p. 76.
40. Agnes R. Burr, *Russell Conwell and His Work* (Philadelphia, 1926), p. 405.
41. *Herald*, July 14, 1845.

42. *Herald,* Aug. 6, 1860.
43. *Herald,* Jan. 19, 1878.
44. Forbes and Greene, *Rich Men of Massachusetts,* p. 80; *Union,* Oct. 20, 1851.
45. *Union,* March 15, 1853. Cf. *Herald,* Jan. 19, 1858.
46. *Union,* Nov. 19, 1851.
47. *Herald,* Oct. 8, 1856.
48. *Union,* Feb. 6, 1852.
49. *Union,* Oct. 1, 1849, Nov. 20, 1851.
50. "Eighth Annual Report of Ladies Charitable Society," *Herald,* Nov. 21, 1857.
51. See the *Union,* Aug. 8, 1849, March 9, 1852, June 10, 1852; and the *Herald,* Feb. 2, 1856.
52. Thus Wyllie writes that "the fundamentals of the success argument, having to do with industry, frugality and sobriety, are invariably the same," and that "the self-help argument . . . explained everything in terms of inner qualities and nothing in terms of environment" (*The Self Made Man,* pp. 199, 141). These two statements are true not because of any evidence Wyllie cites, but because they are tautological. Any nineteenth century argument which took environmental considerations into account Wyllie would rule out of the category of success literature by definition. This methodological decision keeps him from seeing any but the most conservative political implications of the mobility doctrine.
53. Similarly, Eric Goldman has objected to the assumption that Darwinian ideas were given only conservative uses in post–Civil War America, and has called attention to the important phenomenon of "Reform Darwinism." *Rendezvous With Destiny: A History of Modern American Reform* (New York, 1956), pp. 73-128.
54. "The New Nationalism," Speech at Osawatomie, Kansas, Aug. 31, 1910, printed as chap. i of Theodore Roosevelt, *The New Nationalism* (Englewood Cliffs, N.J., 1961), esp. pp. 26-27.
55. *Herald,* Jan. 24, 1845.
56. *Twelfth Annual Report of the Secretary of the Board of Education* (Boston, 1849), pp. 55-59.
57. *Report of the School Committee for 1877,* p. 9.
58. *Report of the School Committee for 1843-1844,* p. 2.
59. *Union,* May 14, 1851, May 19, 1853; *Herald,* March 15, 1853.
60. *Herald,* Jan. 19, 1853.
61. John F. Maguire, *The Irish in America* (London, 1868), pp. 2-3. Emphasis added.

62. Thomas d'Arcy McGee, *A History of the Irish Settlers in North America: From the Earliest Period to the Census of 1850* (Boston, 1852), pp. 233-235.

63. *Pilot*, April 15, 1854.

64. *Pilot*, Jan. 6, 1855.

4. THE DIMENSIONS OF OCCUPATIONAL MOBILITY

1. Information for these cases was drawn from the following sources: manuscript schedules of the Seventh, Eighth, Ninth and Tenth U.S. Censuses; Newburyport Assessor's Valuation Lists, 1850-1880; local city directories; newspapers; a series of manuscript volumes of registrations for the Putnam, Brown, and Female high schools for this period (scattered years). The school registration records are stored in the office of the Superintendent of Schools at the Newburyport High School.

2. *Pilot*, Jan. 6, 1855.

3. Chap. 8 below and the appendix present a detailed critical analysis of Warner's stratification theory.

4. Gösta Carlsson, *Social Mobility and Class Structure* (Lund, Sweden, 1958), pp. 44-45. Virtually every significant theorist of class sees occupation as a central determinant. Cf. Leonard Reissman, *Class in American Society* (Glencoe, Ill., 1959), p. 158.

5. The primary source of data for this analysis was the manuscript schedules of the U.S. Census for 1850, 1860, 1870, and 1880. The sample consisted of all Newburyport residents who listed their occupation as "laborer" on the Census of 1850, 1860, or 1870, and all male children of these men. Errors undoubtedly were made in tracing the careers of these hundreds of individuals. For a variety of reasons such errors are most likely to have led to some overestimation of the extent of migration out of the community and perhaps some underestimation of the frequency of upward occupational mobility. However a cross check against the Newburyport Assessor's lists revealed few mistakes and suggests that the margin of error in gathering data was relatively small. One obvious source of possible error is that some of these individuals may have changed their names during the period of the study, a common tactic of socially ambitious ethnics. I doubt that this was a factor of much significance for this group, though. None of my laborers are recorded on the *List of Persons Whose Names Have Been Changed in Massachusetts, 1780-1883* put out by the Secretary of the Commonwealth (Boston, 1885). Some may have changed their names without legal formalities, of course. But the device itself made most sense for the geographically mobile individuals; a new

name was most useful in a new place (or a different neighborhood in a great metropolis), where people did not know the old one. This subject, unhappily, cannot be explored within the confines of a community study like the present one.

6. The volatility of the population in nineteenth century America has not received the scholarly attention it deserves. A few recent studies report exceptionally high rates of population turn-over in various kinds of communities. Curti found that less than 50 percent of each occupational group remained resident in Trempealeau County, Wisconsin, for as long as a decade in the 1850-1880 period (*The Making of an American Community*, pp. 65-77). The population of Rochester, New York, appears to have been even less stable at this time: only 47 percent of a sample of 500 names drawn from the 1849 city directory could be located in the 1855 edition, and the figure fell to 20 percent in 1859 (Blake McKelvey, *Rochester, the Flower City, 1855-1890*, Cambridge, Mass., 1949, p. 3). For statistical data on the rapid turn-over of workers in the textile mills of Holyoke, Massachusetts, in the 1850's, see Ray Ginger, "Labor in a Massachusetts Cotton Mill, 1853-1860," *The Business History Review*, 28 (1954): 67-91. The whole question requires systematic study by social and economic historians. For some valuable methodological suggestions see Eric E. Lampard, "Urbanization and Social Change: on Broadening the Scope and Relevance of Urban History," in Oscar Handlin and John Burchard, ed., *The Historian and the City* (Cambridge, Mass., 1963), pp. 225-247. Cf. Rowland T. Berthoff, "The American Social Order: A Conservative Hypothesis," *American Historical Review*, 65 (1960): 495-514.

7. Richard Scudder and C. Arnold Anderson, "Migration and Vertical Occupational Mobility," *American Sociological Review*, 19 (1954): 329-334; Ronald Freeman and Amos Hawley, "Migration and Occupational Mobility during the Depression," *American Journal of Sociology*, 55 (1950): 171-177; Lipset and Bendix, *Social Mobility in Industrial Society*, pp. 206-218. A close study of population mobility in Norristown, Pennsylvania, however, shows that a majority of migrants to the community experienced no change in occupational status as an accompaniment of the migration process. And among those who did shift occupational level, a higher proportion were mobile in a downward direction! See Sidney Goldstein, *Patterns of Mobility, 1910-1950: The Norristown Study; A Method of Measuring Migration and Occupational Mobility in the Community* (Philadelphia, 1958), p. 53.

8. *Herald*, May 28, 1858.

9. Carter Goodrich and Sol Davison, "The Wage Earner in the Westward Movement," *Political Science Quarterly*, 50 (1935): 161-185 and 51 (1936): 61-110; Fred A. Shannon, "A Post Mortem on the Labor Safety Valve Theory," *Agricultural History*, 19 (1945): 31-37; Clarence H. Danhof, "Farm-Making Costs and the 'Safety Valve'; 1850-1860" *Journal of Political Economy*, 49 (1941): 317-359.

10. *Herald*, June 22, 1878. Cf. Cole, *Immigrant City*, pp. 132-133. Cole believes that the frontier was somehow a source of hope for the ordinary workman of Lawrence in this period: "For those whose future seemed completely hopeless there was the possibility of moving west." He does not, however, produce any evidence demonstrating that significant numbers of manual laborers from the community actually moved west. It is impressive that sample surveys conducted in Saskatchewan and Alberta in 1930-31 revealed that a significant number of the farm operators of the prairie provinces had some previous experience in unskilled or semiskilled employment; see C. A. Dawson and Eva R. Younge, *Pioneering in the Prairie Provinces: The Social Side of the Settlement Process* (Toronto, 1940), pp. 120-123, 318. But many of these men had been born and raised on farms, and it is probable that relatively few of them had ever worked as laborers in cities hundreds of miles from the frontier. For other negative evidence on this point, see Handlin, *Boston's Immigrants*, p. 159, and the literature cited there.

11. Cf. Handlin, *Boston's Immigrants*, chap. iii, esp. pp. 70-71; Percy Wells Bidwell, "Rural Economy in New England at the Beginning of the Nineteenth Century," *Transactions of the Connecticut Academy of Arts and Sciences*, 20 (1916): 383-391; Shlakman, *Economic History of a Factory Town*, chaps. iii, v, and vi.

12. For a useful guide to the abundant sociological literature on this matter, see Albert J. Reiss, Jr., *Occupations and Social Status* (Glencoe, Ill., 1961).

13. Robert K. Burn estimates that in 1890 the average white collar wage was twice the wage for manual labor; see "The Comparative Economic Position of Manual and White Collar Employees," *Journal of Business*, 27 (1954): 257-267.

14. *Union*, Oct. 30, 1849; *Herald*, April 15, 1856, Sept. 16, 1857, Oct. 29, 1870. Cf. Bureau of Labor, *Fourth Annual Report*, pp. 393-394.

15. It should be noted that the shoemakers of the community— a very large group—were ranked as semiskilled rather than skilled

workmen. The old-fashioned master of the bench has often been portrayed as the archetypal skilled craftsman, but by 1850 the traditional artisan had largely disappeared from the Newburyport shoe industry. A few independent masters still made entire shoes in their shops at mid-century, but the bulk of production was carried on through a putting-out system. The mobile laborers who became "shoemakers" in the fifties, sixties, and seventies seem not to have served any apprenticeship at all. Their task was to perform simple, semiskilled operations on leather farmed out to them by Lynn entrepreneurs. The status of these men, judging from their wages, working conditions, and training, must have been essentially the same as operatives in the textile mills and comb factory, rather than carpenters, masons, and similar artisans. By the 1870's, the local shoe industry had moved into the factory, and most "shoemakers" were simply operatives, except for a skilled minority who did specialized tasks—shoecutting, for example. Such specialized workmen have been ranked in the skilled class, of course. For the shoe industry in Newburyport, see J. D. Parsons, *Newburyport: Its Industries* (Newburyport, 1887), pp. 20-21; *Union*, Jan. 12, Jan. 14, 1853. On the evolution of American shoe manufacture, see Blanche Hazard, *The Organization of the Boot and Shoe Industry in Massachusetts before 1875* (Cambridge, Mass., 1921); John R. Commons, "American Shoemakers, 1648-1895," *Quarterly Journal of Economics*, 24 (1909): 39-84. Warner and Low, *The Social System of the Modern Factory* is a fanciful account of the changing status of the Newburyport shoemaker.

16. Tables 1 and 2 indicate these differences clearly. For comparative evidence supporting this line of argument, see Wilbert E. Moore, *Industrialization and Labor: Social Aspects of Economic Development* (Ithaca, 1951), esp. chap. iv; Charles Booth, *Life and Labour of the People in London* (9 vol. ed., London, 1892-1897), vol. VIII; R. Dahrendorf, "Unskilled Labor in British Industry" (unpubl. diss., London School of Economics, 1956). The only occupational prestige poll which has included a broad range of manual laboring jobs ranked casual laborers, farm laborers, and laundry workers well below ordinary factory operatives; Raymond B. Cattell, "The Concept of Social Status," *Journal of Social Psychology*, 15 (1942): 293-308. See also Michael Young and Peter Willmott, "Social Grading by Manual Laborers," *British Journal of Sociology*, 7 (1956): 337-345.

17. Sociologists have developed elaborate statistical techniques for distinguishing "pure mobility" from mobility caused by overall changes in the occupational structure. Typical applications of

contingency analysis to this problem are found in Natalie Rogoff, *Recent Trends in Occupational Mobility* (Glencoe, Ill., 1953); David V. Glass, ed., *Social Mobility in Britain* (London, 1954); Joseph A. Kahl, *The American Class Structure* (New York, 1957). It was not appropriate to utilize these techniques in the present study, both because of the smallness of the sample and because there were no major changes in the Newburyport occupational structure between 1850 and 1880.

18. These observations about the Newburyport occupational structure are based on my tabulation of the occupations of all Newburyport males listed in the manuscript schedules of the U.S. Census of 1850, and a summary of the occupations of Newburyport citizens in 1875; see the Commonwealth of Massachusetts, *The Census of Massachusetts, 1875: Population and Social Statistics* (Boston, 1875), I, 502.

19. The career patterns of three groups of laborers are traced here. The first of these groups consists of Newburyport residents listed as unskilled laborers on the manuscript schedules of the U.S. Census of 1850. The second consists of men first listed as laborers in Newburyport on the Census of 1860, and the third of unskilled workmen new to the community in 1870.

20. Bowen, *Principles of Political Economy*, pp. 86-87.

21. Lipset and Bendix, *Social Mobility*, p. 168.

22. Cf. the assertion of Warner and Srole that in these years "openings created by the general expansion of the economic system, particularly the establishment of large factories, were filled almost entirely by natives . . . Only unskilled occupations were available to the Irish as farm laborers, stevedores, carters, hod carriers, and domestics" (*The Social Systems of American Ethnic Groups*, p. 31). This is a mistaken judgment for the Irish immigrants of Newburyport, and a grossly mistaken one for the children of such immigrants. Warner's error may in part be attributed to the fact that he based his opinion on an analysis of data drawn from local city directories, and these provide no information on the occupations of young men still living with their parents. For further critical discussion of Warner's analysis of social mobility in Newburyport, see Chap. 8 and the appendix below.

5. PROPERTY, SAVINGS, AND STATUS

1. Max Weber, *The Theory of Social and Economic Organization* (New York, 1947), p. 425.

2. C. Bowles Fripp, "Report on an Inquiry into the Condition of the Working Class in the City of Bristol," *Journal of the Royal*

Statistical Society, 2 (1839-1840): 368-375. Cf. T. S. Ashton, *Economic and Social Investigations in Manchester, 1833-1933* (London, 1934).

3. B. Seebohm Rowntree, *Poverty: A Study in Town Life* (London, 1901); Charles Booth, *Life and Labour of the People in London*.

4. Reverend Leonard Withington, Sunday School Oration, *Herald*, July 13, 1842.

5. McGuire, *The Irish in America*, pp. 5-6.

6. It is difficult, of course, to make precise estimates of the wealth of individuals long dead. No public record is fully satisfactory for these purposes. Local tax figures, for example, notoriously underestimate actual values; only a halfhearted attempt is made to assess savings and chattels, and even real estate valuations are characteristically below market worth. This chapter draws on four primary sources: manuscript schedules of the U.S. Census, Valuation Books of the Newburyport Assessor, Essex County mortgage files, and records of a local savings bank. Despite certain deficiencies in each of these sources, estimates based on figures derived in four different ways warrant considerable confidence. Doubtless there are errors in the totals assigned some individuals, but it is likely that a reasonably accurate impression is conveyed of the economic position of the working class group as a whole.

7. The census-taker furnished the most convenient index of the economic status of residents of nineteenth century American communities. As a part of the Census of 1850, 1860, and 1870, every person in the U.S. was asked to estimate how much property he owned. The question was dropped from the 1880 schedules, unfortunately, so we must rely on assessor's valuations of real property for that year. A comparison of the 1850, 1860, and 1870 census figures with those which appear in the "Newburyport Assessor's Valuation List" for the same years disclosed that the valuation figures tended to run 10 to 20 percent below the census estimates; accordingly, the 1880 figures given here are somewhat biased downward. (The valuation lists are manuscript volumes available at the office of the City Treasurer, Newburyport City Hall.) One further technical detail is that enumerators for the Census of 1850 were instructed to record *real* property holdings. A separate question about *personal* property was added in 1860 and retained in 1870. The total of real and personal property figures was utilized here. Virtually all of the property reported by laborers was in real estate; had personal property estimates been available for

1850 they would have raised the total reported by laborers very little.

8. These conclusions are based on a search through records available at the Essex County Registry of Deeds in Salem. Transactions by workmen in the sample were located in the index volumes, "Grantors 1855-1879," and the text of each of these mortgages was then checked in the detailed records kept in the vault at the Registry. Had the entire period 1850-1880 been examined the number of mortgages might have been 5 to 10 percent higher.

9. The mortgage played a very different role in the West, where, contrary to Populist mythology, the farmer often used it for speculative purposes. See Arthur P. Bentley, *The Condition of the Western Farmer as Illustrated by the Economic History of a Nebraska Township* (Baltimore, 1893); Allen Bogue, *Money at Interest: The Farm Mortgage on the Middle Border* (Ithaca, 1955); Curti, *The Making of an American Community*, pp. 156-162.

10. Phillips, *A Manual of Political Economy*, p. 158; John P. Townsend, "Savings Banks in the United States," *A History of Banking in All the Leading Nations* (4 vols., New York, 1896), II, 439-467, 441; undated clipping (c. 1870) of an editorial from a Lowell, Massachusetts, newspaper, in a scrapbook at the Institution for Savings, Newburyport.

11. Report of the Committee on Banks and Banking of the Massachusetts House of Representatives, 1850, quoted in Emerson W. Keyes, *A History of Savings Banks in the United States From Their Inception in 1816 Down to 1874* (2 vols., New York, 1876), I, 61.

12. Phillips, *A Manual of Political Economy*, pp. 151-152.

13. Keyes, *A History of Savings Banks*, I, 39.

14. Townsend, "Savings Banks in the U. S.," p. 441.

15. Townsend, "Savings Banks in the U. S.," pp. 462, 441.

16. For a perceptive discussion of this setting, see Neil J. Smelser, *Social Change in the Industrial Revolution: An Application of Theory to the British Cotton Industry, 1770-1840* (Chicago, 1959). Smelser's analysis of the social role of the savings bank is extremely suggestive. See also Fishlow's statistical analysis of savings bank deposits by the "provident poor" in England; Albert Fishlow, "The Trustee Savings Banks, 1817-1861," *The Journal of Economic History*, 21 (1961): 27-40.

17. Quoted in H. Oliver Horne, *A History of Savings Banks* (London, 1947), p. 33. See also pp. 25-26, 49.

18. Bowen, *Principles of Political Economy*, pp. 109-110.

19. C. A. Woodward, *Savings Banks: Their Origin, Progress, and Utility* (Cleveland, 1869), pp. 44-45. For a local formulation of this argument, see the *Union*, March 11, 1852.

20. Townsend, "Savings Banks in the U. S.," p. 443.

21. Phillips, *A Manual of Political Economy*, p. 22.

22. Bureau of Labor, *Third Annual Report*, pp. 332-333; *Fourth Annual Report*, pp. 139, 145-146, 198.

23. Representatives of Newburyport's Institution for Savings generously allowed me to examine records which bear on this question. These data relate to only one of more than a hundred savings banks in Massachusetts during this period, and for even that one they are incomplete. The analysis which follows is only a modest case study, based on a small fragment of the research which would be required to settle the Massachusetts savings bank controversy. It does, however, go beyond the mere guesses as to working class patronage of savings banks made by the contending parties.

24. The primary source used was three volumes of "Depositor's Signatures," kept in the vaults of the Institution for Savings in Newburyport. These recorded, for the period July 10, 1856, to January 1, 1876, all new accounts opened. Data included were date of opening, account number, signature of depositor, occupation (often left blank), and city of residence. The fact that occupation was so often left blank accounts for the glaring discrepancy between my findings and the only published evidence on the subject previously available. A questionnaire administered by the Massachusetts Bureau of the Statistics of Labor in 1873 seemed to indicate that the Newburyport savings bank polled—whether it was the Institution for Savings or its one competitor was not disclosed—had only nine laborers among its depositors (*Fourth Annual Report*, p. 189). When one examines bank records carefully, however, it becomes clear that a great many ordinary laborers actually had savings accounts; they simply did not list their occupation in the signature book.

25. Officials at the Institution for Savings felt compelled to respect the privacy of individual depositors. Therefore I was not able to have direct access to account books, but was given limited information on thirty-nine accounts. Twenty of these thirty-nine cases came from a list of laboring depositors who possessed $500 or more in property according to census and tax records; the other nineteen from a list of laborers possessing less than $500 in property holdings. Owners of substantial amounts of property are ac-

cordingly somewhat overrepresented in this sample, and owners of no property at all underrepresented.

26. An intensive study of the oldest savings institution in the country reaches essentially this conclusion; Peter Payne and Lance Davis, *The Savings Bank of Baltimore, 1818-1866: A Historical and Analytic Study* (Baltimore, 1956), p. 65.

27. Shlakman, *Economic History of a Factory Town*, pp. 193-194; Green, *Holyoke*, pp. 44, 105. Edgar W. Martin's *The Standard of Living in 1860: American Consumption Levels on the Eve of the Civil War* (Chicago, 1942) concludes that the typical urban working class family of the period had negligible prospects of saving anything but a tiny fraction of its income.

28. *Herald*, May 2, 1871; Bureau of Labor, *Eleventh Annual Report*, pp. 36-41. For other revealing items on the market situation of the laborer, see the *Herald* for Dec. 27, 1877, Feb. 11, 1878, and April 23, 1878. It is impossible to give any very reliable estimates of changes in the real earnings of laborers in this period. Information on daily rates paid is scanty, and changes in the cost of living and the numbers of days worked annually are even harder to determine. However, the conclusion that there was no dramatic long-term rise in the real earnings of unskilled laborers in Newburyport between 1850 and 1880 seems quite safe. This impression, derived from census wage estimates and newspaper fragments, is in accord with several compilations of wage data for Massachusetts and for the country as a whole. See Bureau of Labor, *Third Annual Report*, pp. 517-520; Edith Abbott, "The Wages of Unskilled Labor in the United States, 1850-1900," *Journal of Political Economy*, 13 (1905): 321-367; Edward C. Kirkland, *A History of American Economic Life* (New York, 1951), pp. 326, 494; Clarence D. Long, *Wages and Earnings in the United States, 1860-1890* (Princeton, 1960), pp. 60, 99; U.S. Bureau of the Census, *Historical Statistics of the U. S.*, p. 90, Series D 578-588.

29. See the *Herald* for Jan. 4, 1878, March 9, 1878, Feb. 17, 1880, Dec. 7, 1880.

30. *Herald*, March 3, 1871.

31. *Report of the School Committee for 1880*, p. 23.

32. This point would appear more clearly in the population figures had the peaks and troughs of the business cycle corresponded closely to the census intervals; they did not, so that the extensive out-migration caused by the Depression of 1857, for instance, had already been compensated for by the time of the

Census of 1860. For population figures see Currier, *History of New-buryport*, I, 161.

33. *Herald*, Dec. 28, 1871.

34. The average annual increase in assessed value of community property was tabulated from figures given in Vale Smith, *History of Newburyport*, p. 232, and George E. Waring, Jr., *Report on the Social Statistics of Cities* (Washington, D.C., 1886), p. 263. For the other generalizations about the Newburyport economy in these years, see Charles J. Brockway, *Business Statistics of Newburyport; with an Introductory Sketch* (Newburyport, 1874); Parsons, *Newburyport: Its Industries;* the *Herald* for Aug. 13 and 24, 1870, Jan. 17, 1871, May 18, 1872, Jan. 15, 1878, May 2, 1878, Jan. 2, 1880, Feb. 21, 1880.

35. *Herald*, May 28, 1858.

36. *Herald*, Jan. 12, 1880.

37. For a general survey of "Distress, Relief, and Discontent in the United States During the Depression of 1873-1878," see Samuel Rezneck's essay in the *Journal of Political Economy*, 68 (1950): 494-512.

38. *Herald*, April 9, 1872.

39. *Herald*, Aug. 3, 1872.

40. *Herald*, Aug. 29, 1856.

6. THE PROCESS OF MOBILITY

1. The distinction between unskilled and semiskilled occupations was ignored in defining the static category, since these jobs comprised an occupational universe, within which there was relatively free movement back and forth.

2. Oscar Handlin, *The Uprooted: The Epic Story of the Great Migrations That Made the American People* (Boston, 1951), p. 88. This finding does not contradict the pessimistic remarks in Chap. 4 concerning the frontier as a source of opportunity for Eastern workmen during this period. To say that agriculture was the most important source of occupational mobility is not to say that, in absolute numbers, movement into agriculture was very large. And in many ways, paradoxically, it was easier for an ordinary workman to obtain a farm on the fringes of the city in which he was employed than it was to venture into the West and make his way there. The attraction of cheaper land was more than offset by the larger element of risk and the need to make a total commitment to farming. The gradualness of the transition from the status of laborer to the status of farmer in Newburyport and the extent of "moonlighting" is striking. The difficulty of finding supplementary

employment of this kind in sparsely populated areas may have been a more important factor than transportation costs in keeping Eastern workmen from moving west.

3. One of the classic vehicles of working class entry into business enterprise—the saloon—was largely unavailable to this group. Probably because they lacked the political influence necessary to obtain liquor licenses, none of these laborers or their sons were saloonkeepers as of 1880. During the sixties and seventies, however, the press complained periodically that dozens of unlicensed rum shops were being operated in the city; see, for example, the *Herald* for July 29, 1872. Perhaps some aspiring laborers had a hand in these. The political situation changed at about the end of our period; several of the tavernkeepers listed in the 1886 city directory were Irishmen from the laboring group. This was just the decade when the Irish were beginning to become a potent force in local elections; see Chap. 7 below.

4. Judgment as to how much property was a significant amount is necessarily somewhat arbitrary. A holding of less than $300, I believe, may be ignored in defining status layers within the working class. Even a tiny shack in the worst neighborhood could not be purchased for less than that sum. Smaller amounts of property represented only temporary insurance against destitution from unemployment; they vanished relatively quickly in an emergency.

5. The quoted phrase is Ireton's famous characterization of the English lower class during the Puritan Revolution; quoted from J. L. and Barbara Hammond, *The Town Labourer, 1760-1832: The New Civilization* (London, 1949), I, 68.

6. For a recent elaboration of the familiar view that the psychology of the American working class has been entrepreneurial, see Gerald N. Grob, *Workers and Utopia: A Study of Ideological Conflict in the American Labor Movement, 1865-1900* (Evanston, 1961), pp. 165-166n, 189. The classic expressions of this approach are to be found in the writings of "the Wisconsin school" of labor history; see John R. Commons, et al., *History of Labor in the United States*, 4 vols. (New York, 1918-1935), and Selig Perlman, *A Theory of the Labor Movement* (New York, 1928).

7. The growing contemporary literature on the sociology of working class life demonstrates the falsity of the simplistic assumption that increased material security is rapidly making the working class indistinguishable from the middle class. See particularly, Richard Hoggart, *The Uses of Literacy: Aspects of Working Class Life, With Special Reference to Publications and Entertainments* (London, 1957); Berger, *Working Class Suburb;* Chinoy, *Auto-*

mobile Workers and the American Dream; S. M. Miller and Frank Riessman, "Are Workers Middle Class?" *Dissent,* 8 (1961): 507-513 and the works cited there; Miller and Riessman, "The Working Class Subculture: A New View," *Social Problems,* 9 (1961): 86-97; Herbert J. Gans, *The Urban Villagers: Group and Class in the Life of Italo-Americans* (Glencoe, Ill., 1962).

8. *Herald,* May 10, 1856.

9. This observation about status is from Norman J. Ware's *The Industrial Worker, 1840-1860* (Boston, 1924), p. 26. Ware employed what later came to be known as "reference group" theory in an effort to show that the American working class was losing status in these years. Centering his attention on artisan groups which were suffering from changes in technology and market organization during this period, Ware implied that the ordinary workman of the 1840's and 1850's judged his present circumstances against the ideal of the independent craftsman of old. My point here is just the opposite. For further critical comments on the dangers of equating the entire working class with the displaced artisan, see the discussion of Lloyd Warner and the Lynds in Chap. 8 and the appendix below.

10. A number of recent studies support this line of argument. See Chinoy, *Automobile Workers,* chap. x; Lamar T. Empey, "Social Class and Occupational Ambition: A Comparison of Absolute and Relative Measures," *American Sociological Review,* 21 (1956): 703-709; J. Kenneth Morland, "Educational and Occupational Aspirations of Mill and Town School Children in a Southern Community," *Social Forces,* 39 (1960): 169-175.

7. LABORER AND COMMUNITY IN 1880: TOWARD SOCIAL STABILITY

1. *Herald,* Aug. 2, 1877.

2. "Anglo-American," *The Labor Problem in the United States* (New York, 1878), p. 24. Cf. Robert V. Bruce, *1877: Year of Violence* (Indianapolis, 1959).

3. C. M. Cornwall, *Free, Yet Forging Their Own Chains* (New York, 1876), p. 225; quoted in George Mayberry, "Industrialism and the Industrial Worker in the American Novel, 1814-1890," (unpubl. diss., Harvard University, 1942).

4. Local city directories also supplied more detailed data about population turnover in this period. Frequently editions of the directory included a note indicating how many families listed in the previous edition were no longer resident in the city, and also how many families were newcomers since the previous edition. Thus some 18 percent of the Newburyport families of 1855 were not

to be found by the time of the 1857 survey; 20 percent of the residents listed in 1857 had not lived in the city two years before. Comparable figures for other periods are:

	Percentage of names dropped	Percentage of new names added
1857-1859	20	23
1859-1863	27	30
1863-1865	18	26
1865-1867	24	23
1876-1878	16	19
1878-1879	12	19
1879-1881	18	21

Turnover rates in the range of 20 to 25 percent for periods as short as two years are certainly striking, even allowing for the crudity of the method used, and even when we note the possibility that many of these moves involved the same families. Goldstein found similarly high turnover rates in Norristown, but discovered that a substantial segment of the population was relatively stable: "The high in- and out-migration rates of each decade were largely attributable to the movement of the repeated migrants into and out of the community . . . There was a relatively large segment of the population which, through its continuous residence in Norristown, provided continuity and stability to the community" (Sidney Goldstein, ed., *The Norristown Study: An Experiment in Interdisciplinary Research Training*, Philadelphia, 1961, p. 90). Cf. Goldstein's fuller report of the study in *Patterns of Migration*. This is an important caveat, but a comparison of the city directories of 1849 and 1879 suggests that Newburyport had a much smaller stable population core than Norristown; a mere 8 percent of the 1879 families could be located in the directory of three decades earlier. Many of the families of 1849, of course, disappeared from the community because of death; even a generous estimate of the number of possible deaths, however, leaves a very large group whose disappearance must have been due to migration out of the city.

5. Oscar Handlin, "The Social System," in Rodwin, *The Future Metropolis*, p. 22.

6. *Herald*, Jan. 19, 1874.

7. Handlin, "The Social System," pp. 22-23, 32-33. Cf. Oscar and Mary Handlin, *The Dimensions of Liberty* (Cambridge, Mass., 1961), pp. 97-98, 107-109.

8. The *Herald's* heart-felt plea for "a renewal of the spirit of

former times" and a "return of the social life" of the preindustrial community appeared in the issue of Oct. 7, 1856. It is impossible to find comparable expressions of this sentiment in the local press of the 1870's; the ideal of an organic community seems to have vanished with the dying out of the old Yankee stock. The Historical Society of Old Newbury was created by the small remnant of old families still present in 1877, but this was patently an organization for the elite, not an instrument for the reintegration of the entire community.

9. See the *Herald* for May 4, 1871, Feb. 6, 1874, May 6 and 7, 1874.

10. *Herald*, Jan. 25, 1879.

11. *Herald*, June 30, 1856.

12. *Herald*, April 24, 1878.

13. See the *Herald* for Feb. 13, 1874, March 18, 1874, March 18, 1878, April 17, 1880, Aug. 9, 1880, Oct. 13, 1880. A religious census conducted in the parish in 1880 found 3417 Roman Catholics in Newburyport, 25.2 percent of the population (*Herald*, Jan. 17, 1880).

14. Reverend E. L. Drown, "Memorial Day Address," *Herald*, May 31, 1878.

15. *Herald*, Dec. 8, 1870.

16. Both quotations are from Robert D. Cross, *The Emergence of Liberal Catholicism in America* (Cambridge, Mass., 1958), pp. 107-108, 242n. Cf. Handlin, *Boston's Immigrants*, pp. 131-132; Kenneth W. Underwood, *Protestant and Catholic: Religious and Social Interaction in an Industrial Community* (Boston, 1957), chap. xii.

17. *Union*, Feb. 10, 1853.

18. *Herald*, March 16, 1878.

19. Immaculate Conception Parish, *Under the Patronage of Mary: 1848 to 1948* (Boston, n.d.), pp. 36-40.

20. Immaculate Conception Parish, *Under the Patronage of Mary*, pp. 41-42.

21. Underwood, *Protestant and Catholic*, p. 211.

22. Daniel P. Moynihan in Nathan Glazer and Moynihan, *Beyond the Melting Pot: The Negroes, Puerto Ricans, Jews, Italians, and Irish of New York City* (Cambridge, Mass., 1963), p. 29.

23. Immaculate Conception Parish, *Under the Patronage of Mary*, p. 34. Eleven leaders of the Benevolent Society for 1871 are listed; their occupations were traced in city directories.

24. *Herald*, Sept. 27, 1880. For the obituary of another of these men, grocer and real estate promoter Patrick Henry, see the *Herald*, Aug. 27, 1872.

25. *Herald*, March 2, 1880.

26. *Herald*, Sept. 29, 1877.

27. *Herald*, Feb. 9, 1878.

28. Warner and Srole, *The Social Systems of American Ethnic Groups*, pp. 161-162.

29. *Herald*, March 13, 1880.

30. For examples of the conservative influence exerted by the priest in labor-management disputes in Holyoke and Lawrence in this period, see Green's *Holyoke*, pp. 21, 71; Cole, *Immigrant City*, p. 53. Mark Karson's *American Labor Unions and Politics, 1900-1918* (Carbondale, Ill., 1958) contains a lengthy discussion of the conservative influence of the Catholicism on the American labor movement.

31. *Herald*, Sept. 29, 1864. The discussion here has focused on the role of the Roman Catholic Church. It would be interesting to know if any of the Protestant sects of the community exerted a similar influence over non-Catholic workmen, but I was unfortunately unable to find out anything concerning the religious affiliations of Protestant laborers.

32. *Herald*, Oct. 16, 1880.

33. *Herald*, Nov. 1, 1880.

34. Richard Hofstadter, *The American Political Tradition and the Men Who Made It* (New York, 1954), p. viii. Cf. Louis Hartz, *The Liberal Tradition in America: An Interpretation of American Political Thought since the Revolution* (New York, 1955).

35. In the absence of definitive historical studies of working class social mobility in other societies, the contrast drawn here is admittedly speculative. It has long been assumed that, by American standards, social mobility opportunities in societies with a feudal heritage have been very low; thus the contrast between the "open" society of the New World and the "closed" society of the Old World. This old belief has recently been challenged by Lipset and Bendix, who label as a myth the notion that the United States has been a uniquely open society. A principal thesis of their inquiry into *Social Mobility in Industrial Society* is that "social mobility is high in all industrial societies." If Lipset and Bendix are correct, none of the traits which distinguish American civilization from that of England, France, or Germany—such as the absence of militant class-based political parties in the United States—can be attributed to national differences in the structure of opportunities. It cannot be said, however, that Lipset and Bendix have successfully established their provocative thesis.

First of all, the evidence on which they base their conclusions is confined almost exclusively to the period since 1900; most of it, in fact, refers to the years since 1945. To extrapolate the findings of such recent studies back into the nineteenth century is obviously questionable. Lipset and Bendix make some use of scattered inquiries which were conducted in Europe, chiefly in the German-speaking nations, toward the end of the nineteenth century. (This literature is reported in more detail in Pitirim Sorokin's classic *Social Mobility*, New York, 1927, chap. xvii.) While these studies effectively undermine the stereotype that occupational mobility in the Old World was extremely rare, they do not suffice to refute the old view that nineteenth century America was significantly more open than the European countries of the age. The evidence concerning social mobility in both Europe and America during the nineteenth century is exceedingly fragmentary. And weaknesses in conceptualization and research design render this early European work much less reliable than Sorokin and the Lipset-Bendix team appear to believe.

Even for the period from which most of Lipset and Bendix's data are drawn, the evidence is not fully convincing. The only form of social mobility Lipset and Bendix consider is occupational mobility; property mobility is ignored entirely. And their measure of occupational mobility is extremely crude; intra-generational movement is not taken into account at all, and neither is mobility *within* the two broad classes of manual and nonmanual occupations. These severe limitations reflect the intrinsic inadequacies of the data available for comparative analysis at the time at which Lipset and Bendix were writing, but this fact does not warrant any greater confidence in the bold and dubious conclusions they drew. S. M. Miller's review of the international mobility literature as of 1960 reveals that evidence which might finally settle the question of American uniqueness is still unavailable, though the somewhat more refined studies reported there point to some substantial variations in occupational mobility rates between nations, with the U. S. ranking generally high—S. M. Miller, "Comparative Social Mobility: A Trend Report and Bibliography," *Current Sociology*, 9 (1960): 1-89.

Until sociological inquiries are conducted on the basis of a broader conception of what constitutes social mobility, and until they are carried out in historical depth, the issue raised by Lipset and Bendix will not be resolved. Certainly it is premature to dismiss entirely the old belief that the opportunity level in the United States has been higher than in Europe. Where convincing evidence to the contrary is lacking, it might be well to accept provisionally the conclusions of Tocqueville, Bryce, and dozens of other perceptive observers who saw a clear contrast between the lot of the common man in the Old World and the New.

36. For a lurid report on the exceedingly intemperate dispute over temperance in Newburyport in the 1870's, see J. E. Wolfe, *How to Fight the Rum Devil; Being a Detailed Account of the Fight against and Victory over the Rum Power of Newburyport, Massachusetts* (Boston, 1877).

37. *Herald*, July 1, 1880, Oct. 15, 1880.

38. *Herald*, Nov. 10, 1870, Nov. 10, 1856.

39. *Herald*, Oct. 27, 1880.

40. *Herald*, Sept. 22, 1880. It is impossible, regrettably, to discuss the question of ethnic and class differences in local voting with greater precision. As noted in Chap. 2, above, Newburyport ward lines were drawn in a way which tended to obscure such patterns. The crude generalizations offered in the text are all that can be made on the basis of the available data.

41. For a very similar analysis of the political scene in New Haven, Conn., during this period, see Robert A. Dahl's *Who Governs?*

42. Immaculate Conception Parish, *Under the Patronage of Mary*, pp. 52-53; *Herald*, Sept. 9, 1877, Jan. 20, 1880. For a description of the Moylan family, see pp. 81-82 above.

43. *Herald*, Sept. 22, Oct. 25, 1880.

44. Immaculate Conception Parish, *Under the Patronage of Mary*, p. 53.

45. Advertisement in the *Newburyport and Amesbury City Directory for 1886-1887*.

46. Fuess, *The Story of Essex County*, IV, 1007.

47. It should be noted that, contrary to expectation, politics was not an important vehicle of occupational mobility for the Irish of Newburyport in the 1850-1880 period. None of the men and boys included in the sample studied had attained a government job by 1880. And from our imperfect knowledge of the situation after 1880 it appears that, at least for high office, political success for the Irish came *after* business success. Dahl reports that in New Haven "the Irish used politics to surmount obstacles to their advance in the socioeconomic world," while groups like the Italians and Jews "more frequently used gains in the socioeconomic world to attain elective positions in politics" (*Who Governs?* p. 42). The Irish of Newburyport, possibly because they never formed quite so large a fraction of the electorate as in New Haven, appear to have followed the pattern Dahl describes for the Italians and Jews.

48. *Herald*, Dec. 23, 1870.

49. *Herald*, Jan. 3, 1880.
50. *Herald*, May 8, 1878, Aug. 26, 1870.
51. *Herald*, Feb. 10, 1879, May 24, 1872. This is not to suggest that local attitudes toward social problems were unfailingly optimistic and humane. In 1878 James D. Parton, Andrew Jackson's biographer and a longtime Newburyport resident, advanced his solution to the spread of poverty and vagrancy: tramps and paupers were to be placed in cisterns, into which water flowed about as fast as a vigorous man could pump it out; "If he worked he was saved, and if he refused he was drowned" (*Herald*, June 14, 1878). See the *Herald*, Feb. 14, 1879, for an editorial similar in tone.
52. *Herald*, Nov. 10, 1880.
53. *Herald*, Aug. 7, 1871.
54. See the *Herald* for Aug. 26, Sept. 2, and Nov. 11, 1871.
55. *Herald*, June 5, 1874.
56. *Herald*, Aug. 26, 1871.
57. *Herald*, Nov. 30, 1880.
58. Hartz, *The Liberal Tradition*, p. 218.
59. *Herald*, Sept. 11, 1877.
60. *Herald*, July 25, 1877.
61. *Herald*, July 31, 1877.
62. *Herald*, Nov. 9, 1880.
63. *Herald*, Dec. 4, 1880.
64. *Herald*, June 12, 1880.
65. *Herald*, Aug. 21, 1877.

8. NEWBURYPORT AND THE LARGER SOCIETY

1. U. S. Bureau of the Census, *Historical Statistics of the United States*, p. 14.
2. For Warner's most extreme claims about the representativeness of the communities he studied, see his general work, *American Life: Dream and Reality* (Chicago, 1953). Cf. Warner, et al., *Democracy in Jonesville; A Study in Quality and Inequality* (New York, 1949), p. xv: "Jonesville has been our laboratory for studying Americans . . . We can say that Jonesville is in all Americans and all Americans are in Jonesville, for he that dwelleth in America dwelleth in Jonesville, and Jonesville in him . . . To study Jonesville is to study America." A similar assumption about the representativeness of Newburyport recurs throughout the Yankee City volumes, despite one uncharacteristic disclaimer to the effect that Yankee City was only *"one of the thousands"* of communities which had to be studied in order to construct a comparative sociology (Warner, *Social Life of a Modern Community*, p. 22).

3. Warner, *Social Life*, pp. 1-5, 38-39; *The Social System of the Modern Factory*, p. 2.

4. C. Wright Mills, review of *Social Life of a Modern Community* in *American Sociological Review*, 7 (1942): 263-271. Cf. Mills, *The Power Elite* (New York, 1956), chap. ii, for a general attack on social stratification studies conducted in small towns.

5. Florence Kluckhohn, "Dominant and Substitute Profiles of Cultural Orientations: Their Significance for the Analysis of Social Stratification," *Social Forces*, 18 (1949-1950): 376-393.

6. For comments on the impropriety of generalizing from the Newburyport case or from any small community, see Paul K. Hatt, "Stratification in the Mass Society," *American Sociological Review*, 15 (1950): 216-222; Kahl, *The American Class Structure*, p. 49; John F. Cuber and William F. Kenkel, *Social Stratification in the United States* (New York, 1954), pp. 23-28; William Peterson, review of Sidney Goldstein, ed., *The Norristown Study* in *American Sociological Review*, 28 (1963): 477-478.

7. Oscar Handlin first pointed out some of the chief distortions in Warner's portrait of Newburyport in early reviews of the Yankee City volumes. See *New England Quarterly*, 15 (1942): 554-557; *New England Quarterly*, 18 (1945): 523-524; *The Journal of Economic History*, 7 (1947): 275-277. Cf. Henry F. May's review of vol. IV of the series in *New England Quarterly*, 21 (1948): 276-277.

8. Curti, *The Making of an American Community*, chaps. v, vii-ix. Though the Curti volume was conceived as an effort to test Turner's frontier thesis, the authors are somewhat cautious about attributing to the influence of the frontier conditions which might have existed in communities far from the frontier. They carried out a very interesting comparative analysis of the distribution of property in their frontier county and in 11 Vermont townships, and found that the property structure in the two areas was "strikingly similar." (78). Comparison of the present study with the Curti volume should serve to further undermine the simplistic contrast between the supposedly closed social order of the East and the supposedly open communities of the West.

9. McKelvey, *Rochester*, p. 3; Ginger, "Labor in a Massachusetts Cotton Mill, 1853-1860," *The Business History Review*, 28 (1954): 81-88; Knowlton, *Pepperell's Progress*, p. 59; Shlakman, *Economic History of a Factory Town*, pp. 146-150.

10. Weber, *Growth of Cities in the Nineteenth Century*, pp. 266, 249-251.

11. Shlakman, *Economic History of a Factory Town*, pp. 193-

194. For a valuable critical review of some of these pessimistic estimates see Ginger, "Labor in a Massachusetts Cotton Mill." For evidence which suggests patterns of property mobility similar to those in Newburyport, see Cole, *Immigrant City*, esp. pp. 53-54; David Brody, *Steelworkers in America: the Nonunion Era* (Cambridge, Mass., 1960), pp. 86-87, 107-108; Sam B. Warner, Jr., "Residential Development of Roxbury, West Roxbury, and Dorchester, Massachusetts, 1870-1900" (unpubl. diss., Harvard University, 1959), Appendix C; Walter Wyckoff, *The Workers; An Experiment in Reality: The East* (New York, 1897), pp. 127-128.

12. E. P. Hutchinson, *Immigrants and Their Children, 1850-1950* (New York, 1956), chaps. vi-viii.

13. Otis Dudley Duncan and Stanley Lieberson, "Ethnic Segregation and Assimilation," *American Journal of Sociology*, 64 (1959): 364-374. The Irish probably represent this pattern in its most extreme form. See Handlin's discussion of the differences between the Irish and Jews in nineteenth century New York; *The Newcomers: Negroes and Puerto Ricans in a Changing Metropolis* (Cambridge, Mass., 1959), pp. 26-27. Curti found interesting evidence of Irish land hunger in the Trempealeau County study; see *The Making of an American Community*, pp. 183-187. Possibly a cultural pattern common to Roman Catholics in the United States is at stake here; the most recent survey of religious differences in social mobility, Gerhard Lenski, *The Religious Factor: A Sociological Study of Religion's Impact on Politics, Economics, and Family Life* (rev. ed., Garden City, N.Y., 1963), chap. iii, reaffirms Weber's stress on the connection between the Protestant Ethic and occupational success.

14. Lipset and Bendix, *Social Mobility in Industrial Society*, p. 219.

15. If the data on occupational mobility for the six cities were reported city by city it would be possible to say more about the variables at work. Albert J. Reiss and Evelyn M. Kitagawa, who had access to the original data, have reported that there were distinct differences between the crude *job mobility* rates for the six, but they unfortunately do not discuss *occupational mobility* rates. About half of the intracity differences in job mobility rates, they conclude, were due to differences in the age and migrant structures of the cities; see "Demographic Characteristics and Job Mobility of Migrants in Six Cities," *Social Forces*, 32 (1953): 70-75. Sidney Goldstein calls attention to another important variable—whether or not those coming into a city have high or low occupational qualifications. If the latter, and if many of the emigrants are of

high occupational status, a vacuum is created in which hometown youths of low status are necessarily drawn up the occupational scale; "Migration and Occupational Mobility in Norristown, Pennsylvania," *American Sociological Review*, 20 (1955): 402-408.

16. On the distribution of the urban population and patterns of urban growth see U. S. Bureau of the Census, *Historical Statistics of the United States;* Weber, *The Growth of Cities in the Nineteenth Century*, pp. 34-38.

17. Handlin, *Boston's Immigrants*, p. 88.

18. Warner, "Residential Development of Roxbury," Appendix C.

19. For this formulation on the question of representativeness I am indebted to Maurice R. Stein's valuable discussion in *The Eclipse of Community: An Interpretation of American Studies* (Princeton, 1960), chap. iv, esp. p. 94.

20. Warner, *Modern Factory*, pp. 182-185, 87-89. For other characteristic expressions of the view that social mobility opportunities in the U. S. are on the decline see Elbridge Sibley, "Some Demographic Clues to Stratification," in Bendix and Lipset, *Class, Status and Power*, pp. 381-388; J. O. Hertzler, "Some Tendencies Towards a Closed Class System in the United States," *Social Forces*, 30 (1952): 313-323; C. Wright Mills, *White Collar: The American Middle Classes* (New York, 1951), chap. xii; August B. Hollingshead, "Trends in Social Stratification: A Case Study," *American Sociological Review*, 17 (1952): 679-686.

21. Newman Smyth, *Social Problems: Sermons to Workingmen* (Boston, 1885), pp. 12-13. Several of the labor leaders who testified before the Blair Committee in 1883 made similar assertions; see U. S. Congress, Senate, *Report of the Committee of the Senate upon the Relations between Labor and Capital* (Washington, 1885), I, 49, 256, 757. Cf. Edward Young, *Labor in Europe and America* (Philadelphia, 1875), pp. 177-179.

22. Robert S. and Helen Merrell Lynd, *Middletown*, pp. 65-66, 51; *Middletown in Transition: A Study in Cultural Conflicts* (New York, 1937), pp. 67-72, 471.

23. Warner, *Modern Factory*, chap. x.

24. See, for example, L. J. Carr's review of Warner's factory volume in the *American Sociological Review*, 12 (1947): 727-728, and Oswald Hall's review in the *Canadian Journal of Economics and Social Science*, 14 (1948): 277. Maurice Stein has recently presented an entirely sympathetic restatement of the Lynd and Warner theses in *The Eclipse of Community*, chaps. ii and iii. It should be said, however, that Stein aimed not at a detailed critical

evaluation of these works, but attempted rather to extract from these and other sociological field studies a general theory of American community life. The critical analysis which follows, therefore, does not necessarily apply to the hypotheses Stein derived from Warner and the Lynds, though at some points it does.

25. In the past decade or so the blocked mobility notion, unchallenged orthodoxy in American sociological writings of the 1930's and 1940's, has frequently been called into question; see, for example, Gideon Sjoberg, "Are Social Classes in America Becoming More Rigid?" *American Sociological Review*, 16 (1951): 775-783; Ely Chinoy, "Social Mobility Trends in the United States," *American Sociological Review*, 20 (1955): 180-186; William Petersen, "Is America Still the Land of Opportunity? What Recent Studies Show about Social Mobility," *Commentary*, 16 (1953): 477-486. These excellent criticisms, however, have been inconclusive; hard data to support the authors' assumptions about the mobility implications of various structural changes in the society have been regettably scarce. The now abundant literature on the social origins of "the American business elite" indicates that though mobility from the bottom to the very top of the class ladder is very rare in present-day America it is apparently no less rare than it ever was; see the evidence cited in Chap. I, note 2 above. The business elite studies, however, are not sufficient to refute the blocked mobility hypothesis. Access to a few positions at the very top of the social pyramid seems a poor index of the openness of a social structure. Rogoff's survey of occupational mobility in Indianapolis is not open to this objection, for the sample included all occupational levels; see *Recent Trends in Occupational Mobility*. But Rogoff's concern, as the title indicates, is only with *recent* trends—trends since 1910. The Rogoff study, therefore, does not challenge the assumption that the opportunity level was higher in *nineteenth century* America. And both Rogoff and the authors of the business elite inquiries deal exclusively with mobility of an inter-generational kind. By no means all of the important issues raised by proponents of the blocked mobility hypothesis, therefore, have yet been settled.

It is noteworthy that Warner himself has partly reversed his position on the blocked mobility issue. In 1952 Warner and James C. Abegglen conducted a study of the social origins of some 8000 American business leaders; see *Occupational Mobility in American Business and Industry, 1928-1952* (Minneapolis, 1955), and a popularized report of the findings, *Big Business Leaders in America*

(New York, 1955). In comparing their data with the famous Taussig-Joslyn study in 1928 (*American Business Leaders*) Warner and Abegglen found no trend toward increased inheritance of elite business positions. Some of the evidence even pointed to a slightly higher rate of upward mobility in the more recent sample, and the authors were quick to conclude from this that the American class system was becoming increasingly open. Warner's new-found optimism about mobility trends in the United States seems as open to question as his original pessimism. The differences on which his judgment about trends was based were very small to sustain such weighty conclusions, as Morroe Berger points out in "The Business Elite: Then and Now; From Entrepreneur to Executive," *Commentary*, 22 (1956): 367-374. And the extent of elite mobility, as previously observed, is only one and by no means the most important measure of the openness of a class system.

26. Warner, *Modern Factory*, pp. 4-7.

27. Warner, *Modern Factory*, p. 87.

28. Warner, *Modern Factory*, pp. 88-89.

29. A possible explanation of this startling shift in Warner's image of the community would be that though he never overtly replied to his critics in later writing, Warner was stung by the charge that the Yankee City he portrayed was static, "trendless," entirely unrepresentative of changing industrial America. Certainly this was a criticism which could never be made of *The Social System of the Modern Factory*, for here Warner pursued trends with a vengeance, and elaborated not only the national but the "world implications" of the dramatic changes he now perceived taking place in Newburyport.

30. Warner, *Modern Factory*, p. 5. For some previous strikes in Newburyport see the *Herald* for the week of April 6-13, 1858 and for May 2, 1871; Bureau of Labor, *Eleventh Annual Report*, pp. 36-41.

31. Handlin, review of *The Social System of the Modern Factory*, pp. 275-277.

32. Warner, *Modern Factory*, chart i, p. 65.

33. Parsons, *Newburyport: Its Industries;* Brockway, *Business Statistics of Newburyport;* various items in the *Herald* of the 1870's. Mechanization and absentee ownership were standard features of New England industrial life long before the Civil War; see Shlakman, *Economic History of a Factory Town* and Green, *Holyoke*. It is ironic that Warner, in discussing the idyllic craft order in shoe manufacturing, alludes to the efforts of the Knights

of Crispins to preserve stringent apprenticeship requirements and to prevent the use of "green hands" in the post–Civil War decade. Not only had the Knights everywhere lost this struggle more than half a century before the "successful" Newburyport strike; it was precisely in Newburyport that the craft order was so weak as to permit capitalists from the great shoe center, Lynn, to set up "runaway shops" as a means of avoiding "Crispin trouble." See the *Herald* for Sept. 17, 1877, and Jan. 2, Feb. 11, and April 23, 1878.

34. Lynd, *Middletown in Transition*, p. 471.

35. The Lynds were too careful observers to overlook migration from rural areas into the community; see, for example, *Middletown in Transition*, p. 52. They failed, however, to see how vitally this movement of unskilled men affected the adjustment of the Middletown working class to mechanization.

36. Calculated from the table "Actual Mobility of All Sons, 1910, Detailed Occupational Categories," in Rogoff, *Recent Trends in Occupational Mobility*.

37. The failure to consider possibilities of this kind and to delineate with care precisely what elements of the population were affected by particular economic changes has been a central defect of many important works in labor history, including such classics as Norman J. Ware's *The Labor Movement, 1840-1860* and J. L. and Barbara Hammond's *The Town Laborer, 1760-1832*. It is undeniable that some of the changes associated with industrialization have harmed large groups of workmen, but the fate of the glass blowers or the Hammond's weavers cannot be assumed to epitomize the fate of the entire working class in industrial society.

38. Warner, *Modern Factory*, p. 185.

39. See Mills, *White Collar*, and the literature cited there.

40. The high concentration of sons in the low-skill occupational universe in New Haven was probably due largely to the fact that the sample included many more very young men than any of the others; the minimum age for inclusion in the New Haven Sample Family Survey was only sixteen, and all the youths examined were unmarried and living at home. The San Jose inquiry, by contrast, was limited to respondents at least thirty years old; the Indianapolis data, since they were drawn from marriage license applications, similarly underrepresent the very young.

Another variable which may have influenced these findings is race. None of the Newburyport working class families were Negro, and only a few nonwhites were included in the San Jose study. The Indianapolis, Norristown, and 1945 U. S. figures are for whites only. The other inquiries included nonwhites, but the lower mobility rates of nonwhite groups do not seem to have influenced the results very much, except perhaps in the case of New Haven and Norristown. A separate sample of Negroes married in Marion County, 1938-1941, was drawn by Rogoff, and comparison with white sons revealed very low rates of Negro mobility into high status occupations; *Recent Trends in Occupational Mobility*, chap. v.

41. The relatively low mobility into nonmanual occupations in New Haven was probably due to the age composition of the sample, as explained in the previous note. Both of the San Jose estimates seem high, but the 1900 figure warrants little confidence for reasons advanced in the note to Table 16. It is quite possible, of course, that California attracts a disproportionately ambitious and talented migrant population and this may be reflected in both San Jose figures.

42. Again, it can be objected that the trend toward somewhat greater access to nonmanual jobs for men of working class origins has been accompanied by a decline in the relative status of nonmanual as against manual occupations; see Mills's *White Collar* for a discussion of the dramatic expansion of menial white collar occupations in recent decades and the consequent blurring of income and other status differentials between blue collar and white collar work. This is indeed an important point, but it may be doubted that many white collar workers evaluate their status as negatively as Mills does. Certainly in present-day America most shifts from manual to nonmanual positions would still be considered upward mobility by most observers.

43. Chinoy, *Automobile Workers*, p. 124. On this point, see also Bennett Berger's *Working Class Suburb*.

44. The reader on social stratification edited by Bendix and Lipset, *Class, Status and Power*, is the best introduction to this literature.

45. For full discussions of this, see Michael Harrington, *The Other America: Poverty in the United States* (New York, 1962); Gabriel Kolko, *Wealth and Power in the United States: An Analysis of Social Class and Income Distribution* (New York, 1962).

APPENDIX. FURTHER REFLECTIONS ON THE YANKEE CITY SERIES: THE PITFALLS OF AHISTORICAL SOCIAL SCIENCE

1. For a useful discussion of the impact on historical writing of some recent developments in the social sciences see two essays by H. Stuart Hughes: "The Historian and the Social Scientist,"

American Historical Review, 66 (1960): 20-46; "History, the Humanities, and Anthropological Change," *Current Anthropology,* 4 (1963): 140-145.

2. Edward Hallett Carr, *What Is History?* (New York, 1962), p. 84.

3. For a suggestive discussion of the general issue, see Barrington Moore, Jr., *Political Power and Social Theory: Six Studies* (Cambridge, Mass., 1958), esp. chap. iv; Asa Briggs, "Sociology and History," A. T. Welford, et al., ed., *Society: Problems and Methods of Study* (London, 1962), pp. 91-98.

4. For a useful summary of the abundant Warner literature as of 1953, see Ruth Rosner Kornhauser, "The Warner Approach to Social Stratification," in Bendix and Lipset, *Class, Status and Power,* pp. 224-254.

5. E. R. Leach, *Political Systems of Highland Burma: A Study of Kachin Social Structure* (Cambridge, Mass., 1954), p. 282; see also pp. 6-9, 227, 283-286.

6. Warner, *The Status System of a Modern Community,* p. 13; *Social Life of a Modern Community,* p. 90.

7. These are but a few examples to suggest the monumental scale of the Yankee City venture. For a full account of "The Field Techniques Used and the Materials Gathered," see *Social Life,* pp. 38-75.

8. Warner, *Social Life,* p. 40.

9. Warner, *Social Life,* chap. ii.

10. Warner, *Social Life,* p. 14.

11. Warner, *The Living and the Dead,* p. 4.

12. Cf. Robert Bierstadt, "The Limitations of Anthropological Methods in Sociology," *American Journal of Sociology,* 54 (1948): 22-30; Oscar Handlin, review of vols. I and II of the Yankee City series.

13. Warner, *The Living and the Dead,* p. 110.

14. Warner, *Social System of Modern Factory,* p. 139.

15. Warner, *The Social Systems of American Ethnic Groups,* p. 28. In his excellent study of Burlington, Vermont, Elin L. Anderson found a similar myth, particularly among the upper classes. Anderson was unwilling to accept their claims without investigation, and discovered that in fact the "pure" Yankee stock made up less than a third of the population (*We Americans: A Study of Cleavage in an American City,* Cambridge, Mass., 1937, chap. iii, "The Myth of a Yankee Town." For a similar finding in another Vermont community see the unpublished study by Martin and Margy Ellin Meyerson described in David Riesman, *Faces in the Crowd: In-*

dividual Studies in Character and Politics (New Haven, 1952), p. 274.

16. Warner, *Social Life*, p. 209.

17. Warner, *Social Life*, p. 5; *Modern Factory*, p. 2. John P. Marquand's savage lampooning of Warner as the "Malcolm Bryant" of *Point of No Return* (Boston, 1949) should not be allowed to obscure the fact that the two men viewed the community from a very similar perspective. Marquand appears to have felt that Warner betrayed the confidence placed in him by Marquand himself and other upper class respondents. Whatever the merits of this accusation, Warner seems to have reproduced the views of this group with considerable fidelity.

18. For examples in addition to the previously cited works by Warner himself, see Allison Davis, Burleigh B. Gardner, and Mary R. Gardner, *Deep South; A Social Anthropological Study of Caste and Class* (Chicago, 1941); August B. Hollingshead, *Elmtown's Youth: The Impact of Social Classes on Adolescents* (New York, 1949); Robert J. Havinghurst and Hilda Taba, *Adolescent Character and Personality* (New York, 1948).

19. Warner, *Social Life*, pp. 81-82.

20. Warner, *Social Life*, pp. 83-86, 227-251; Warner, Marchia Meeker, and Kenneth Eells, *Social Class in America: A Manual of Procedure for the Measurement of Social Status* (Chicago, 1949), p. 129.

21. Warner, *Social Life*, p. 74.

22. Warner, *Social Life*, pp. 74, 81-84.

23. Warner conceded that "not all the people in Yankee City are aware of all the minute distinctions made in this book" (*Social Life*, p. 91). At another place he admitted to relying heavily on the judgments of "all the better informants" (*Social Life*, p. 84). The "minute distinctions," it is reasonable to suspect, were made by "the better informants." And it seems evident, both from the image of the city projected in the series and from quotations given to illustrate the rating procedures—"she does not belong"; "they belong to our club"—that "the better informants" were not uneducated laborers. The Davis and Gardner study, *Deep South*, pp. 71-73, and Warner's own manual, *Social Class in America*, pp. 60-62, supply evidence that Americans from the lower class levels see fewer classes than upper class respondents, and that they see class "as purely a matter of income and power." For further observations on this question, see Lipset and Bendix, "Social Status and Social Structure: A Re-examination of Data and Interpretations: II," *The British Journal of Sociology*, 2 (1951): 259.

24. Warner, *Social Life,* pp. 90-91, 200-201.
25. Warner, *Social Life,* pp. 73-74.
26. Warner, *Ethnic Groups,* p. 69.
27. The reclassification of the 1933 data by generations is in Warner, *Ethnic Groups,* pp. 70-77.
28. Warner, *Ethnic Groups,* pp. 35-41.
29. Warner, *Ethnic Groups,* p. 60.
30. A comparison of the 1849 and 1851 city directories with the names of laborers listed by the local census-taker in 1850 showed that these directories were a highly unreliable source—less than 60 percent of the families recorded in the census schedules were in either directory. A similar comparison for 1860 makes it appear that later directories were sufficiently inclusive to be an adequate source for a study of this kind. At best, however, the directories of this period supplied data concerning *heads of families.* Warner's mistaken assertion that the Newburyport Irish rarely found factory employment was partly due to this deficiency in the source he relied upon; Irish youth, it was shown in Chap. 4 above, were employed in local factories in large numbers.
31. This is not to suggest that knowledge of the "average occupational status" of the members of particular ethnic groups at various times is without value. An index of this kind can certainly contribute to an understanding of acculturation processes. Such an index, however, is easily misinterpreted when the changing composition of the group is ignored and inferences are made concerning the likelihood of individual mobility.

INDEX

This book is one of a series published under the auspices of the Joint Center for Urban Studies, a cooperative venture of the Massachusetts Institute of Technology and Harvard University. The Joint Center was founded in 1959 to do research on urban and regional problems. Participants have included scholars from the fields of architecture, business, engineering, city planning, economics, history, law, philosophy, political science, and sociology.

PUBLICATIONS OF THE
JOINT CENTER FOR URBAN STUDIES

PUBLISHED BY HARVARD UNIVERSITY PRESS

The Intellectual versus the City: From Thomas Jefferson to Frank Lloyd Wright, by Morton and Lucia White, 1962

Streetcar Suburbs: The Process of Growth in Boston, 1870-1900, by Sam B. Warner, Jr., 1962

City Politics, by Edward C. Banfield and James Q. Wilson, 1963

Law and Land: Anglo-American Planning Practice, edited by Charles M. Haar, 1964

Location and Land Use: Toward a General Theory of Land Rent, by William Alonso, 1964

Poverty and Progress: Social Mobility in a Nineteenth Century City, by Stephan Thernstrom, 1964

PUBLISHED BY THE M.I.T. PRESS

The Image of the City, by Kevin Lynch, 1960

Housing and Economic Progress: A Study of the Housing Experiences of Boston's Middle-Income Families, by Lloyd Rodwin, 1961

Beyond the Melting Pot: The Negroes, Puerto Ricans, Jews, and Irish of New York City, by Nathan Glazer and Daniel Patrick Moynihan, 1963

The Historian and the City, edited by Oscar Handlin and John Burchard, 1963

The Joint Center also publishes monographs and reports